TOUCHSTONE

GROUPS IN SCHOOLS

BY

Ruth G. Newman, Ph.D.

A Touchstone Book
Published by Simon and Schuster

SBN 671-21698-8 Casebound
SBN 671-22032-2 Paperback
Library of Congress Catalog Card Number: 73-22780
Designed by Irving Perkins
Manufactured in the United States of America

1 2 3 4 5 6 7 8 9 10

ACKNOWLEDGMENTS

I AM much indebted to many people for this book's existence. In practical terms, I am indebted to Michael Korda because he believed in it from its inception, so long ago, to its completion, and to Barbara Masser, Ph.D., whose editorial comments and suggestions were intelligent, perceptive, tasteful and helpful. I am indebted to the Small Grants Division of the National Institute of Mental Health for allowing me to do the basic work. I am much indebted to Barbara Hitchcock and Beverly Dempsey for their struggles with my impossible handwriting and impatient nature. Likewise I am grateful to Tut Jordan for her summer typing help and to Marjorie Keith for proofreading.

On more philosophical grounds, I am, as the dedication tells, deeply indebted to Fritz Redl, who taught me so much about disturbed children and their life in schools and in groups. I am grateful too to the late A. Kenneth Rice, to Margaret Rioch, Sir James Sutherland and Pierre Turquet for introducing me to the Tavistock method of thinking about groups and social change, and to many of my colleagues in the A. K. Rice Institute in the Washington School of Psychiatry, with whom I learned painfully and happily. Let me name a special two: Garret O'Connor, M.D., and David Singer, Ph.D. I am grateful as well to my colleagues of the past, William Morse and Nicholas Long. I want to acknowledge here the importance of shared ideas, support and friendship with James B. Mackie, Ph.D.

More personally, I am grateful to my son Jeffrey, his wife, Killian, and my daughter, Brooke, and her husband, Andrew, for simply being around and being available in their own ways, and for their providing material for good school groups in each of their children, my grandchildren—Andrea and David Newman, and Nikos and Samantha Hecht, in order of their appearance.

One last acknowledgment as important to me as the rest: I am most indebted to those patients, supervisees and students from whom I have learned much and who have sustained me in rough times more than they could imagine, and to Re Reiger, Ph.D., and Elma Denham, M.S.W., of Hillcrest Children's Center.

DEDICATION

To three people from whom I have learned much:

Winifred G. Whitman, M.D., Psychoanalyst,
who taught me who I was,

Fritz Redl (teacher, philosopher and clinician),
who taught me how to search and sometimes find,

and

The Late A. Kenneth Rice, Ph.D.
(once Director of the Tavistock Human Relations Institute,
London, England),
who taught me how to put it all together

A NOTE

In a book that discusses children, teachers, parents—people, in short—the lack in our language of a genderless, singular personal pronoun creates problems. To avoid constant repetition of "his or her," "he or she," I have taken the old-fashioned way of letting the masculine pronoun do the work for all, except where sex is specified or significant.

Contents

Introduction: Why a Book About Groups in Schools

THERE ARE several major reasons for a book about groups in schools. The first one is that while human beings are, like many other creatures, group animals, they are unlike most other animals in that they consciously organize their attempts to transmit their knowledge, beliefs, attitudes and means of communication to their offspring. They do this in order that their experience of life may survive. Over the centuries, they have developed schools to accomplish this task. To establish schools, adults have had to form groups to portion out and administer their accumulated lore and learning so as to make possible the communication of increasingly complex sets of learnings to increasingly large groups of children and young people in increasingly bewildering sets of interrelated societies. As a result, one cannot understand schools without understanding both the groups of adults and the groups of children and young people, and seeing how they relate to one another.

As one among society's many institutions, the schools have inherited a large share of responsibility for transmitting our past and present so that we may have a viable future. By nature, and also because of their numbers, groups are the means by which schools either succeed in accomplishing the mandate they have received from society or fail. One way of evaluating what has

been done is to look at the process of education as one might at
any other institution or industry. Looking at it so, we distinguish
three elements in the school process: input of raw material, transformation of that material, and creation of the end product. The
"raw material" is our children; the transformation is the educative
process—carried on primarily in and through groups—and the
"product," the emerging "educated" youth or young adult.

Putting it in bald terms, we may say that the goal of education
is to create "products"—people who have the abilities and skills
needed to cope with present-day society and—since change is a
vital condition of society—to be instrumental in bringing about
necessary change. Judging by the uproar we are hearing these
days from old and young, the school as an institution is failing in
this task. Its critics claim it has succeeded neither as a guide to
society as it now exists, nor as a catalyst for creative adaptation
or constructive change. Older critics among us, of the left as well
as of the right, add that it has not even been successful in its
primary role of transmitter of past values, attitudes and knowledge. The schools themselves have, with some justice, defended
themselves by pointing out that the impact of others of society's
institutions—housing, welfare, health, government, industry, the
family and so on—has been such that the input population of the
schools has changed, so that the subject matter and methods used
in the past no longer work. The schools, in reaction to the criticism and turmoil around them, are now being pushed to try one
desperate plan after another, few of them well thought out, well
prepared or well executed. Each plan thus born of desperation is
tried for a time and then dropped, often without objective evaluation of why or how, or in fact whether, it has failed.

Thus the schools have been engaged not so much in their primary task of educating children as in defending themselves and
trying to maintain at least the status quo. It is not surprising, we
realize as we consider the situation, that an institution embroiled
in its own turmoil, and beset by demands and catcalls from
other institutions of society, should be so entrapped in its present
difficulties that it cannot countenance change from within its
structure. Since it is difficult, if not impossible, to teach what
one does not experience, the school finds it cannot fulfill its man-

date to transmit values of stability from the past, for these have been swallowed up in the confusion; it cannot transmit skills for coping with the present, for it has lost those skills itself. Certainly, in its present condition of imbalance, the school cannot possibly teach its charges the means to bring about thoughtful change.

If one looks at the schools as one institution within the group of institutions that make up society, the interdependence of the various institutions becomes clear. One can see that the forces operating in the entire group of institutions that impede getting society's work done are precisely those that one can see in minuscule, and under far more controllable conditions, within small groups as they relate one with another—the school board with the administration; the staff with the P.T.A. and the community representatives; and the students with the teachers and counselors.

One can then ask about certain constants among group forces. There is the problem of group roles, for instance. How is it that one person in a group, or one group among many, gets selected to play a role for the whole group? How or why does a group allow itself to be selected for a particular role? Once frozen into the role, can it get out of the role if it wants to? What does the particular role assigned to a group and accepted by it do to the group? Can a person or institution chosen for a role mobilize itself out of the assigned role without the aid of the rest of the group and the help of the leadership? Although, as applied to some of our institutions, these are problems of international importance, they can all be found in miniature in the school, for the school is an institution whose job affects the fate of all of us, and whose methods necessarily depend on groups to plan, to carry out, and to apply whatever action is offered.

It is in school groups—which include those informal groups formed by the children themselves to meet their own agenda of learning how to live and play and learn together—that one may see group forces as they develop, much as one can see under the microscope the multiplying cells that make up a total organism. One may see the variety possible in the handling of the role of leadership, see how leadership works, and as well study the art of followership—its purposes, its dangers, its rewards. One may study the methods of group learning—what models are imitated, what errors prove damaging, what ones useful. One sees basic human needs operating in all groups—dependency, flight-and-fight, the pairings that are formed within groups—and one can find ways of using these human needs for learning or for exploitation. One sees how rebellion grows; where it can be constructive, and where it may lead to violence and chaos. From third grade to budget hearing committee, one can see how the stated purpose of a group may get lost, or be waylaid, because of undercover issues in the group that must be dealt with before the group can set to work on its agreed-upon task. And again, one can see how one person or one group can be made to play a role—say, that of scapegoat—even if his playing that role prevents the accomplishment of the group's task. In studying that situation, one may get some understanding of the purpose a particular role serves for the whole group.

This brings us to a third reason for a book on groups in schools. Let me set up the hypothesis that among society's institutions the school has been selected to play the role of scapegoat. From what we know about groups, we know there must be reasons why the school is the institution selected for this role, and reasons, too, why the school allows itself to be so selected. Further, from what we know about groups we may reason that there is a price to be paid for playing any role within a group. That price may be too high for a particular individual to pay. He may be destroyed, or at least immobilized, to the detriment not only of the individual involved but also of the entire group.

My conviction is that the price of having the schools play the scapegoat among society's institutions is now too high. I believe that the very reason for the selection of the school as scapegoat among society's institutions, the reason for society's maintaining it in this role, is found within the task allotted to the schools: the task of producing people who can, given the set of values, knowledge and skills that we have accumulated, bring about change as change becomes necessary. And change is frightening.

There are few groups of any kind—even among revolutionary groups whose goal is change in the outside world—who can, within their own structure, by action, accept change without a struggle. Witness the inflexibility and fanaticism of the most effective revolutionaries. Human beings always struggle to get to a balance position; change is a process that by its very nature causes imbalance. People resist the discomfort and the uncertainty of that imbalance.

Most people react to change as if they were saying, "However bad it is, we know what we've got—and who knows, what is to come might be worse! Moreover, even if the next thing is better, how do I know whether I as an individual can adapt to it?" This phenomenon of resistance to change can be seen even in a subgroup of first grade children who, as they are learning to read—which many of them do want to do—still hesitate to give up the reward of dependency on adults who tell them, read to them, show them. The pressure of the group and teacher, if there are no hurdles, will usually succeed in showing such children the rewards of independence and the joy the skill itself may bring. They will indeed then learn to read, and with satisfaction once the step has been taken—but there is sure to be an internal struggle first. A group of teachers who are asked to teach in a new way—let's say, in a learning center, instead of in separate classrooms—will resist, even if some are excited about the prospect, and even if the decision of the administration is firm. Some among them, representing greater resistance to change, will struggle, will do the job in form but not in fact, and some indeed will probably represent resistance to the new to such an extent that they will ask for transfers to an old-time school, or worse, will stay and sabotage, or try to sabotage, the program. A group of administrators who have got together to redesign a curriculum may know the penalties of sticking to the old texts and the old plan, but somehow the meetings will go on longer than scheduled—because, though they all agree on the need to change, they all have different views on what, when, and how. Somehow, the result is that the introduction of the new curriculum and the new texts is postponed to "a later date," which really means to a time when the group can grapple with its own anxieties about dealing with the changes involved.

In other words, the undercurrent resistance to change, regardless of the fact that all, or most, group members agree that change is necessary, is such a basic force in groups that *unless it is understood and recognized, along with the many ways it exhibits itself*, a task which engenders change will not get done. More than any other institution, except possibly the family, the school is a microcosm of the larger society, and as such represents society's resistance to change. Insofar as the school concentrates only on the past without regard for the present or the future, it becomes irrelevant, not because of the particular content it teaches, but because it fails to use history as a bridge to life today. Insofar as it deals only with the present, it is deaf both to the messages from the past and to the imperatives of the future, and so becomes ineffective as well as irrelevant. The problems of the schools thus become a mirror for the problems that exist to a greater or lesser extent, though usually not so comprehensively, in each of society's institutions. It is for this reason that among social institutions, the school is a logical choice for the role of scapegoat.

The inability of the school to encompass change and to bring about ways of changing becomes a good excuse for the blindness of other institutions to the same faults and lacks in their own subgroups. If these institutions fully recognized the imperatives guiding their own future, they might have to change, too, for we know from the study of groups that change in one member brings about change, large or small, in all. The very threat of that change is enough to cause a group to find covert ways to avoid looking at what it is doing and so seeing why it is not achieving its stated and agreed-upon task. This house-of-cards effect is the same as that seen in a family where a wife or husband or child is deterred from changing because of what the change might mean to the whole family. It is seen in a classroom group where, when the bully becomes reformed, the class either creates a new bully or finds a way to reconcile itself to being without a bully by causing each member of the class to accept the part of himself which might at times like to become a bully. We see it too in a staff group in which a member who has customarily followed makes a strong bid for leadership and dethrones the incumbent leader. To freeze people into allotted roles is a way of agreeing, covertly, not to get the assigned task done. And this is true too for an institution among institutions. If the schools organized to try to change, other institutions would have to do so too. For that reason, all collude to resist change.

Indeed, if the school found ways to mobilize itself out of the scapegoat position, its doing so would affect housing, the family and health institutions, to name but a few. Take without argument, pro or con, the mandate for busing. This one controversial school issue loomed large enough to be a major issue in many '72 political campaigns. It affects and is affected by housing, health, mental health, the family, the status of minority groups, etc.

That is why all the institutions have a stake in keeping the school in the scapegoat role, and why the schools, in addition to defending their vested interest, find it so difficult to get out of that role. Knowing the force of groups, one wonders what would happen in society if some of the fantasies of the radicals who suggest shutting down the schools were to come to pass. The other institutions of society would join forces to bring the schools back: their own survival would be at stake. Thus the freezing of schools into a scapegoat position can be seen as a means of defending all the other institutions from too great a threat of change. (Besides, schools themselves have taught people to be "good," to stay in line and make no trouble, so most people are easily brought to heel.) The process is probably a conscious one on the part of some people within certain institutions, but for most people in positions to guide their institutions it remains covert—that is, it is a process they are unaware of.

What can be done? For the schools to cast off the scapegoat role requires that they shall themselves understand the processes, both covert and overt, that operate in groups sufficiently clearly to be able to see what is happening to them, to know to what extent they are in fact responsible and to what extent they are being burdened with responsibilities that should be shared by other institutions in society. When these demarcations are clearly seen, it becomes possible—however difficult within a group as complex as the group of social institutions—to bring about change without toppling all of the institutions involved.

Considering that schools are not only made up of groups, and do their work in and by means of groups, but also are the institution chiefly responsible for educating society, we can no longer afford lack of sophistication about groups. To survive and be useful schools need to be aware of the varieties of groups and of the forces that operate within them, of the various aspects of leadership and followership, and of the kind of tasks to be done by different groups, as well as of the meaning and effects of responsible decision-making and the delegation of authority.

To help them achieve this understanding of group dynamics, schools have within their own structure a prize laboratory, for the school is a microcosm of all society. Schools can find in their own home territory every kind of group that is represented in society at large. They can see and come to understand the varieties of group dynamics that exist in all groups from the treatment group to the international conference. Groups can be found in the classroom, the counselor's office, the staff room, the playground, the locker room, or the faculty cafeteria. They can be found in the principal's office, the superintendent's conference room, the board room or the auditorium where community and school meetings take place.

Understanding these groups can help schools with their primary task of education—enabling the young to emerge into society with ability to cope with and ability also to inaugurate necessary change in society. An understanding of groups can, further, give schools the ability to change within themselves, and thereby to force other institutions of society to do whatever is needed to effect change in their own bailiwicks. Instead of remaining society's scapegoat, trapped in maintaining the status quo, schools must have the tools and materials to enable them to be what they are supposed to be—educators—that is, leaders out of a state of ignorance into a state of knowledge.

RUTH G. NEWMAN

Washington, D.C.

I

If Three's a Crowd—
What's a Group?

SCHOOL IS for learning. School is made up of groups. Anxiety is an ingredient both of learning and group life. To understand the forces behind all kinds of groups in schools, one must understand something about the anxiety attendant upon a group. There is much evidence to support the thesis that anxiety is necessary to learning. That evidence comes not only from experiments in human and animal psychology but also from the studies of biologists such as Lorenz and of physiologists such as Cannon. True, because the theory of groups in sociology, anthropology and psychology is comparatively new, there is not yet as much firm evidence in these fields as one might wish, but even there the data suggest that anxiety generally accompanies entry into any task-oriented groups—also into many that are not task-oriented. Indeed, anxiety is a continuous force, sometimes latent, sometimes active, in all group life.

Unpleasant associations are linked with the word anxiety. And well they may be, for in its more severe forms anxiety is akin to terror; it may lead to panic or immobilization, and may even take on the quality of nightmare. Even when it is not so severe, the appearance or recall of anxiety may block learning, temporarily or permanently. Yet, in its milder forms, anxiety may not only be an aid to learning, but may and indeed does cause learning to occur. It is in one way not unlike alcohol: in small doses it is beneficial, sometimes even medicinal; in large doses it may confuse and cause trouble; as the quantity mounts, so does the risk of ending in disaster.

As with alcohol, it is difficult to determine precisely what amount of anxiety is beneficial, what amount can be tolerated without harm and to what extent it may set in motion forces destructive both to the person experiencing it, and too often to others as well.

Some individuals assimilate large doses of threat of one kind and yet quake at the injection of a minuscule dose of another kind. For instance, some people adore the scare of a roller coaster and yet quaver at the thought of being ridiculed. One's constitution, personality, upbringing and life experience determine the kind and amount of anxiety that may help or hinder or even stop learning altogether.

One way to find out about a child's ability to take anxiety in group life and to deal with it is to examine his reactions to the first experience of school. That first experience may be in nursery school or kindergarten, or it may come later. In some societies— in Israel and Russia, for example—this would be no test, since many of the children there have been living in institutional groups from infancy. In our own country this experience, properly studied, provides a good index of an individual's ability to tolerate anxiety. From a study of such data we might arrive at a far more sensible system of grouping than one that depends on chronological age for instance, or on IQ level. Placement would depend on the child's ability to learn in a group. A judgment might be made as to the amount of anxiety the child could benefit by without experiencing distress.

To understand better the role of anxiety in groups, let us consider what study of that first day of school can tell us. For many children the first day of school is a muddle of muchness. This is

true even for those children who have looked forward to school,
and those who enjoy school soon after entering. Those who have
been exposed to groups of children in their families and in neighborhoods may take the first day in stride. For others, the array
of stimuli that confronts them comes like a stunning blow. For
both groups it is unlikely that with so much going on there will be
any clear recollection of the event. There are people, big and
little. The room is at once as large as a hall and as small as a
closet. Many even of the well-adjusted and school-ready children
may be shy or tentative when beginning new things; such children
are likely to feel small and alone in a mass of unknown live and
unlive objects and shapes. Such feelings are characteristic of those
one may have all one's life in entering new groups. One temporarily loses the ability to differentiate one stimulus from another,
one person from another. Indeed, if anxiety is severe, ability to
differentiate people from things is impaired, and it becomes
difficult if not impossible to recall the experience as a whole—
one recalls only impressions which reveal the quality or intensity
of the anxiety, but not a unified experience. This tells us something about some ways in which severe anxiety may hamper the
learning process: It may confuse perception, it may curtail ability
to differentiate, and it may block recall—all three essential to
learning.

Because the first day of school seems to be such a synthesis of
the experience of anxiety people feel in entering groups, I once
asked 250 seventh, ninth and eleventh grade children to tell me
or write me their recollections of the first day of school. From this
mini-survey, I realized that at most a kind of montage of impressions remained:

"There was Mother—then there wasn't Mother."—"We sat
down on the floor, no, on chairs."—"A big person with a shelf of
a bosom hung over me and I didn't know where the door was."—
"I wet my pants and they laughed at me, and I started to cry."
—"A big, fat girl with black braids took my purple crayon and I
grabbed her braids and pulled and wouldn't let go till the teacher
held me."—"A tall boy with big feet stepped on my painting. I

couldn't stop crying and they told my mother I was insecure."— "We had to go along a kind of a brown hall and then down wide, gray stairs to get to a playground, but when we got there we couldn't use it and had to go back and be quiet all the way."— "There were children and more children. It seemed to me some were the size of giants. They swept down the corridors as if they knew where they were going."—"I remember noise, so much noise that I wanted to throw up."—"I don't know. I guess it was all right."—"The first thing I remember was the kindergarten Halloween party and that was two months later."—"Gee, I don't know, my mother said I was always good in school, but I don't remember myself."—"It seemed to me the lights were always so bright and I kept blinking."

What really happened that day? Is anyone sure? Why so much anxiety?

The experience of anxiety upon entering groups goes on throughout the lives of most people. It may be greeted with anticipation or with pit-of-stomach-sinking dread, or a bit of both. It goes on, yes, but it is unlikely that it does so in quite the same way as that first time when all was strange and one had no way of being certain how, or even if, it would end. This kind of anxiety accompanies the transition of a person from one group to an-other—in this case, a very small, inexperienced person. It may be he yelled and screamed in protest and did not want to come back, but when he did so, found it not so strange and really quite okay, even fun. It may be he was not able to come back at all— that he was too immobilized; or that he came back in body only, safely keeping part or most of himself detached and out of reach. In these responses the child is not much different from adults entering a brand-new group. He has simply less means of con-cealment or camouflage.

As a child (or adult) gets used to a group, he will be able to take in experiences that caused anxiety the first day but are now growing to be no threat at all. When this happens, he can assim-ilate sufficient doses of anxiety to find himself challenged to take on new things, risk himself a bit and stretch his world. This kind of anxiety, easily offered in a group, is a "growing" and beneficial experience. Since looking at the child in this situation will lead us to some understanding of what a group is and what it does, it is worthwhile to consider the child's original group and see what he has learned from it that enables him to deal with his first institutional, away-from-home group—his first classroom group. Whatever its foibles and deficiencies, however organized, whether cushioned by financial ease and an ambiance of open affection, or bone-hungry, with lack of food and clothes and comfort, a child's first group—the family—is a group experience in which the child has come to feel relatively safe.

During the first few years of life, a child, simply because he finds himself in a group, no matter how small, learns a thousand things about himself and his family—things he doesn't know that he knows. Already, in the months before speech, before locomotion, he has listened to voices, has felt sureness or ambivalence in the arms that held him, the fingers that bathed him and diapered him, has sensed the nipple (breast or bottle) that nourished him. He has heard fear or warmth, anger and passion, in his mother's and father's voices, smelled it in their skins. He has seen how and when he could evoke a smile, a yell, a slap. He has known how long and how loud he must cry to bring about some response in his family group. He has learned when silence is necessary, and with whom he may giggle and play, and whom he must avoid. He has learned, so far as his own life is concerned, who is the real boss of the family and on what occasions whoever it is will intervene to determine his immediate fate. He has learned some ways to please, and often how to start a row among the others. He has become fairly competent in handling himself in the role the family has allotted him, even if that role turns out to be an unsuitable or destructive one. He has begun to find a place for himself—he is the bad one, the good one, the bright one, the dumb one, the clown, the sad one, the loved one, the nuisance, the burden, the sick one, the fixer-upper, the baby.

As clearly as a lion cub learns its territory, a child learns about the boundaries and the geography of his family group. He becomes aware of those objects—moving and still—that get in the way, and somehow come up and hit you, or fall down on you, or lick you, or scratch you or growl at you or burn you or send you hurtling to the floor. To an infant, the animate and inanimate together form a primary group, undiscriminated from one another. As adults we think we have left this consciousness of the furniture and physical environment of a group behind us, but to a larger extent than we like to think, that is not true. Seldom does a person of any age describe a group without mention of the atmosphere, the weather, the furnishings or décor, whether he is talking of an army group or a church meeting, a classroom or a political powwow.—"It was hot in that room and smoky," we say, in explaining our bewilderment. "The chairs were so soft I kept falling asleep until the guy next to me pushed me awake." —"My regiment had to be quiet in the bush and the weeds kept tickling my nose."

A sense of trust or distrust develops from a child's contacts with this undiscriminated world peopled with sensations and signals. The way people in his world handle the child, and especially handle betrayals of him, will determine his ability to cope and his style of maneuvering within his group. This is true whether he feels he has been betrayed by a falling cabinet, a hot burner, a jealous brother or an overprotective grandfather. If he is too trusting, he may not survive. If he has no experience of anger, or of expressions of joy, he will not know how to recognize anger or joy in himself or in others. If he is severely distrusting, he may never learn to discriminate between animate and inanimate, and may end up relating to the one as if it were the other. (In its extreme form this inability to discriminate is a major aspect of autism, and many of the efforts that are exerted in attempting to treat the autistic child are aimed at helping him learn to trust a particular person and to discriminate an object from a person.)

By the time the child goes to real school—or to kindergarten— his response to the family group is usually pretty well differentiated: he can tell objects from persons, persons from animals, and persons from each other. He may kick a chair and call it names when he's stumbled over it, but then so do we adults sometimes, and somewhere basically we do know it's a chair we're kicking and not an evil spirit in the chair. Insofar as this is not so, the child will have a difficult time in his first school group. It is probable that he will be less able to join future groups without an at least momentary reversion to the total feeling of lostness and helplessness. For this reason, a major teaching goal in kindergarten and first grade is to help the child learn what the patterns of life are in the school room and what is and what is not acceptable; he sees what is different here from home, and when the two groups get mixed up.

What the child experiences in going to real school for the first time is in microcosm what each of us experiences in joining any new group that carries with it demands for joining in, exposing oneself, stretching one's brains and body and feelings and one's view of the world. The whole process is, in fact, *learning*.

But the child comes not wholly unprepared. He has been able to move outside and sample bits of other amorphous groups before entering school, groups such as those in the supermarket, bus, yard, block or playground. He has learned to recognize, much as a dog does, the voices and smells of visitors to his house, those he likes, and those he shuns or fears—and those he can handle. Hopefully, he has experienced some other children his age at one or more of these outside arenas. So long as the leader of his group —usually mother, or a delegated leader, such as sitter or caretaker—is familiarly by his side, he is within a boundary he understands, and finds it is usually not too frightening.

However, when he makes the transition from home to school that first day, and for some more timid souls, even later on, the door that closes on him in the school for the school day shuts out mother, sister and brother, and he is left alone with a new geography to get used to, a new group of little people of his own age and strange new big people.

To be new and alone in a group, with neither cues as to the kind of leadership he will have to live under nor knowledge of which aspect is a lure to danger and which a gate to pleasure, is an experience a person has uncountable times in his life, but it is most unlikely that he will ever again be quite so unarmed again as he is that first day in school. Sometimes, depending on his ability to tolerate or use anxiety, the experience may have been so damaging that he views each new group he encounters as a threat; sometimes it is so exciting that it appears a happy or challenging opportunity, and he wants more and more of it.

Essentially, our adult experiences of fear about entering new groups has enough likeness to that first day of school to make it possible for us to enter into the child's feeling. When you are three, four, or five, you don't know for sure that you'll survive. Later on, each person, according to his temperament, his needs and the patterns he has seen, will have found some defenses with which to enter new groups. Some will clown, others will sit in a corner. Some will engage one person and avoid or block out all others. Some will turn nasty or aggressive. Some, if the going gets rough, will get sick. Some will be coy or ingratiating. Some will make a bid for all the attention by tears or tantrums or sulks. Some won't show their fears and some will flee. But at three, four, or five, the defenses are rarely fully organized, and so one can see the response to anxiety and to group participation as, or even before, defenses get mobilized.

We have identified anxiety as an essential component of group life. Let us now consider just what a group is so that we may come to understand the effect of such anxiety for good or ill.

"Two's company, three's a crowd." Two is a pair, and in a pair each person needs only to relate to one other. Take a pair of lovers: the boy may relate to the girl as if she were his mother, and she to him as if he were an earlier boyfriend, but the two have only each other to test what happens between them. Two then is not a group. Three or four or eight or ten may be a group, or it may be a crowd or even a gang. Twenty or fifty or one hundred may be a large group or a mob or an infantry company. Whether four or forty-four, individuals may simply be people in the same place at the same time, without any interest in each other and with only the slimmest of common threads linking them. For example, when one hundred people on a busy avenue are all moving in the same direction, they may seem a mob to an observer in a bus, but they are neither a group nor a mob—their relationship to one another is purely one of coincidence: they happen to be on the same street at the same time.

It is only a shared task or goal that makes individuals into a group. Sometimes, of course, the actual shared goal is different from the stated or conscious goal of the group. This may happen because of the strength of the leadership, or because of the covert (unconscious) needs of the group, or because of both. Take a staff meeting called for the ostensible purpose of redesigning the school schedule. Underneath the stated agenda there is a covert purpose: to see if the group can so corner the director of curriculum that he will be forced to resign or at least to transfer to a different job. Some members of the group may be aware of this underlying purpose, others may be in the dark; but when it turns out that the announced task of revising the schedule is never directly addressed, it becomes fairly clear that some more pressing group business has to be attended to before the group can get on with its work. In a particular group, the leader may have a real agenda quite different from the reason he has given for the meeting. The plan may well include keeping the followers in the dark until it is too late to withdraw or refuse to act as desired, or too hard. Often, the followers allow themselves to remain unaware of the real task until they reach a point of no return. This kind of phenomenon is found everywhere, but it is particularly dramatic and often tragic in the political arena. Hitler and Mussolini are prime examples of such calculating leadership and the history of their countries is a classic example of irresponsible acquiescing followership. It may be that Watergate alerted us to covert agendas.

On a shuttle flight once, I was one of the passengers landing in a plane threatened by a bomb scare. The seventy-odd passengers were asked to disembark as hurriedly as possible and go a safe distance from the plane. The crew was busy helping the firemen spray the plane and get out the baggage, searching the plane for the hypothetical bomb. The passengers had the experience of fear and uncertainty in common. We shared being rushed from the plane and walking in the cold rain and sleet to an assigned point presumably out of danger; we shared the relief of not being in the plane, and concern about how to get back to the air-port from the place where we had landed. All of us depended on the airline for leadership in making decisions and arrangements, but chatter and hypothesis, fantasy and the recounting of past experience began to be exchanged, along with the details of asso-ciated experiences some people had had. Some blamed the airline for inefficiency (a common group activity—"let's get together and blame the management"). Some laughed too loud, or talked too heartily—a sign of common anxiety. Others withdrew in-wardly into themselves, but were forced to stay with the group by circumstances—the common experience of the non-belonger.

Leadership in the group began to develop through competition among the members. The more aggressive complainers attracted one faction, the patient-waiters lined up behind another leader. Some did useful things like wrapping coats around children or thinly dressed women, or making umbrellas of soggy newspapers. Time was too short for leadership to develop to the point where leaders could adequately handle the task of taking care of a group of scared people deserted on the outskirts of a city airport on a wet, cold night—but a group it had indeed become.

Then an airline representative announced the end of the scare, and directed the passengers to line up to have their baggage searched and then to get into buses to go to the airport some fifteen minutes away. Suddenly, as quickly as it had formed, the "group" deteriorated into a mob, everyone now pushing to be first to get his baggage searched in order to get a bus-seat ahead of other people. Women and children, protected minutes before, were now shoved back, and the mild complaints that before had been merely defenses against fear now became raucous accusa-tions of the airline. The group was a group no more, it became merely a number of weary travelers eager to get to their destina-tions and have a drink—not together, but separately—expressing their post-anxiety reactions as individuals no longer concerned about how others of their number would react to their behavior, rude or courteous. Before, they had thought they might have to remain together for an unknown length of time; now, desire for anonymity from the others returned and personal goals super-seded common group awareness.

A group then is more than two people who come together, or find themselves together, with an overall common goal or task. How they achieve their end depends only in part on the nature of the task. How the task changes in the doing depends on the type and quality of the group and on its leadership. Whether a leader can keep himself aware not only of the stated agenda or task but also of those covert goals that impede the group's work will, at least in part, determine the group's success in its job.

We come here, then, to the essential question for all groups: the question of leadership. Observing groups directly or as recorded on tape, one can see at once the mutual interdependence of group and leader. It is a two-way street; one cannot function without the other. Some groups demand a certain kind of leadership to accomplish a particular task; or they may put the leadership under pressure to fill needs that exist in the group which have to be attended to before the work can get under way. If the leader does not recognize the group's need or mandate, the group will disperse, come to a standstill, or transform itself into something else. While it is true that certain types of leadership bring about certain specific effects, a group may in its actions insist upon a certain type of leadership, even while it complains bitterly about getting the very thing it is asking for. Often a group is not consciously aware that by its own behavior it has often chosen in the person of its leader the very one who will deter the work rather than further it. This is particularly true in adult groups. With groups of small children, of course, the leader or teacher is foisted upon the group; it is the administration, and by extension, the part of the community in power, that selects for the children the kind of leadership it approves of. How this selection is made, or not made, and how the leader selected may be bypassed, is another fascinating problem, related not only to the personal predilection of the selecting principal or superintendent, but also to the forces in the community that get themselves expressed through the people who get chosen to teach or to decide what teaching the children are to receive.

So far as schools are concerned, what does anyone—a teacher or administrator, or community representative, or student, for that matter—need to know about himself as a leader? The fact that a teacher is older and bigger than his students may or may not give him authority; it does give him much responsibility, whether he takes it well or not. But size, and age and even position do not in themselves automatically bestow leadership. Any group-wise fourth-grader can get the group to test the teacher's limits, and demonstrate whether they've got a title or a leader, and what kind of leadership the leader provides.

Ideally, the leader should be a person suited to accomplishing the given task or able to delegate leadership to those who can get parts of the work done while the leader retains responsibility for making final decisions. But all too frequently, a leader is chosen for irrelevant reasons—popularity, charisma, looks; he may be chosen out of nepotism, or out of fear of some higher-up, or even because no one else asked or was willing to lead. He may be chosen because in-fighting in the group has dethroned effective leaders and no one more suitable was left. With adults, the leader—good or poor—can lead only so long as the group or system lets him and no longer.

Children, however, must accept whatever leadership is assigned them. They get handed their parents, and sometimes nearly as irrevocably, they are assigned their teachers—good, bad or indifferent. When a child learns techniques, he can sometimes defeat a teacher, but he may also be defeated by him, and by the institutions—school, school board or union—which support the teacher, as well as by the corporate state for which all of these stand—one authority, indivisible, from principal to superintendent. This is true unless the community via the parents has found a way to get heard: the child himself is indeed as helpless as he may feel.

It is no wonder that by adolescence, when a youth no longer feels so helpless, the frustration of years emerges, sometimes appropriately and sometimes inappropriately, and there is often a healthy wave of rebellion directed against the "oppressors," i.e., adult society. It is rarely the troublemakers of our early classes who are the rebels in education; those troublemakers have dropped out, or been pushed out, actually or spiritually, years before. The rebels now are the ones who have suffered through and have become aware of the frequently witless decision-making surrounding them.

Leadership sounds enticing, but once having got it, few are happy with it—and of these few, some become drunk with it and behave like drunks. Others are stampeded and behave like a headless herd of sheep. For leadership can be a burden, not only because of the responsibility and the extra work demanded of the leader, but also because it carries with it the penalty of being adored, envied and hated, often simultaneously. None of these feelings are easy to bear. Probably in part because of the attitudes taught in school, we Americans are not too good at bearing hatred. As a group, we want everyone to love us; many of us, as parents, teachers or administrators, in order to avoid being hated, sometimes resort to bribery, wheedling or selling ourselves short. Adoration can be a trap for leaders in every field of endeavor, in the classroom as in the capitol. The fickleness of the crowd is no less true for being a cliché—and the headache known to the wearers of crowns has found no aspirin, buffered or straight. As for the hate and envy that may be engendered by the leader because of unworked-out personal dynamics more properly directed towards fathers, mothers, teachers, and authority in general, we know only too well from our current history (the assassinations of John and Robert Kennedy, of Martin Luther King and Malcolm X) that leadership is fraught with danger. On a mini-scale, this is as true for student leaders in the classroom as it is for the teacher or the principal. Metaphorically at least (and, tragically, once in a while also in a literal sense) leaders are struck down in our classrooms and schools as they are in our society. By analysis of group life and group forces, we may be able to arrive at some clues as to what makes for these occurrences, and also as to what makes for responsible followership, and responsible leadership.

School is the field where leadership and followership grow or wither. How they grow depends on the kind of nourishment that is given by teachers, administrators and taxpayers in the form of models. Take, for instance, one type of leader—the gang leader. If he is successful, he is doing a hard job well, for success means discipline, knowing when to give orders and when to offer freedom of choice. It means organization and imagination, projection and planning. Did the leader show this talent in second or fifth grade, or in seventh or ninth grade, before he dropped out, or was pushed out? Did he find his model for leadership in the school or the street? What did his teachers do about it? Could they have exploited his ability for the use of society and for his own good? Or did they, in fear and trembling, rage and frustration, send him packing outside the school doors? And how many followers followed him out when he went?

We shall study those followers too—followers who permitted themselves to be led either passively or actively. We shall examine the roles each one plays and how each role can come to have its own satisfactions, however perverse. It is interesting to explore how one's role in a group can become the core of one's sense of his own identity: the scapegoat, the silent observer, the yes man, the no-sayer, the cynic, the troublemaker, the initiator who cops out, the reluctant one who follows through, the drone, the P.R. man, the peacemaker and conciliator, the "let's blame someone else" guy, the always hurt one, the violent one, the baby, the tough guy, the martyr, the outsider, the clown, etc. One can see each of these roles in the second grade, in the seventh grade or the seventeenth, and one asks how a person gets to be so frozen in his role that he takes it again and again as the years and the groups participated in accumulate.

In learning about a person as he develops in a group throughout his school years and thereafter, we see that it is the freezing of a personality into one or another group role that deteriorates his ability to adapt to new experience in new ways, his ability to free himself to try new modes of thinking, communicating and behaving. Although our talents and abilities differ considerably, it is possible through awareness of ourselves in a group to recognize the forces pressing us to take and retake the same role in group after group. It is by such awareness and personal decision-making that one often can free oneself and take a more palatable or useful or satisfying role than the one assigned and accepted in the past, for reasons perhaps logical enough then, but now no longer operative. Each of us is capable of taking a number of group roles, some diametrically opposed to those we think of ourselves in and those people think of for us. This should be a happy, liberating thought. But it is often, and with good reason, a frightening thought that may run like this: "What? This is me? Can it be that I, the mild, gentle, sweet mouse if let loose may, it turns out, be an aggressive taunter, a baiter, and a fighter?" For educational purposes, this range of human capability—this ability of a single person to play many surprising roles—is a salutary thought. For despite the evidence of the school's cumulative record, despite the reputation a child has achieved in the school, the child may still, with group-wise teachers and well-formed groups, be encouraged to try many different roles, to grow and learn in the variety of the repertoire school groups offer. Scratch any one of us and you find the capacity, however it disturbs our narcissism to think so, to take on many different—and some none too pleasing—roles at some time, if a group requires the role or our own needs require us to accept it. We shall study these role-playing leaders and followers and watch how their manner changes in relation to the personal dynamics and interests of their age and background; we can then see what light these roles throw on school people and their use or misuse of the forces that exist in a group to aid or impede a specific goal.

We shall consider also the forces that operate in school-group meetings, large and small, structured and free, in classes and in cafeterias, in staff meetings and ladies' lounges, in girls' rooms and boys' rooms, in board meetings and small group discussions. We shall search these dynamics to see what helps a group become more effective, what counteracts the forces that paralyze a group and keep it from acting constructively on its own behalf.

We shall inquire also into that everyday paradox of group life—the fact that to act on what one says is such a rare phenomenon in our society that when one does so consistently in a group people become confused and disbelieving; they have to rearrange their total defenses. So that in contrast to the manipulative wheedling that so often goes on to get children to do our bidding, the most powerful force in discipline and one of the hardest to stick to is to say exactly what one means and do exactly what one has said one will do. This is especially true for children in classroom groups; it is also true for adults in administrative offices and union arbitration meetings and community programs. It is the essence of discipline in education. But for all the use made of it by most of us, doing as one says one will do appears to be a secret weapon unknown to most people and distrusted by those who encounter it.

School is made up of a myriad of groups. To join a group creates anxiety; to deal with oneself in a group takes awareness; to negotiate with others takes initiative, tact and political awareness. To be responsible for oneself in leadership or followership takes learning and skill. Yet, since we are human, and live and work in groups whether we like it or not, we must learn how groups operate and useful ways of operating within them or we shall be unable to transmit any significant body of information to each other. If we cannot do this job, society will in fact be in as bad a way as at this time it seems to be.

This book then is about group life in school. Its purpose is to explain the dynamics of groups that occur within schools and also those of groups outside the school whose activities bear directly on the fate of the school and the course it takes. It is surprising that there has so far been so little study of school group structure. I hope to throw some light in this study on the classroom group and its subgroups, on the informal groups children form and on task-oriented groups. We shall discuss too staff groups, administrative groups, parent and community groups, therapy and counseling groups within the schools, consultation groups and community groups affecting the school. In studying these groups and their interrelationships we shall analyze the similarities and differences between child-oriented and adult-oriented groups. We shall of course be giving a great deal of attention to the nature of leadership and followership. To understand the need for differences in group structure, we need to take a hard look at the initial task a group sets out to do; we need as well to look at the covert processes that may defeat the group in its task or help it succeed.

Since schools are always a microcosm of the society they reflect and seek to perpetuate, they cannot change unless society is ready for change. Yet the school is the very instrument which can hold back change or further it. To understand the nature of social change and to make useful change possible requires a sophisticated understanding of group dynamics. Teachers, parents, and school administrators desperately need that understanding. What I hope to do in this book is to throw more light than we now have on the group life of adults and children as they experience school.

II

The Core Group

THE CLASSROOM group is the center of the child's and the teacher's school universe; it has as much variety as life itself. Presumably, regardless of age, the students who are grouped together in a classroom, under the guidance of one or more teachers, are there to learn how to live in the world in which they find themselves, and to learn the skills which are necessary to them—skills which we hope will be personally enriching as well. For the student, this last clause is the seasoning which despite tears and turmoil and frustration makes the whole thing palatable. To accomplish even a part of this task, the students must learn to live together as a group. For good or for ill, the lives of the students and teacher in the group are inextricably bound together until the end of the school year. Although the students will very likely learn more about their own strengths and weaknesses from each other than from the teacher, just how this learning is transmitted, whether to benefit the student's growth or to distort it and so perhaps cause his immobilization, is, in large part, in the teacher's hands.

A teacher plays multiple roles in the classroom. His roles change as children develop from toddlers to young adults.

Ideally and overall, his first job is to facilitate the learning process, but in doing so and as part of the educative process, he becomes proof to the child that the world is bigger than his family, and that the adults in it react, to some extent, differently from members of his family. On the basis of these differences and similarities, the child's world comes to include hypotheses about contrasts and comparisons.

The teacher is thus the testing laboratory in which the child measures other adults of the outside world. "My teacher says," "My teacher does it this way . . ." "But Mr. Wallace says that's not so . . ." are phrases one hears in one form or another from second grade through college. It is in this role far more than in the more familiar one of hander-down of the tablets of school-laws that the teacher becomes in fact a mini-god and a window on the world. Too frequently, alas, it turns out that the window offered looks out on an arid and eroded landscape. The personal style of the teacher—his personality, his life-experience and training—will, along with the cultural characteristics of the people being taught, determine the kind of image the teacher will present. He may be a herder of sheep, a field sergeant, a power behind the throne, a mother hen, a "Come-on-pals" scout-troop leader, or a prestidigitator, who, by skilled practice in attention-holding, can transform chaos to order, implant a hunger for learning, sow seeds of self-esteem to harvest the fruits of competence, without the group's ever realizing how carefully it has been guided. Or the teacher may be only an example of the living dead, no matter what his chronological age, a humorless, joyless, harried or constricted automaton in clothes.

There are also times, more frequent in the earlier grades, when a teacher becomes a substitute parent—but that is and needs to be a temporary role. At such times the teacher often is lured into becoming the "good" mother or father and acting in opposition to the actual parent, simply giving whatever the child demands instead of filling unmet needs. Then there are times when to facilitate learning the teacher must be an arbitrator, others when he is the policeman, and still others when he is the friend or the dragon.

The way in which a teacher is able to use his style of leadership in the classroom will be greatly influenced by colleagues, representatives of the "school system," parents and particularly by the principal to whom the teacher is responsible. For one of the themes that gets conveyed to the class very early is the fact that no group, no matter how autonomous it wants or seems to be, can long exist without relating to other groups. The pressures and boundaries that are exerted on the students are often as stringently, or even more stringently, exerted on the teachers. When Miss Greene's engrossing project on planets which everyone is interested in and excited by must be dropped because the supervisor insists that reading be taught not by the project method but by the guide book on phonics and visual recognition, the children are quickly aware that teacher is not the top boss. The children's recognition of this kind of fact brings with it the recognition that the mini-god is, like them, subject to influences, boundaries, and controls within which his degrees of freedom are limited, and often in fact thwarted or distorted, by the type of leadership that comes down from above. It would seem then that for learners and teachers alike there is always an "above"—even Moses the Teacher got his mandate from God.

The boundaries for children are different boundaries and imply different privileges, but that is because the tasks of teacher and student are different, as the tasks of administrators and teachers differ. The student's task is to learn; the teacher's task—though, hopefully, he learns too—is to provide opportunities for students to learn. To what extent the teacher's abilities are interfered with from above or by other staff members will depend on the leadership ability of the principal, who is himself also bounded by the reality of the groups that surround him. And so it goes: freedom of choice is so bounded that the teacher often feels helpless. Complete freedom of choice is a dream, and not always a happy one. But even within the boundaries set forth, there is more freedom to choose than most of us use. To the extent that the principal is a self-aware leader, able to negotiate, to fight when a fight can be won, to balk when balking can pay off, to give in when giving in makes sense, and to take the responsibility for his stands and their outcome, the teacher's degree of freedom to teach is increased. If the teacher has learned to use the autonomy he has, his students cannot help but learn something, however osmotically, about being, in some basic way, master of one's fate within the limits of group life—probably the most important lesson for living anyone can learn.

We have postulated, then, a pyramid of power. At the base of this pyramid rests the classroom group. In its own way it affects the entire superstructure. If it collapses, the levels above it are often immobilized—for it is indeed the cornerstone, and if it fails, the entire structure grows shaky.

Formal and informal groupings as well as leadership differ from age group to age group. What is appropriate for one stage of development, may still be necessary, though now inappropriate for another. Frequently, a group, whether of twelfth-graders, college sophomores, or graduate students—or even of parents or congressmen or businessmen—will behave in such a way that the only leadership possible is that appropriate to the kindergarten. But we all tend to develop unevenly and as we grow, our needs, even more than our demands, require an increasing variety of leadership. We shall see later what kinds of leadership are appropriate to different developmental needs, but first there are elements common to our needs at all ages that are worth looking into, for they are necessary at all levels.

Within a group larger than five, there are always subgroups. Since nearly all classroom groups are a good deal larger, their subgroups loom even greater in importance. The fate of the entire group, including that of the teacher, can be determined by a subgroup. A teacher who is unaware of the subgroups that form, break up and re-form in new patterns, is as much at the mercy of events as a general who does not know that one of his divisions has surrendered to the enemy, while another has withdrawn behind the lines, and a third is planning a coup. To be aware of the changing tides of subgroup splits and realignments, of the purposes for which they form and what they achieve, is in itself a task essential to successful classroom management, yet that subject is a gaping vacuum in the training of most teachers. Fortunately, there are teachers who seem to have an inborn talent for spotting alignments and for putting the leadership that emerges to good use. Such teachers have fingertip awareness about which pairs should be separated and which encouraged, and about which subgroup has become destructive to the task of the whole group and has to be stopped, even though it costs a lesson plan, a dose of extra energy, the scratching of a planned schedule. They know also which subgroup rebellions will wear themselves out without interference, no matter how flamboyant they look for the moment, and which will not. But such teachers are rare and the rest of us less gifted souls need experience and training.

A basic primer concerning subgroups might include the following rules:

Rule 1   The larger the class, the more naturally formed subgroups there are, and this is a good thing, for it facilitates getting work done. Any administrator knows the hopelessness of getting any job done—even the licking of envelopes—if a large number is involved; we all know small communities function more effectively than large. The difficult task for the teacher is to know what the subgroups are, how they interact with one another, how they function and for what purposes, overt and covert. The smoothest functioning subgroup may be one the teacher is unaware of, a sub-rosa group formed specifically for the purpose of sabotaging work. If a teacher can recognize the reasons behind the natural subgrouping, he can skillfully make use of this awareness to get work done in the variety of group tasks occurring in a school day.

For instance, when a teacher discovers, by having collected notes being passed between Connie and Tess, that a girls' club—The Secret Six—has been formed for meeting in lunch and play periods daily for the purpose of prying loose other people's secrets, she may be able to interest the girls in studying the history of secret service and spying in the American Revolution or Civil War or at present.

Rule 2 Out of the subgroups emerge child or youth leaders with varying capacity to lead. Any leader may make bad mistakes that will defeat him or the group's mission. Any leader, by virtue of his having taken on, or been given, leadership, will be the target for attack—obvious or subtle, conscious or unconscious. Rivals will appear and either vanquish or vanish. Frequently, the most talented leaders have a quite different agenda from the teacher's. If the work of the group becomes too frustrating or too chaotic, too hard or too easy, or even just too boring, it is likely the teacher-approved leader will be dethroned and another one chosen. The new leader may be more effective—he may well divert the group to a task counter to the work in hand.

The most remarkable examples of leadership sometimes come from delinquent gangs or street groups. How leadership emerges, how it is challenged and tested, and how to deal with its impermanence is developed is something that appears to be close to instinctual among animals, as Lorenz points out in his book *On Aggression*. Among humans, perceptions of the sort are dramatically documented by Piri Thomas in his autobiographical account of his youth in the barrio, *Down These Mean Streets* (Alfred A. Knopf, 1967). Since Thomas brings out dramatically all the basic elements of the emergence of leadership, the passage is worth quoting:

> We were moving—our new pad was back in Spanish Harlem—to 104th Street between Lex and Park Avenue.
>
> Moving into a new block is a big jump for a Harlem kid. You're torn up from your hard-won turf and brought into an "I don't know you" block where every kid is some kind of enemy. Even when the block belongs to your own people, you are still an outsider who has to prove himself a down stud with heart.
>
> As the moving van rolled to a stop in front of our new building, number 109, we were all standing there, waiting for it—Momma, Poppa, Sis, Paulie, James, Jose, and myself. I made out like I didn't notice the cats looking us over, especially me—I was gang age. I read their faces and found no trust, plenty of suspicion, and a glint of rising hate. I said to myself, *These cats don't mean*

nothin'. They're just nosy. But I remembered what had happened to me in my old block, and that it had ended with me in the hospital.

This was a tough-looking block. That was good, that was cool; but my old turf had been tough, too. *I'm tough enough. I am tough enough. I've got mucho corazon, I'm king wherever I go. I'm a killer to my heart. I not only can live, I will live, no punk out, no die out, walk bad; be down, cool breeze, smooth.* My mind raced, and thoughts crashed against each other, trying to reassemble themselves into a patter of rep. I turned slowly and with eyelids half-closed I looked at the rulers of this new world and with a cool shrug of my shoulders I followed the movers into the hallway of number 109 and dismissed the coming war from my mind.

The next morning I went to my new school, called Patrick Henry, and strange, mean eyes followed me.

"Say, pops," said a voice belonging to a guy I later came to know as Waneko, "where's your territory?"

In the same tone of voice Waneko had used, I answered, "I'm on it, dad, what's shaking?"

"Bad, huh?" he half-smiled.

"No, not all the way. Good when I'm down."

"What's your name, kid?"

"That depends. 'Piri' when I'm smooth and 'Johnny Gringo' when stomping time's around."

"What's your name now?" he pushed.

"You name me, man," I answered, playing my role like a champ.

He looked around, and with no kind of words, his boys cruised in. Guys I would come to know, to fight, to hate, to love, to take care of. Little Red, Waneko, Little Louie, Indio, Carlito, Alfredo, Crip, and plenty more. I stiffened and said to myself, *Stomping time, Piri boy, go with heart.*

I fingered the garbage-can handle in my pocket—my homemade brass knuckles. They were great for breaking down large odds into small, chopped-up ones.

Waneko, secure in his grandstand, said, "We'll name you later, *panin.*"

I didn't answer. Scared, yeah, but wooden-faced to the end, I thought, *Chevere, panin.*

It wasn't long in coming. Three days later, at about 6 P.M., Waneko and his boys were sitting around the stoop at number 115.

I was cut off from my number 109. For an instant I thought, *Make a break for it down the basement steps and through the back yards —get away in one piece!* Then I thought, *Caramba! Live punk, dead hero. I'm no punk kid. I'm not copping any pleas.* I kept walking, hell's a burning, hell's a churning, rolling with cheer. *Walk on, baby man, roll on without fear. What's he going to call?*

"Whatta ya say, Mr. Johnny Gringo?" drawled Waneko.

Think man, I told myself, think your way out of a stomping. Make it good. "I hear you 104th Street coolies are supposed to have heart," I said. "I don't know this for sure. You know there's a lot of streets where a whole 'click' is made out of punks who can't fight one guy unless they all jump him for the stomp." I hoped this would push Waneko into giving me a fair one. His expression didn't change.

"Maybe we don't look at it that way."

Crazy, man. I cheer inwardly, the cabron is falling into my setup. We'll see who gets messed up first, baby!

"I wasn't talking to you," I said. "Where I come from, the pres is president 'cause he got heart when it comes to dealing."

Waneko was starting to look uneasy. He had bit on my worm and felt like a sucker fish. His boys were now light on me. They were no longer so much interested in stomping me as in seeing the outcome between Waneko and me. "Yeah," was his reply.

I smiled at him. "You trying to dig where I'm at and now you got me interested in you. I'd like to see where you're at."

Waneko hesitated a tiny little second before replying, "Yeah."

I knew I'd won. Sure, I'd have to fight; but one guy, not ten or fifteen. If I lost I might still get stomped. I took care of this with my next sentence. "I don't know you or your boys," I said, "but they look cool to me. They don't feature as punks."

I had left him out purposely when I said *they.* Now his boys were in a separate class. I had cut him off. He would have to fight me on his own, to prove his heart to himself, to his boys, and most important, to his turf. He got away from the stoop and asked, "Fair one, Gringo?"

"Uh-uh," I said, "roll all the way—anything goes." I thought, *I've got to beat him bad and yet not bad enough to take his pres-tige all away. He had corazon.* He came on me. *Let him draw first blood,* I thought, *it's his block.* Smish, my nose began to bleed. His boys cheered, his heart cheered, his turf cheered. "Waste this chump," somebody shouted.

Okay, baby, now it's my turn. He swung. I grabbed innocently, and my forehead smashed into his nose. His eyes crossed. His fingernails went for my eye and landed in my mouth—crunch, I bit hard. I punched him in the mouth as he pulled away from me, and he slammed his foot into my chest.

We broke, my nose running red, my chest throbbing, his finger —well, that was his worry. I tied up with body punching and slugging. We rolled onto the street. I wrestled for acceptance, he for rejection or, worse yet, acceptance on his terms. It was time to start peace talks. I smiled at him. "You got, heart, baby," I said.

He answered with a punch to my head. I grunted and hit back, harder now. I had to back up my overtures of peace with strength. I hit him in the ribs, I rubbed my knuckles in his ear as we clinched. I tried again. "You deal good," I said.

"You too," he muttered, pressuring out. And just like that, the fight was over. No more words. We just separated, hands half up, half down. My heart pumped out, *You've established your rep. Move over, 104th Street. Lift your wings, I'm one of your baby chicks now.*

Five seconds later my spurs were given to me in the form of introductions to streetdom's elite. There were no looks of blankness now: I was accepted by heart.

"What's your other name, Johnny Gringo?"

"Piri."

"Okay, Pete, you wanna join my fellows?"

"Sure, why not?"

But I knew I had first joined their gang when I cool-looked them on moving day. *I was cool, man,* I thought. *I could've wasted Waneko any time. I'm good, I'm damned good, pure corazon.* Viva me! Shit, I had been scared, but that was over. I was in; it was my block now.

Not that I could relax. In Harlem you always lived on the edge of losing rep. All it takes is a one-time loss of heart . . .

This excerpt indicates a number of sophisticated aspects of leadership worth examining. For one, there are the nonverbal cues that Piri picks up in casing the group he wants to enter and eventually lead or co-lead—walk cool, be smooth, play down emotion—"I turned slowly and with eyelids half closed" . . . "with a cool shrug of the shoulders," etc. Secondly, we note throughout the restraint and the discipline Piri shows, despite his desire for the struggle, his fear of it and his full awareness of the possibility of defeat and damage, both physical and psychological. Thirdly, there is, even in the heat of confrontation, the knowledge that feelings and strength are not enough—"Think man . . . think your way out of a stomping." There is, fourthly, a mastery of timing: Don't make a grab for leadership—don't do it all in one day. Wait till the moment is ripe and the circumstances optimal. Develop patience—wait, and outwait, but not too long. Finally, note the mastery of strategy—"I'd left him out purposely . . . I had cut him off. He would have to fight me on his own." These are the elements of a true leader. They emerge in the classroom, often to be knocked down by the authorities, sometimes permanently. If recognized and used in class or at home, they may not have to be used in antisocial ways.

How can a teacher use the leadership chosen by the children? If that leadership is unusable or destructive, how can a teacher channel it or counter it effectively without destroying talent or setting up more dangerous resistance? The example from Piri Thomas is as notable for implicit tact and the respect it shows for the other guy as for successful performance. A teacher or parent could well take lessons.

Since no leader can lead a group that will not follow, it becomes the teacher's job to support and strengthen leadership that can be harnessed in the service of learning or growth. For instance, one might allow a group to elect a popular even if not well-organized boy to manage and arrange a class trip, giving help when a skill is needed, and making suggestions, but not interfering or taking over when sins of omission and commission appear. Carried out in a nonpunitive fashion, such an experience could teach more than a thousand "but you must" interventions. It could show the popular lad selected that it takes more than charm to lead. It could teach him to organize, or at least to delegate well. It could teach the class group that popularity in itself does not get a necessary task done, and that charisma is not the best basis for choice, not a substitute for skill. The fact that that trip may be less than perfect, or that it may need first aid from others or even have to be postponed, disappointing as that may be, is frequently less a learning loss than a teacher-patched trip in which the implicit lesson is *"No one but adults can really do anything"* (which is a myth we adults often contribute to perpetuating).

The lesson is leadership can, if openly received by the class, indicate where leadership has messed itself up. Ultimately, learning leadership and its duties, burdens and satisfaction is a major need in our society, and teaching it is teaching for the future. More immediately, if student leadership is given leeway for experimentation and error in the classroom, it can become a teacher's primary aid, more effective than any adult leadership can be.

Corollary to Rule 2   Often the best bet for leadership material is the defiant fellow or independent lass who can and sometimes will cause mayhem in the class by gathering willing followers for the purpose of disruption or sabotage. Another good bet is the one who seldom comes to the front, but somehow is always where the action is, the one who feeds the series of toppled leaders his ideas and program for group procedure. Lust for power is an easy motivation—we all have it, whether we use it or not. Therefore, it is not hard to capture the attention of a power-seeking child and get him to become more effective in his use of his personal resources. The results are often not what the teacher intends, but the learning that results is no less valuable. What is hard is to teach the penalties of the responsibilities that come with authority—pain usually teaches that. (See *Autobiography of Malcolm X, Jesus Christ, Super Star, Thirteen Days*, or the life of Robert Kennedy.)

Rule 3   A teacher who wishes to make up teacher-selected subgroups for particular work-tasks such as reading or arithmetic, physics or shop, mural-making or current-events discussion, would do well to note within a particular class not only the leadership choices, but the character and form of the subgroups and know how they have evolved. One can find out where leaders are—in the cafeteria, the bus, the playground, the halls, or among the cliques and clubs of girls who cluster in the locker rooms, the teams and gangs of boys who hang around the playground after school.

To discover something about leadership and followership it is useful, surprisingly enough, to study the ones who are always, no matter how groups combine, "out of it," or on the precipitous edge. It is not enough simply to observe; one has to notice what temporary or basic needs are being met or left unmet by the various combinations that are made; what pace, what level of communication exist; what caring for and being cared for; what forms of rejection and bullying and scapegoating are being sought out, and what talents are consistently being overlooked by one particular class that might well be sought after in another. A group has a style or temperament as much as an individual. It just takes more work to determine it. Some children get lost in one group and are found in another. Some are too committed loners or too internally tied up or too ignorant of social skills to join any group. A teacher can help a child within a group to see in what ways he asks for the role he is assigned and show him how he can gain the confidence and the skill to alter his role if he wishes to. Hard and painful though this changing of roles may be, it is through that suffering that one grows up. A teacher can, if he has recognized the force of the group, decide to switch a child out of a subgroup in which the child has either been "out of it" without hope of change, or been compelled to follow in sheep-like fashion without stretching his mind or behavior patterns, or one in which, perhaps, he has too easily won leadership and is experiencing no challenge. A teacher can teach a child the social skills needed to achieve a group role useful to him and others.

The usual arbitrary grouping based on IQ or achievement is often self-defeating. To function properly, a group requires a bit of everything. What does not work is a homogeneity of personality, where either everybody or nobody wants to lead; where no one can help anyone else because everyone knows everything or nothing; and where no one can be helped without belittling his own competence because he doesn't really need help; where everyone talks at once, or where everyone is withdrawn or a passive dreamer or a hesitant mumbler. There is nothing about IQ or achievement level per se that arranges for the various members of the group to be different enough to complement each other. True, one ought not hold a gifted fellow back because another child hasn't begun to catch on to a concept and may never do so, nor ought one try to push a slower child beyond his ability to cope—but between these extremes, within an average class of 25 to 30 children there is an infinite variety of talent not discoverable by IQ or AQ (Achievement Quotient). If one observes carefully how children select one another, one sees they do not exclusively pick leaders of their own kind, but that as in many surprising marriage combinations that work, they pick people who may have some things in common with them, but are in personality, behavior, and mental bent quite different from themselves. Such focused observations on the part of the teacher help him to be free to use trial and error as a means of group selection. Heterogeneous grouping adds seasoning to replace the boredom that sooner or later occurs in homogenized groups.

Rule 4 The periodic switching of members from subgroup to subgroup is sometimes a good way to break up stultifying cliques or embattled rivalries, as well as to minimize the erosive effects of the upper, middle and lower strata-levels that set in and become fossilized among children and teachers alike, so that somewhere about the fourth grade it is likely that a child, his parents, and his teachers all collude in setting him in a niche as hard to get out of as it is hard to climb out of the poverty class in our society. Moreover, there is for young and old an unstated lesson to be learned from the experience of finding oneself in new groups. Here are some quotes from twelve- and thirteen-year-olds after two switches of groups a month apart from each other:

> I'm always quiet the first couple of days in a group. Maybe I'm shy or maybe I need to know where the land lies before I risk myself.

> I can't stand the silence. I have to barge in no matter how much of a fool I make of myself.

> I guess I like to take over—I always see what's up and then get someone to join up with me and I'm off—every group I'm in.

I must be a loner. I don't know what happens. They always seem a tight little group and I end up outside. Oh, I make a few stabs at joining, but if anyone rejects me—that's the end and I'm back on the benches alone.

I feel terrible. I always manage to shine up to the teacher—as if I need her to protect me or something. I know the kids hate me for it, and I hate myself—but I always do the same darn thing.

You know, I think it's fun. I'm pretty quiet in groups, but I find I can always find someone whom I can egg on. Sometimes I just grin, or poke someone or hand them something and soon he gets into trouble or starts some action. The teacher nearly always blames the other guy, but I'm the one—and she doesn't know it.

When a person becomes aware of his own repetitive behavior, he can begin to do something about it, especially if he has the help of a teacher who can arrange groups on the basis of the need of a child not to feel trapped into a derogatory image of himself, or conversely, not to be carried away with his own importance.

IQ and achievement groupings not only fail to give opportunity for such help, but also pigeonhole the child, often inaccurately. And these inaccuracies often have irreversible effects. Certain children have struggled and strained to the breaking point because, with an IQ of 87, they were set in a high school Honors Group on the basis of having been placed, in elementary school, in A-level reading and arithmetic groups and having caused no trouble there. Likewise, and more frequently, I have known very alert, quick children to be forever doomed to C and D groups, either because they took tests poorly, or because their pace of development was not what the teacher expected, or simply because they had once been fidgety, restless, naughty children within their subgroups and so had been placed in low-achievement groups on the basis of an unwritten nuisance rating. There may even have been nothing wrong in the original placement; the child might have done well in his assigned group and contributed well to the group's progress. But what was wrong was that the teacher had come to look at the subgroup assignment as a diagnostic truth, and so had seen the child as delivered to the school in a given box, packaged, wrapped and labeled. Once he had been so labeled, his peers, his parents, his other teachers and, far worst of all, he himself had come to accept the label assigning him to a permanent role in life.

A recent innovation in teaching may help solve such problems of group placement—the "open classroom" or "learning center." In the "learning center" two to four teachers are stationed in a central place to be available to children in their various tasks— Social Studies, Arithmetic, Language Arts, Sciences, and Expressive Arts. Architecturally, centers are set up for home-room groups made up of children of approximately the same age. But in many learning centers, pupils from any of the adjacent classes, roughly grouped within three or four grade levels, may go to any one of the center teachers to get help with tasks in specific areas. In many cases, where the teachers are content with the situation and can adjust to the variety of ages and to the demands made upon them, this is a most successful innovation. Such open centers literally stand or fall on the teacher's ability to use subgroups, not as they have been set up beforehand but rather as they relate to the specific tasks at hand. This is indeed an idea for grouping that should be investigated further. Time and again we have found that success in putting learning centers or "open classrooms" into effect requires that the teachers themselves be carefully oriented, not only to their new tasks, but also to experiences of large and small groups. Without such experience, many are too uncomfortable to give the plan the chance it deserves.

To put it another way, no classroom with more than ten children can fully meet the children's needs or serve the aims of the teacher, whether these involve subject matter or human relations and behavior, unless the teacher understands the nature of groups and subgroups. To achieve real understanding teachers need not only insight, observation skills and common sense, but personal experience of the underlying nature of groups themselves. This kind of training has been so far rare and spotty. Methods of providing it are discussed in Chapter XII.

III

A Framework of Theory
About Group Life

To COME to understand the specific problems of school-related groups in and out of the classroom, we need to look at some of the forces that make groups do what they do—to themselves and to their leaders—and to see how they let what is done to them be done. What theories of human behavior have we to explain the subtleties and complexities that make up group behavior? Let us first visit a few groups, see what happens in each, and then explore some theories as to the basic forces that impel groups in general.

Group 1—A Science Class

First day in a seventh grade chemistry lab. We note the usual witch's array of boiling glass globes, the blue flame of the Bunsen burner, the acrid smell of sulphur. Instruments lie on the zinc desk. Instead of chairs there are stools, and the teacher has on a white lab coat reminiscent to the students of the doctor's office. The children's postures, as they file in, express emotions that run the gamut from curiosity and excitement—cover-up signs of fear and awe—to total lack of interest. There are some giggles and some holding of noses about the smell, some pointing of fingers at the jars of blue and yellow bubbling substances. There are the smart alecks who have chemistry sets at home and rightly or wrongly are labeling everything. Some, as their defense against the strange, new experience, are talking of Frankenstein and the making of monsters. The teacher is a good teacher, aware of the anxiety aroused by the beginning of new things—the strange and the threatening. He describes what the children see before them. Five boys reach out to touch the bubbling blue jar. He tells them about what they may touch, and what may burn or poison or explode. He points to the containers and tools on the desks. "What would that be for, Johnny?" he asks. "How do you think we could use this? How would you lift it if it were half full of carbolic acid?" "Let's act all that out now and pretend to be scientists," he suggests, demonstrating tool after tool, material after material.

And so, by careful specific directions, with limits carefully defined as to where and how and why one uses this or that tool or material, he transforms the strange into the understandable and takes on a full measure of leadership. He repeats what he has said and done again and again, not only because everyone forgets, but in order to familiarize the class with the purpose of all this apparatus. The children are, this first time at least, utterly dependent on the judgment of the teacher to tell them, to warn them, to show them, and to supervise their moves and rescue them when things get too risky or out of hand. When children clown or horse around, they are reproved or sent packing. Thus, the boundaries are clearly defined, with the responsibility clearly placed on the teacher; both the danger and the excitement of learning new concepts and the use of the new tools are made as clear as any new experience can be made. Later, the children will be expected to do more on their own. Since today and for the next few times they are novices, it is expected that as a group they will be dependent on the teacher for their safety in the work at hand. What is taken in will vary according to particular talents of each individual group member as he listens and experiments. Since these tools can be dangerous, the margin for error is sharply limited; there cannot be as much freedom of exploration as there might be in an English or history class. Still, a wise teacher prepares within the bounds of safety a certain margin for error, knowing that learning occurs this way too.

This type of teaching job is based on instruction and rehearsal for doing. The class's job for the present is to be dependent—dependent not only on the teacher's knowledge but also on his judgment concerning his use of language, his apportionment of time, all in relation to the age of the children. Leadership in an English, French or history class can, of course, be as educative and appropriate, but the danger of bodily harm being absent, the English or history or language teacher's leadership can allow a greater margin for error and a wider range of initial independent exploration. In other words, a science teacher and a language arts teacher may each be exhibiting a full measure of appropriate leadership and still be quite different from one another. The content and materials of the task determine how and to what extent each one will assume control to get the work done. This type of group teaching—where the teacher imparts information and skill—is the major, though not the only, method of teacher leadership. The teacher is aware of the class's dependency and uses it consciously in the service of the work.

Group 2—A Busing Experience

In a school in which a great deal of busing was going on, certain black children were being bused to what had before been a very clique-y upper middle class school. The bused-in children tended to be late because of transportation difficulties. Day after day, by the time they got to school the limited number of textbooks available already had been given out. Class seating was such that few of the bused-in children were situated so they could share a book with the non-bused-in students. The teacher, though her words denied discrimination, acted out her actual feelings by criticizing or punishing students who hadn't done their work for the day, and these were almost invariably the bused-in blacks. These black bused-in students came from middle-class homes as well as ghetto homes, so that they were as different from one another as the original middle-class white students were from the ghetto students. The bused-in students got together to protest. Fearing the punitiveness of the teacher and believing their protest would not be heard by the principal or their classmates, they planned and carried out a fight after school between themselves and their white classmates. Enough chaos came out of this fight to cause many of the bused-in students to be temporarily suspended and severely criticized. Even so, their complaints were heard. The solution, interestingly enough, came through the seeming objects of the fight—the white children. Some of these children, when the smoke had cleared and the sense of outrage diminished, learned what that particular fight had been about. They too got together as a group, and, with some of the black bused-in students, decided to challenge the teacher who they agreed was biased. They re-seated themselves in such a way that bused and non-bused students sat together in alternating rows and side by side. Thus, they could share the limited number of texts, and uncompleted work decreased to the usual expectation, across the board, for black and white, bused-in and walk-in students.

Though this togetherness of the group became more real and less dramatic as time went on, it remained clear that what had made the group come together in the first place was their recognition of a common enemy—the teacher. The leadership in this case was in the children; it was motivated by a negative force, the teacher. It was appropriate leadership for the purpose of getting the work done. The mode chosen was planning because in this instance that seemed the way to get at the teacher whose ways were militating against work getting done.

Group 3—A Faculty Revolt

A committee instigated by the teachers of a school got together in order to present to the principal a list of grievances against his management; they wanted to show him how his behavior affected their teaching. Up to that time, the faculty of this particular high school had been notably uncohesive, but now the attack on the principal unified it. The principal had long been known throughout the community as an exceptionally bright, creative innovator. But the faculty objected to his efforts to upgrade the school, holding that he, though a black man, was taking over white values and deserting his own people. They said he was using the school as a political stepping-stone and forgetting the welfare of students and teachers alike. They complained that he was seldom available to the staff because he was so busy reforming everything that he had forgotten his first loyalty—loyalty to his job, to the school. The immediate plan of the committee was to send a petition to the principal, and then, if it went unheeded by him, to forward it to the school board; this eventually was done. On some of the issues raised the faculty had much evidence, especially in regard to the principal's unavailability to them.

However, as the staff was finally getting together at a meeting where the sole task was to draft a resolution, subterranean antagonisms broke out. The fight was led by two people, a man and a woman. The man was bitter that the principal had been appointed over his seniority and felt personally vindictive. The woman, a counselor, had once been close to the principal, but now felt personally neglected because of his political life; she resented others claiming the attention of her old friend. Other individual grievances, too, both major and minor, had been accumulating, without proper outlet or communication with the principal. If the principal had allowed earlier meetings to express anger and annoyance as they arose, that might indeed have caused him temporary anguish, but it would probably have prevented the group's final getting together as a "lynch mob" that in the end did indeed have the principal removed from the school for which he had tried to do so much good. The staff group, on the other hand, lost without firm and appointed leadership, had found itself unable to get together in unity even when they had anger as a common bond until leadership for expressing this anger became apparent. The pairing of two who had been rivals before, the jealous assistant principal and the hurt counselor, now not only allowed the group to unify around them, but also to place the task of ousting the principal in their hands. The product of their union was revolution and new leadership. The counselor and assistant principal were, however, only temporary leaders who could retain their roles only while the task was ousting the principal; they did not have the skill to maintain leadership in the job of administering the school. Eventually their leadership gave way to that of a newly appointed, much more conventional, in-house principal whose program threatened no one. The school now settled back into being the mediocre, unimaginative place it had been before the advent of the reforming, now ousted principal.

Group 4—An Experience in School Mismanagement

Because of poor administration in a center which included a five-class treatment school for disturbed children, the overall agency director had left, and his experienced principal soon decided to follow him. He left on Labor Day when it was too late for the newly appointed school director to find a replacement. The assistant principal took over the post of principal; he was a young man full of defenses, inexperienced in supervisory skills and clinical knowledge of disturbed children. He did not foresee the anxiety-provoking effects of the total situation on the teaching staff. The school director's job was complicated by the fact that many experienced teachers had left with the original director and principal, leaving only a few experienced teachers among many brand-new ones. As the year progressed in that five-classroom school, each class containing very disordered children who needed stability, sophisticated understanding and special methods of education on the part of the adults around them, four teachers resigned, one in January, one in February, one in March and one in June.

The leadership in this school at that time was in flux and unpredictable. New panaceas—each differing markedly from the one before it—were desperately grabbed at and tried out, sometimes monthly, sometimes even weekly. There were nine children in each class. The difficulty of teaching and managing disturbed children required that more than one adult was needed in a class of nine children. Yet a single teacher had all nine. When this arrangement failed, as it inevitably had to, the failure caused the exodus of more than one teacher and much turmoil and upset to the children. It was then decided to hire aides—after the horses had run from the barn, so to speak. Instead of having expert and intensified supervision of aides and teachers to replace staff casualties as they began to mount, the remaining staff was criticized and taken to task in front of the already upset children. The new director, though educationally sophisticated himself, had by now given this year up as a loss and was concentrating largely on providing for the future—probably rightly. By the end of the year, the director had a clean sweep of staff to start anew, for nearly all the original teachers had by then resigned. Personnel decisions were complicated by unresolved racial issues which muddied administrative, clinical and educational policies.

These four vignettes illustrate a number of points about leadership in schools. The story of the science teacher illustrates a leadership appropriate to the task of education—a leading of children out of naïveté to knowledge by a person secure in his knowledge of his subject and his audience. The genuine dependency needs of the children being taught were met in the service of the work-task. This sort of leadership makes for a successful work group.

The story about busing tells of a leadership that emerged from the student group itself as the effect of a negative factor: An important nucleus representing the disparate black and white upper and lower income groups got together against a common enemy—the biased teacher, and after a fight, prevented the appointed leadership from destroying the work-task: that of giving everyone in the class an equal opportunity to learn in accordance with the individual's ability. Here by means of a fight and subgroup dialogue, the leadership in the student group took over, defeating the counter-work leader—the teacher.

In the third vignette we saw a staff, who as a group resented abandonment by their absent leader. This group produced a leadership-pair who reflected the animosity felt by the whole group, both because of the changes demanded of them, and because of feelings of desertion in the group. The pair chosen united the group and succeeded in leading it to free itself of the original leader, who, creative as he was, had proved unable to exert leadership in the particular arena where he was supposed to be leading.

In the fourth vignette, we saw how poor agency administration filtered down, bit by bit, to destroy the possibility of accomplishing the assigned work-task—that of directing teaching and treating disturbed children in a special-education treatment school. The overall agency administrator had shown himself ignorant of psychological and educational needs; his behavior had interfered with school policy. The new director, though himself educationally skilled and group-wise found he had inherited a mess. A special problem of leadership focused on the defensive inexperienced, assistant principal who had taken over as principal. Through his lack of knowledge, and his inability to delegate duties, his failure to trust or support his staff, he lost four out of his five teachers in the course of the school year through resignation. The fact that racial problems were part of the pie, made it more difficult for the black school director. As a result, work for one year was sacrificed. Still a clean sweep of staff was attained, making possible a fresh start. Some children were hurt; many staff members were rendered incompetent—in fact, some with good potential were so dismayed that they left the special education field for good. The leadership offered here in the school part of a center illustrates the unhappy fact that when top management in an agency is inept, the confusion engendered will seep downward to each branch, bringing in its wake destructive and sometimes tragic consequences.

The questions raised here—questions of goal, task, work, unconscious forces, leadership and followership—involve the basic forces that control the work of all groups—children's groups or adult groups, self-study groups, or learning groups or management groups, treatment groups or politically oriented groups.

When we talk of groups in schools, however, we must consider with special attention the question of how human development affects the character of a group, and what kind of leadership is required in each of the various stages of development.

One convenient and useful theoretic framework for the study of groups comes from Wilfred Bion's *Experiences in Groups*. The concepts Bion formulates are based on his World War II work with RAF casualties in groups where the purpose was to get the men back from the hospital into the air. These concepts have been most useful in helping us to understand the various levels of group life: what a group thinks it needs to do, what forces operate in reference to its leadership, what forces block it from working to achieve its goals, and what goals are actually being pursued, in contrast to the stated goals of the group. Bion's concepts have been concisely summarized by Dr. Margaret Rioch in *Psychiatry*, Vol. 33. They have been amplified and applied in many different settings by many people, particularly noteworthy among them the late Kenneth Rice of the Tavistock Institute. The theoretical ancestors of Bion and Rice are many: among them we may name especially Lewin, Freud, Jung and Klein. In this country, Harry Stack Sullivan's thought has been influential in its application of the concepts we are discussing. Where groups that include age differences are involved, I have found Erikson's concepts, when translated into Bion group insights, especially valuable.

Bion's theories rest on the hypothesis that a group differs from the individuals that make it up though it is of course affected by those individuals. A group gets together for a particular purpose—educational, therapeutic, political, managerial, etc. It thus has a goal. When the group is working well, it pursues its goal effectively, the group members behaving cooperatively and rationally, each taking responsibility for his own part of the work task, each taking leadership when that is appropriate and delegating leadership to other leaders when the task is furthered by so doing.

Any of us who have ever gone to meetings know that this is an ideal—that that is not at all the way groups operate most of the time. On the contrary, much of the time the group appears to

avoid, obfuscate or defeat the work it is presumably trying to
accomplish. Bion and his followers explain this phenomenon on
the basis of the concept that a group is more than the sum of its
parts—that it is a *Gestalt*, a whole, operating within the forces
that influence it. (This idea can be attributed to Lewin's "field
theory.") One of the factors influencing it—a factor the group
often rails against—is the problem of where the boundaries lie—
where this group ends and the other groups begin. Sometimes
boundaries, though they exist, may be "open": a country that has
open immigration, as the United States did in its earlier history,
seems to have "open boundaries." Another force that acts on a
group is time; a group has time boundaries—it begins and it ends:
it has its own mortality. Each session, each class, has its own
beginning and end. But the group often tries to extend these
boundaries. One can see that in such phenomena as the fact that
it is sometimes only in the last five minutes that the real work gets
going, or the fact that some meetings extend far past their scheduled time, or begin long after the announced time. The "Marathon" group is a purposeful extension of time boundaries. But
boundaries are as inevitable as death and taxes! (Rank's theories
are useful here.)

Within the boundaries a group gets together for a work-task or
purpose, but it may behave *as if* the purpose in getting together
was not to do the agreed-upon task but rather to deal with the
problem of leadership. Who is the leader? What will he do for
us, or to us? Shall we let him lead? If not, who will lead us? And
what will happen to the new leader? The work of the group
often, for long periods, becomes focused not on what it has met
to do, but rather on testing what Bion calls "Basic Assumptions"
about the group's relation to its leadership. *All of these assumptions are unconscious*: the group behaves *as if* it had met not
for its stated purpose but *as if* to do quite other things.

One Basic Assumption is that a group is meeting to make the
leader feed its needs, to take care of it, make decisions for it, give
it love and knowledge, and protect it from outside harm or inside
conflict. This Basic Assumption mode Bion calls *Dependency*. If
a leader fails to satisfy the group in this, a group acting in this

mode will try to make the leader do so. If he will not, it may try
to pick one of its own members to give what the appointed
leader will not give. Of course, since the demands are unconscious and unlimited, no leader can meet them, and the energy of
the group is taken up trying to make this un-do-able thing come
to pass. Result—the work task is forgotten. The Dependency
group's purpose is to "*make* George do it." The mode of a group
acting in Basic Assumption Dependency is docile, though there
may be squabbles. It acts *as if* no one but a leader had any skills
or knowledge to contribute to the task. No matter how bright or
competent its members, it acts more stupid than it is in order to
force the leader to take over.

A second Basic Assumption, "*Fight-or-Flight*," has a different
mode. A group acting in this mode behaves as if it had got
together not to do the task at hand but rather to fight or to flee.
It acts *as if* there were a common enemy which it must vanquish
or be vanquished by, escape or be imprisoned by. If it can find no
outside enemy, it will turn upon itself and create civil emigra-
tions. Its mode is suspicious, paranoid, sleuthlike or militaristic.

Bion postulates a third Basic Assumption, which he calls the
"Messianic" Assumption: acting in this mode groups behave *as if*
they had got together for the sole purpose of finding or making a
pair, who will by their pairing create a Messiah. This Messiah is
to save them from themselves; he is to take over for them and do
the job of the group without the members of the group having to
work themselves; they will not need to bear frustration, error,
failure or disappointment or the arduous task of learning. In such
a group the appointed leader is given up as unsatisfactory, and a
pair is chosen to produce the new leader. It is in fact a group
fantasy that proceeds as if it believed that "a little child shall lead
them." In this mode the group behaves in a reverential, optimis-
tic, hopeful fashion . . . until it becomes clear that, of course, no
Messiah will appear, and then the group either reverts to one of
the other Basic Assumptions, or gives up its *as if* life and really
gets to work.

Bion says there may be other Basic Assumptions in which
groups act as if they have met together not to do the task they

consciously know they have met to do, but for some other purpose, one dictated by the group unconscious. Kenneth Rice suggests that one further Basic Assumption of Group Life is that they can all become homogenized, that their individual boundaries will disappear so that they are, or eventually will be, lost in an oceanic amorphous oneness.

It has to be kept in mind that all Basic Assumption life is unconscious. However, although it runs counter to the work task, and is in fact independent of it, a Basic Assumption can be harnessed and put to use by a skilled work-leader. For instance, a military group or a football team, to do their assigned work, might well use Basic Assumption Fight (-or-Flight?) to accomplish their ends. A religious group might use Basic Assumption Pairing, etc.

The Basic Assumptions we have listed may be charted on a developmental scale. For example, our last addition, the "Oceanic Mass" Assumption, in which people are not individuated from one another, would probably be the most like infancy where objects and self, others and self, are undifferentiated. In infancy, life is all one amorphous need, and the adult is seen as an extension of oneself. When a group is acting in that mode, it does not need to challenge the leadership, since the leader is seen as indistinguishable from the followers. Some classes and some therapy groups are led and run in this fashion. They frequently fail to get their work done, for the leader, often unsure of his own identity, so identifies with the group mode that he wants closeness for himself more than he wants to have the work accomplished. Everyone becomes mixed up with others in the group, and the group work, which requires differentiation and different skills, suffers.

Basic Assumption Dependency, which nearly every group exhibits at one time or another, is akin to the early developmental years when Mother and Father are realistically depended on to feed, protect, shelter, and teach, where in fact all answers come from one source. When a group leader fails to be Mother or Father—that is, fails to provide what is asked for—the group becomes depressed, passively hopeless and unable to cope. They then either take to another Basic Assumption mode, or they try to make one of their own members the all-giving parent, or they realistically begin to work.

Bion couples the "Fight" Basic Assumption with "Flight." Biologically, it is true that animals are equipped either to fight or to flee for survival purposes. With humans, however, Fight techniques and reactions usually appear earlier than Flight reactions. One might say that on a developmental scale. Fight is typical of the 9-to-12-year-olds, and that Flight is more characteristic of the 12-to-14-year-olds.

The Basic Assumption Pairing mode we have described matches the developmental phase of adolescence, where sexuality as a power is made manifest biologically and psychologically.

This is not to say that a group sticks with any single kind of unconscious Basic Assumption life. What usually happens is that the group shifts from one to another mode, alternating these modes of retreat with periods of work. A teacher or leader may by style bring about a reaction of one Basic Assumption rather than another; this tendency in the leadership Bion calls having a *valence* toward one mode more frequently than another.

In the early grades, children *are* in fact more dependent than they are later. To do their work, a fourth grade group needs to depend on the adult to show them, to tell them, to indicate how and why and where. Dependency of that sort is conscious and real; it is not part of *Basic Assumption life*. The group here is work-oriented at its own age-level of need. If, however, the fourth grade children behave more like kindergarten children in helplessness and lack of ability to cope, and try to make the teacher satisfy and reassure them, as a smaller child needs to be fed, the group's work will be slowed or stopped, and we may then say they are acting in a Basic Assumption Dependency manner. True, when they are working well, they may indeed be dependent on the teacher to tell them, show them and help them, but that sort of dependency is a *conscious* need in the service of the task; it is quite unlike the Basic Assumption behavior.

From what has been said, it will be clear, I believe, that Bion's concepts derive from a belief in unconscious forces that operate within individuals and determine their behavior. But this behavior is not the same for a group as for its individual members. A group's behavior is more extreme. It might be said that individual dynamics appear as similes—"I feel *like* a murderer"—but a group dynamic exhibits itself as a metaphor: "I *am* (We are) the murderer of the leader." The concept of these joint unconscious forces is reminiscent not only of the teachings of Lewin, but also of those of Jung and Klein. The concept that personal history affects present behavior and decision-making of course owes its origin to Freud. So does the conviction that unconscious forces work simultaneously with conscious forces. The defenses that arise in the personality to keep the conscious ignorant of the unconscious were originally described by Freud and Anna Freud.

Looking at the development of children as they grow from kindergarten through high school or drop-out time, we note that group forces, the reactions to leadership, the readiness or ability to stick to work and complete a task, can be fitted into the Erikson chart of the stages of human behavior (see pages 76–77). Erikson was interested in groups as a natural habitat for the study of growth and development. He followed Freud's formulations but extended them further by seeing the child in his social milieu, affected by his parents' values, income level, and cultural background. Study of the group forces for and against work, forces directed toward or against apparent leadership, must of course include study of the inner dynamics of individual members of the group; but for Erikson, as for Bion and Rice, study of the group had to include also awareness of the impact of the group's social values.

The developmental scale Erikson offers is more like the Cathedral of Coventry than like the Walls of the Old City of Jerusalem: instead of the newer structure being superimposed upon old ruins as in Jerusalem, the old and the new exist side by side, as at Coventry, encompassing at once the then, the now, and the hope for tomorrow. Erikson's formulations exist securely side by side with Freud's. He elaborates Freudian concepts to express what he thinks happens in the social life of human beings as, from birth through life to death, they use their energy to grapple with the conflicts of growth. Like Freud, Erikson uses symbols as a shorthand means of describing a large collection of hypotheses drawn from clinical data. In Freud's schema, the concepts of ego, super-ego and id are metaphors derived from clinical experience with the ill. Erikson's data are based on experience with the normal as well as with the deviant in samplings of different cultures. Erikson emphasizes the impact of the culture on the expression of inner conflicts and the struggles of men through the stages of growth from crib to deathbed. Erikson describes the ways people learn to cope with the groups they live with from childhood on—the family they grow up in, the school, their peers and colleagues, the families they generate, and society at large.

As individuals we know only too well that we never quite leave our infantile and childish longings and modes of expression behind. They crop up in irrational, insistent claims to be taken care of beyond our real needs, in temper tantrums as uncontrollable as those of any three-year-old (if better concealed), in fights over who is best, and in sulks and withdrawals when we fail to get our way. But since a group becomes in force of expression more than the individuals who make it up, participation in groups shows us up to ourselves, graphically, and sometimes most unpleasantly, as the infants we often are or as the two-year-olds or ten-year-olds we carry within us. We may be able to conceal and control this primary self when alone or with one or two others, but in a group of any duration there is no way of permanently hiding the primary self beneath. We may, as adults, flatter ourselves and insult adolescents by calling our behavior adolescent. In a group we are sometimes lucky if we find ourselves up as far up as adolescence on the developmental scale. For this reason, it is essential to see what the forces are down there that can get whirled into motion in any group.

Because of the pressures of group life in all its variety, none of the stages of development one has passed through ever wholly disappears. Different basic core conflicts exist at different stages around which all else flows. The behavior and feelings consequent on these conflicts make human needs, demands and reactions at each stage different from those which prevail at other stages of development, but the needs and reactions of all the stages are always there in the wings, ready to emerge, given the proper stimulus, both before and after the period of growth in which they are the central aspects of development.

For instance, as Erikson points out, an infant whose basic need is trust may nevertheless be wriggling and doing back flips to get loose from the hold of his mother, thus indicating the presence (though as yet undeveloped) of a need for autonomy and the expression of personal will. Or a mature man may in time of crisis wisely, or unwisely, consciously or unconsciously, decide to yield the major decisions of his life to a leader for the purpose of achieving some goal he shares in. He may, perhaps, give control of his destiny to a Hitler, or to a religious leader, or even to his wife. Such dependency and trust may prove well placed or disastrously misplaced; whichever it may in the end turn out to be, it is nonetheless an abdication of decision-making. The step may be undertaken for a brief time or a long time; because of a personal necessity or because of a social edict such as a military draft or life on a battle front. Whatever the case, to abdicate decision-making results in a return to a more infantile mode—a dependency stage of followership appropriate and necessary for an infant, but not for an adult—at least not most of the time.

Each stage of development carries with it a mandate for the kind of leader who will satisfy the needs of that stage. If the assigned leader of a group does not fill those needs, the work of the group is in jeopardy. For that reason, it is essential that a school team take pains to study the style of leadership proposed, and see what kind of followers that style is likely to attract.

All the various theories, then, are needed. Let me sum up my own methods of putting them to use: In working, as one must do in schools, with the growing and grown human beings in groups, I have found it useful to think first of the Bion and Rice formulation of group life, of the problems of leadership and authority and responsibility that are involved in getting work done. I have found it useful next to consider Freud and Jung's concept of unconscious forces as determining behavior, and to recognize that group behavior, which often seems to go counter to the work-task and against what the group thinks it wants, is always in fact based on the need of the group members to act out the group's own collective formula or history, especially in relation to the appointed leader of the group, the teacher. If one then takes into account Sullivan's and Erikson's contributions, one sees the impact of the social forces on personality development, and thus the picture of personality development in the individuals and in the group. As we combine all these theories, the many and often confusing aspects of group life, as it goes from one stage to another, become clearer. Fritz Redl contributes one of the best pragmatic theories of children's group life.

Application of all these ideas would help us in the selection of teachers to fit a specific age group and situation. For instance, an accepting and giving teacher—a Mother Earth figure—might be exactly what is needed for a first-grade class on whom inordinate demands for performance have been made, and for whom too high standards have been set. But such a person would be an inappropriate choice for a college-preparatory class, or a vocational class where precision instruments are being used and high standards of performance are really essential. Children who lack trust in adults have to achieve that trust before they can learn; thus, the first work-task of their teacher would be to instill a measure of trust. For such children a teacher who was inconsistent, unstable or often absent would be disastrous, especially to the very distrusting, the disturbed, the very young, or those traumatized by earlier negative experiences. But that, in fact, has been in large part the black experience with white teachers. So traumatized have black children been by the distrust engendered by whites, that a white teacher is, per se, suspect; the white teacher who is to teach blacks has to be selected for double doses of reliability. Indeed, it may be easier to have blacks teach blacks at the early stages, though later on the inclusion of stable whites becomes an essential part of the black experience.

Further, knowing what forces control a child at different stages of his growth and then making critical self-evaluation, a teacher may come to see that he is better suited to take on leadership of one particular age group than of another, or to handle the task that is more appropriate to one particular developmental stage, or one particular kind of job, than to another.

But the business of growth is curious. In children emotional growth as well as physical growth often takes place in spurts. A teacher with a given style might not have been able to reach Pete in the beginning of the year, but in July, Pete is ready for that style, and work proceeds surprisingly well. On the other hand, Lucy and her teacher got along together very well in the fall, but by spring Lucy has grown and needs another type of leadership, so she and the teacher are far apart at several points. The well known "class slump" at the end of the year is not always only spring fever, or weariness; it is often caused by the fact that a group has outgrown its teacher's leadership style, and, snake-like, is trying to shed that leadership like so much dry skin.

It is essential to underline too the fact that no stage, however well established, is attained for good; the mountain crest, once reached, eternally slips under our feet and we slide back. Perhaps we fall less far and less chaotically after we have once achieved the summit, but we climb personal and social Himalayas every day. Although we may not need to fall back as far as Sisyphus, life for us is as it was for him, a continuous struggle upwards on the very paths we scaled but yesterday and will scale again tomorrow.

The chart reproduced on pages 76–77 presents a group-focused amplification of Erikson's Epigenetic Chart of the Eight Stages of Human Development. In the chart are noted those aspects of group leadership especially or predominantly necessary at a given developmental stage. A chart, of course, is always simply a convenience. In thinking about the dynamics of the successive stages, one must always keep in mind the constant flow of conflict between the presumed negatives and positives of each stage, and remember that in each stage the negative aspect has its own assets for human growth, which are just as useful as the positive aspects. Many positives can be overdone to the point of grave damage. For instance, trust is the sine qua non of any relationship, but to trust without testing the trustworthiness of the person trusted is prime foolishness. Willfulness makes for autonomy, but it also makes for trouble with authority and interferes with the rights of others. As to negative factors—guilt is usually a destructive feeling, yet without it sensitivity and the sense to know one has hurt someone or has wrecked something may be lost.

Erikson's chart has been expanded to include the Bion concepts. Bion and Erikson would agree that the force of groups may evoke all things in all members. Since each of us keeps those conflicts within us at all times, no one in a group, no matter how objectionable he may seem, no matter how "out of it," or how embarrassingly gushy, can speak or do anything in a group without speaking not only for himself but for a part of each member. The amazing thing is that while no one consciously believes this, if one sticks around and sensitively observes and listens, it always turns out to be true. That unthinking, angry monster opposite one and that simpering soul next to him both speak for something inside oneself and inside the group. At a given moment, moreover, horror upon horror, one finds oneself grateful to either person for acting and expressing those very things one wouldn't be caught dead doing and saying oneself, but that one nevertheless does feel. It may be a part of oneself that one hides from oneself and would rather not see. So much more convenient, then, to be able to push one's own individual unacceptable thoughts or feelings onto someone else! Incidentally, this may help one to understand the need a group has to have people take given group roles—the scapegoat, the bad boy, the on-the-fringe sitter, the monopolizer, the silent critic. Each role has a bit of everyone contained in it. If this seems unbelievable, one need only keep in touch with one's feelings next time one is at a meeting where a group is grappling with an upsetting issue; one finds out rather amazing things about the variety of one's fantasied participation in the group, even if, overtly, one acts much as usual.

One can always tell when a group is playing the group projection game (often with the teacher or leader colluding): "*He* feels that or thinks this or did that; it's not me. How could you think *I* could feel or do anything like that?" But, though one can as a rule feel whether or not the group projection game is being played, there is also a way of testing: Remove the "bad one." Many teachers do this all too readily; it is a major use they like to make of school psychologists: "Get rid of that horrid boy with the vile tongue and the ready fists in my group." Two weeks later, another "bad boy" of like dimensions appears—one who up to now, while the other "bad boy" was there, had not had to be "bad." The trick in handling this game is to be able to accept within oneself the unacceptable, to take on only those roles one can and wants to play, not those the group decides it needs. One does not as a grownup need to experience every role. In exploring group experience, a child may need to try all sorts of remarkable roles on for size. An effective teacher helps the child to take those roles that lead to good rather than poor self-images, but that do not deny the aspects of a child that he may himself not like, that he pretends exist only in other people—not in himself.

Here is another example of group projection: Phil has managed to stop begging the group to make him the fall guy, the excuse. He is no longer the scapegoat. But now we see the group rejoice in the fact that Charles will step into that role. Why do they need a scapegoat? Because a part of each person in that group feels the need to be what the scapegoat represents, even the fellow who is first to "dish it out." If Phil or Charles takes the role, no one else has to see the scapegoat part of himself.

Again, consider the case of Larry. Larry, who was mostly out of the group—the loner on the fringe—has worried the teacher enough so that he has been transferred to another section. The group is now preoccupied with the question: "Where is Larry?" He is far more important to the group in his absence than he was when present. Because he is gone, there is now talk of how Ginny would like to be in Section One too; her friend Mary is there. There is talk of Sam's leaving early for piano lessons, and the group can't seem to get to work dealing with its needs to be out as well as in—until, thank heavens, Lucy, who was in the group before, but not very *in*, offers herself up to the group as the fringe hanger-on, more out than in—and the group can go on.

It is the group itself that requires someone to play this role to take care of the members' own need for withdrawal, to conceal from themselves the fact that each has a section of himself which is a fringe hanger-on, though no one likes to admit it. What happens to the person because of the role he takes is another story; at this time we need only recognize that the need of the group is at the bottom of the group pressure. It is a group means of coping with inner conflicts. It is a group defense against pain, fear, and shame, against a group sense of guilt and inadequacy, that forces it to do this to its members. If we can elect one of us to take on the role of being the bearer of an uncomfortable feeling, the rest of us can be free of the feelings the role represents. Unless one is group-wise, one can find oneself boxed into a role by a group.

Another note about developmental dynamics as they relate to the structure of groups: We have seen that certain differing modes of leadership are needed to fit different kinds of groups. Since a group is more than a collection of individuals, the group usually appears more prone than many of the individuals in it to behave at levels somewhat younger than the chronological age of its members in terms of individual development. With individual children, for instance, willfulness and containment take over a focal position at an early age—the age of toilet training. (This varies considerably of course with the individual.) However, in a classroom, though conflicts around willfulness and boundaries are prevalent at kindergarten or first grade level, they become even more so in second and third grade. This is the time of the scatological joke which causes a group uproar, the horror burned in memory forever of loss of bladder or bowel control while in a group.

That teacher's delight, the period of industry and outward curiosity, tends to come not in second and third grade, as Erikson's chart implies for individuals, but rather, for groups in the fifth, sixth, and sometimes, if pubescence is not too overwhelming, even in the seventh grade. In other words, the teacher gets his teaching reward, if TV and overeager parents permit, before the furies of adolescence upset the whole system and make for a repetition (with a difference) of all the stages children have just gone through. It is true that the repetition of inner dynamics adolescents live through brings about not only the difficulties adults talk of—rebellion, lack of consideration, a false sense of dependence or of independence—but also the excitement of contact with new ideas. The ability to put together information and come out with a new insight for oneself comes with adolescence. If the culture allows enough leeway, adolescence is of all stages the one in which the pupil is most eager to learn—if we have or can achieve the imagination to group him well and to teach the group instead of singling out the individual at a time when he doesn't feel "single."

What have all these perceptions to do with the classroom? If one includes the focus of it all—the work-task and the work group—nearly everything. Is what we have said about classes true also for therapeutic groups? If the group is looked at not as a conglomerate of individuals but as a true group, our understanding of group dynamics provides the basis for therapy as for all group work. What about staff and management groups? If it is indeed true that all groups waver between the reality of their needs (in relation to the maturity and skills of the group members) and that "as if" life we have postulated, where unconscious behaviors take over until they become nearly the total group reality, we already know a good bit about what we shall find in those adult groups, and what their general needs for leadership will be.

If we were wiser than many people on staff-selection boards seem to be, these hypotheses could be, as we have pointed out, tremendously useful as criteria for selecting teachers who would suit the ages they teach, and who would enjoy teaching these ages. But, even more, we would also be able to judge better where, in the process of working on any task, the teacher could expect and use aspects of Basic Assumption Life in the service of the work-task. Out of his observations, the teacher, by diagnosing whether a group is in a work mode or a Basic Assumption mode, might learn when to expect blocking of a task and might find ways to understand the blocking that occurs in terms of a group, rather than pointing the usual blaming finger at one Wicked Willie, or one "negligent parent," or "poor Mary-Lee who is making my work so much harder."

To discover what living in a group arouses in oneself enables one to see how it may be the group that is expressing some need by creating a problem, rather than Mary-Lee or her parents, or Willie, or one's lesson plan or one's textbook. Any or all of these may indeed be the springboard of a clue to group interaction; but if one sees troubling forces in a group only as caused by an individual problem, solving that problem probably will not enable one to get at the underlying issue—how to help the group learn in accordance with the individual capacities of its members. One must learn and not get stuck on an instant of individual behavior management and so lose sight of what the group is doing to bring it about. Understanding group forces enables one to see what kind of leadership is being asked for and what kind is appropriate for the group at a given stage of development. But it is a rule of thumb that a group may behave in any mode at any time, whether appropriate to its age or not. If one recognizes the underlying forces, one is less apt to get caught up in immobilizing and self-defeating maneuvers, but will rather be able to focus one's own and the group's talents and energy to productive ends. This is as true of administrative groups and their relation to each other as it is true of classroom groups and their relation to other classes and school groups.

The chart below is a shorthand way of translating Erik Erikson's epigenetic chart concerning the factors affecting human development. It indicates those that come about through the internal dynamics of a child and his relationships with people significant to him and those that exist because human beings are group animals whose development is affected by the groups they find themselves in: nuclear and extended family; school and play groups, peer groups and work groups.

In reading this chart, keep in mind two points already made: (1) The chart is simply a convenient scheme for looking at the way children develop both individually and in groups; it shows us how social or group relations fit into the particular needs of a period of growth, and how certain kinds of leadership are more

CHART OF LIFE CYCLE DEVELOPMENT—DERIVED FROM ERIKSON AND BION CONCEPTS

Conflicts Occupying the Energies of Humans at Different Stages of Development

And the Predominant Modes Required for Leadership Dealing with Groups Who Are Working on These Dynamics Covertly *and* Overtly *along with Unconscious Basic Assumptions*

GROUP MODES AT GRADE LEVELS		STAGES
Consolidation, retirement, transmission of knowledge and goods; preparation for death, dying	VIII	Late Middle and Old Age
Marriage, child-raising; focusing on work; plans for separation from children and from work; own lives	VII	Middle Age
Twelfth grade through college or work, graduate school; marriage, child-raising	VI	Adulthood
Ninth through twelfth grades	V	Adolescence and Young Adulthood
Sixth through eighth grades	IV	Pre-Adolescence and Puberty (Latency)
Third through fifth grades	III	Middle Childhood
Kindergarten through first and second grades	II	Early Childhood
Pre-school, nursery, day care, home care	I	Infancy

Predominant Modes of Group Leadership for Stages of Development

Work Pairing	*Ego Integrity vs. Despair Dynamic* Supportive and human connection-type leadership, offering chance to let go without giving up
Fight-Flight Dependency	*Generating vs. Stagnation Dynamic* Leadership offering opportunity to review past dynamics and reevaluate goals and values in relation to identity; leave room for change
Inner controls assumed; leadership consultative in nature	*Intimacy vs. Isolation Dynamic* Leadership required offers opportunities to work on all past dynamics; core dynamic here expresses loneliness, sex relations and commitment
Dependency Pairing Work Fight-Flight Struggle for inner controls	*Identity vs. Role-Confusion Dynamic* Requiring all the former types of leadership, plus distinct boundaries in which there is free rein to experiment; tryout by self and with adult
Work Group Dependency Fight-Flight Inner and outer controls	*Industry vs. Inadequacy Dynamic* Requiring teacher-learner leadership; adult and peer for learning skills, socialization, competition
Dependency Fight-Flight Groups Emerging inner controls	*Initiative vs. Guilt Dynamic* Requiring combined controls with loose reins—dealing with fight-flight drives
Dependency	*Autonomy vs. Shame and Doubt Dynamic* Requiring mothering and fathering, acceptance; limit setting, controls from without; leadership
Groups Controls from without	*Basic Trust vs. Mistrust Dynamic* Requiring mothering, nurturing, limit-setting leadership

easily assimilated at one period than at another. (2) Since, as we have seen, growth can never be portrayed in a smooth straight line, but rather goes up and down and back and forth in zigzags, so too does affinity for one kind of leadership rather than another. This back-and-forth movement may fluctuate in a matter of minutes, or days, or months. The portrayal here is a generalized summary of expectations, not a neat step-by-step progression.

Let me explain further how the Erikson formulations can be translated into Bion terms. Bion's three "Basic Assumptions"—Dependency, Fight-Flight and Pairing—may be seen as paralleling specific stages of human development. There are in fact stages in which human children are genuinely dependent for survival on adults—namely, infancy and early childhood; to a lesser extent, in all the rest of one's life, too, there are occasional periods and situations which evoke real dependency. There are also stages of development and situational periods of adult life in which the Fight-or-Flight response may be essential for survival in body or personality. Likewise, there is a stage of human development where Pairing is an optimal mode of behavior for the survival of the human race. These developmental stages are real, and group leadership which evokes any one of these phases at the appropriate time can be said to be in the service of work, of accomplishing the work-task of the group. Thus at each given stage of life, a leader or teacher should be chosen who exhibits the kind of leadership appropriate to work with the particular phase.

Bion is using the concept of Basic Assumption to show us that in a Basic Assumption phase the group is avoiding or defeating its work by retreating to an assumption that insists the group has got together *not* for the purpose of work, but to make the leader be Mama or Papa; or to make him be General, or Sergeant; or to make him be God who brings forth a Messiah to answer all questions and save the group from having to work. These processes he sees as *unconscious* and the behavior as *as if*, not correlating with the facts. They are anti-work and directed at, or against, the leader as representing authority; they try to make him take responsibility for getting work done and themselves abdicate it.

But behavior may be either "real" or "as if." A group of

second-graders, for example, may be in a *real* dependency stage, where the leader has the answers and the skills to teach, and where the work is to learn those answers and skills. In that situation the group is a work group. If, however, the group behaves not like a second grade class but like toddlers with few social skills to apply or ability to listen, it is behaving in a *Basic Assumption Dependency* mode inappropriate to its work-task and actual developmental age. It does so because it unconsciously wants teacher to be Mama or Papa, not Teacher.

The leadership modes outlined on the chart indicate unconscious needs which force a group to behave inappropriately toward its leader, defeating its work-task. This behavior is sometimes caused by group needs of the moment, sometimes by the leader's need not to stick to the work, but rather to be loved, revered, seen as Savior or deliverer. The demand on the leader, then, is complex and difficult. He must fit in all the real stage-level needs of the group—very important for teachers—and yet distinguish those needs from the unconscious needs which defeat the work and make the leader into something other than a person who is there to further the task. No chart can reflect this essential dilemma. It is important to keep this in mind.

IV

Paradoxes of Group Life

BEFORE PROCEEDING to a study of those elements of group dynamics which are part of the life of every teacher, counselor and Board Chairman, it is worthwhile to explore briefly the compelling and often contradictory forces that occur in individuals when they are members of groups. Operating on the theoretical base sketched out in the last chapter, we recognize some common attributes that exist in group life and affect individual members of the group. As we note these, we can observe and perhaps explain some of the puzzlements and surprises, some of the seemingly unpredictable turns of events, that make the history of any group both so like the history of every other group and yet so uniquely different.

Any group at any moment includes within itself a series of contradictory—in fact, paradoxical forces. Here are some examples:

Paradox 1—Individual Comfort versus Group Discomfort

Most people are more comfortable relative to each other in a one-to-one interaction. Yet they join groups to learn, to play, to wield power, to protest, to do business, to facilitate courtship, to experiment, to debate, to worship, to baptize, to wed and to bury. Moreover, except for schoolchildren, prisoners, and the military, they do so in general out of choice.

Paradox 2—To Do or Not to Do a Task

While everyone agrees that a group comes together to do a task, the definition of that task, among adults at any rate, often takes as much time as getting the task done, or more. In the case of small children, the power to agree upon the task to be done is vested in the educators. But the educators themselves are swayed in defining the hows and whats of the task the children should perform by pressures from the outside world of politicians, budget-wielders, the organized or unorganized community, and the fashions of the time. The vectors of all these pressures often becloud the task itself and thus confuse the teacher. This situation frequently results in the children's not knowing what is expected of them except in very concrete minuscule assignments and overall purpose. It is clear that what is often a subject for general controversy is seldom translated into specific decisions.

Paradox 3—Conscious versus Unconscious Goals

When everyone has agreed that there is a task to do, and also on what that task is, and after that on how it is to be done, then, as we have seen, unconscious processes—the Basic Assumption Life—may militate against getting on with the work and doing the job. A corollary of this paradox is that often at the very moment when rational forces take over, the group's energy appears to vanish, and then the situation frequently requires that the teacher capitalize on some of the unconscious primary group processes, such as Dependency, Fight-Flight, or Pairing, to mobilize the group to get the work underway.

An example will make clear how this happens: Jean has come to school feeling miserable and deserted. Her mother has gone on a business trip with her stepfather. Last week her real father telegraphed from England that he was coming back with a new wife

whom Jean had never seen. During this weekend Jean's older
sister has taken advantage of her mother's absence to stay out
overnight with her best friend, while Jean's own best friend is
"mad at her" and won't talk to her, and her one other real friend
is quarantined with the measles. Despite having time to spare,
she has been too miserable to prepare her homework for Miss
Tucker's history class, and Miss Tucker, she knows, is a stickler
for homework.

As fate always seems to have it, Miss Tucker calls upon Jean
to report on the factors leading up to the Civil War. Hopelessly,
Jean opens her book, stalls for time, and then begins with an
improvisation from her imagination. Miss Tucker stops her. The
girl and boy in the desks next to hers giggle, and Jean bursts into
sobs.

"I don't care if you don't like me," she bursts out, seemingly
inappropriately. "I know I'm dumb and no one wants to sit next
to me," and her sobs rend the room.

Miss Tucker is not unkind, but she has seen Jean break up the
classwork before by her "dramatics." "Stop crying," she says to
Jean firmly, but not unkindly, "and go to the nurse's office. She'll
do something for you."

"No," shouts Jean, "I won't. She's never there when I go. No
one is ever there when I need them and Miss Tucker's mean and
you're all mean." And with this she runs from the room.

Miss Tucker and the group are silenced by mass guilt and/or
anger. Jean's deskmate to her right is crying, and the boy to her
left is chewing his pencil nervously. All look to Miss Tucker, who
is feeling none too happy herself and wishes she had said something before class to Jean, who had, in fact, been hanging about
her desk, acting lost and woebegone. She realizes that until the
group's needs for comfort and cherishing are expressed, no work
will get done. She takes care of the group by sending Sue, a
mature eleven-year-old, to see where and how Jean is, and if she
can help. Miss Tucker is a bit ashamed of her relief, when, from
the back row, Charles blurts out, "Oh, Jean makes me so mad,
she's always crying." The class anxiety is handled both by Miss
Tucker's showing she'll take care of Jean's needs and by Charles's
expression of irritation.

Now, perhaps the class can get to work. But it has exhausted its energy by this drama. Now that they are ready to work, Miss Tucker calls on Jerome. Jerome is a Civil War buff and has brought into school some props for the anecdotes he plans to tell, but even he, well prepared as he is, now answers in a flat voice. Miss Tucker is aware that the class, emotionally drained, is experiencing nothing but words. She has her lesson plan, and she wants to get on with it, especially since the specter of her supervisor's visit tomorrow is in the back of her mind. She tries to get a little life into the recital.

Don and Sylvia in the middle row are fighting over a box of crayons. The class looks on at this fight spellbound, as if it were a Civil War in itself. They are united in looking from one to the other of the protagonists as if at a Ping-Pong match. Miss Tucker lets the children fight for three minutes or so, and then calls a halt. By the time the two have, at Miss Tucker's command, moved their seats away from each other and subsided, the class paralysis has been overcome. Miss Tucker now uses the fight within her class to make a point about the Civil War. The class is alive again, and Jerome waves his hand, "Hey, Miss Tucker, I brought in these books with pictures on the Civil War . . ." Unconscious processes had broken the class up. Now they have also brought it together.

Let us analyze this incident to understand some of the unconscious processes involved: Jean's personal weekend trauma came to school with her that morning. She entered her class group apprehensive that she would be called on to do a work-task she was unprepared for and that she would thus be found wanting. Her sense of abandonment and rejection, her anger at expectations placed on her to do and accept things beyond her emotional capability, while arising out of her family dynamics, were set off by her being called on in class. Her initial brave little effort to "bull" her way through by making up an answer was a last-ditch effort to keep her surface behavior above the level where despair and rage had placed her. The normal giggles of her deskmates in response to her effort sent her over the brink to a primary-process tantrum and flight. Such a display touched off in the group their own primary-process needs. For her, they acted the role of the rejectors, jeerers, the seemingly uncaring people in her family group, with Miss Tucker as the one who would put her on the spot and show her up. Jean now acted for the group the disarray children experience when they feel put on the spot and made to feel helpless by adults. The class offered up two of their members—Don and Sylvia—to deny the response of them would dread—being laughed at or made ridiculous. The fact that Jean fled rather than staying to fight or weep, probably had something to do with the fact that Miss Tucker had told her to go to the nurse's office; while she had to defy Miss Tucker, she still had to obey her and the group's mandate—to take her misery out of the room. Misery is often handled either by contagion to others in the group, or by denial by them; it is a kind of impervious quarantine mask intended to insure against catching the pain that is not so far from any of us when it is evoked in a group by emotions such as fear of rejection or reaction to ridicule and betrayal. Jean's outburst set off these feelings because she, for good reason, was experiencing most of them. She was not ready or prepared to work because she was too loaded with them. The leader, Miss Tucker, unknowingly precipitated the retreat to unconscious forces by calling on Jean. For all one knows, Miss Tucker may have had a pull to do so because of feelings of her own, feelings that she too had brought with her into class. For now she rued the fact that when she had noticed a needy Jean hanging about her desk earlier, she had denied the urgency of the need. If she had talked with Jean at that time, she might have satisfied enough of Jean's need to avoid the dramatics, and she probably would not have called upon her to do a work-task for the group, recognizing that Jean was unable at that moment to do the work. Thus her subliminal message to the group by calling on Jean was that the Civil War was less a major issue for the group than the emotional experiences occurring within the group.

Once the incident had occurred, Miss Tucker's attempt at getting the class back to its task failed because the feelings of rage, sadness, and helplessness, still rife in the group even with Jean out of the room, had to be dealt with. The group was not in such bad shape it needed surgical help, but it did need "First Aid." It needed rest and a period of re-energizing—an attempt to do the work—calling on Jerome—at that moment was futile. The group then offered up two members to have a minor fight, expressing for the group their need to deal with primary processes and to re-energize themselves before they could work. Miss Tucker showed great leadership wisdom in allowing the fight to go on for three minutes without stopping it too soon, but then stopping it before further group deterioration took place. For it was the fight that brought the group together again. The two fighters united the group's attention. The action revitalized the group, at the same time expressing as anger, as fighting so often does, its rebellion against helplessness and sorrow. Many teachers are not wise enough to use a fight for their own purposes while keeping it within bounds. Miss Tucker was. As a result, the group was able to pull itself together. Since she had taken care of the group casualty by sending out a competent delegate, Sue, without herself deserting the group in panic as some teachers (or group leaders) are tempted to do, she was able to keep the respect of her group. She had cared for both the needs of the casualty and of the others. The group could, therefore, after the "First Aid" of the fight get to work. Many people would have considered the fight diversionary; those who know groups find it useful to see that fight as potential First Aid.

To get the group on task again, Miss Tucker wisely did not call on another questionable group member who might or might not have been prepared, but allowed a member of the group expert in this particular work-task to take over with his enthusiasm and information. Thus, while Jerome, the Civil War expert among the group members, had been for a time waylaid by a primary process, by the time the unconscious processes of the group had pulled the group together, the group was ready to listen and he to give forth.

Paradox 4—Loneness versus Loneliness

While people often join a group or stay in one to mitigate against loneliness, they are often as lonely in a group as when alone, or even more so.

From recent studies on wolves reported in the April 1971 issue of the magazine *Natural History* and from a record called "Wolf Music" issued by the magazine, it seems clear that wolves are a most sophisticated type of group animal. They have developed long, mournful howls, the howl of each wolf in a pack differing from all the others in harmonies and notes, and each easily recognizable by every other wolf in the pack. Wolves howl, it is true, when they are in danger or when a tragedy—such as the death of a pup—has befallen them, or when they are hurt or sick. They are heard over miles of wilderness, and other wolves of their pack come great distances to comfort, to help, to rescue them, and even to mourn. But mostly wolves howl because they are lonely; they ask for an answer, and get one if any wolf from their pack hears. When wolves are deserted (even by a human they know) they howl all night until he returns. Motivation to howl in the continuous way they do, of course, is founded on survival; but it is clear that their need to communicate is motivated also by loneliness. The lone wolf who howls is not, as myth has it, seeking a kill—he is seeking companionship. Thus it would seem that the wolf bears out Frieda Fromm-Reichmann's conviction that loneliness is so terrible that it is a motivation to action—in human beings, to nearly any action—to mitigate it. Harry Stack Sullivan points out that one function of loneliness in adolescence is to motivate the young to overcome isolation and join others, despite the anxiety involved.

The wolf calls his group. The human being joins a group. His howls may not be as effective, as personalized, or as readily answered, but the motivation is the same. "Come—I need others." (Unlike human group action, the wolf, it seems, uses his howl, too, to *avoid* fights. He can recognize his pack-members by their howls, and with territories well-defined, he does not answer the howls of wolves of packs other than his own in order to avoid fights over territory. We cannot say as much for man, but we can recognize and empathize with the wailing, unutterably desolate call of the howl of loneliness. Like the wolves, we use groups to mitigate loneliness and use our voices to communicate with members of our group—who may or may not come at our call. (See Farley Mowbry, *Never Cry Wolf.*)

Paradox 5—Oceanic Fear versus Fear of Isolation

While people have a driving urge to be part of a group, they fear and dread being swallowed up by the group, losing their identity, their autonomy, their own boundaries. Yet often a group made up of individuals all of whom fear a loss of themselves and a blurring of boundaries acts as if all resented even the temporary withdrawal of any member. Often they further isolate the person who keeps his distance from a group, the one who does not readily join in, who keeps himself on the fringe. Such people, though they represent the fear in us all, are often punished for being "snooty," or "queer," or "cowardly."

Paradox 6—Who Leads? The Leader or the Group?

To learn what goes on in a group, we look at its leader—teacher, youth, counselor, student activist, therapist, or principal. Yet to know what goes on with the leaders, we must look at the group. A leader, no matter how sure he is that he wants to teach or lead a group in certain ways, will not be able to do so if the group will not let him. "Yes, sure we want to learn," they say—but not this, not that, not if you speak like that, look like that, have white skin, have black skin, use that material, etc. If the group, whether for constructive or destructive reasons, doesn't want the leader to "do his thing," it can block or immobilize him. If the group members are adults, they can kick the leader out, or they can leave. If they are children (even adult-children) they can manage not to hear or to understand what he asks of them, even though their conscious intelligence understands perfectly. They can violently manhandle their leader or passively ignore him. And they can, if they act in concert and in cooperation with other groups, get him removed.

A group can devote its time to doing its task or to destroying its task. A curious twist is that while thinking it is doing either one, it may actually be doing the other. The group often behaves as if it were absolutely innocent of sabotage, and often believes it is, too. But if one inquires carefully, the resistance emerges, much like one of those drawings one had as a child, where, if one painted a blank page with water an entire scene emerged. It is at that point, when the resistance is out in the open, that the work can at last get underway. The concept then that a group is thoroughly dependent for its destiny on its leader is a myth—a beautiful self-whitewashing myth in the case of all but small children, and enforced groups such as those in prison camps. With Hitler, lynch mobs, Mylai, gang rapes, wherever guilt follows, the whitewash is always: "It was he, not we who did it!" In 1974 U.S., it is Nixon, not we who elected him.

Paradox 7—Competence versus Mindlessness

Many people join groups to raise their level of adequacy and so differentiate themselves from others—it is a kind of quest for identity. However, the level of anxiety in a group tends to be higher than in one-to-one relationships, and while greater individual competence may be achieved in a group, and in fact, has to emerge for a group to be successful, subjective reports indicate individual feelings of far less adequacy and competence in a group than when alone.

Paradox 8—Roles in Reference to Free Will and Coercion

Many people in a group come into it with the conviction that they are acting out of free will: "I can do as I like, come or go, be active or sit back. I do not have to be a leader, a yesman, a manipulator, a clown, or a scapegoat." Yet, if a group at a given moment, to work out its own development, requires that certain roles be played, there will always be someone in the group to play each role. Whether because of that someone's personal past history, or his role in other parts of his experience; whether he rises to the bait willingly or without knowing it—someone will always take each role required. A particular person may indeed be skilled enough in social relations to get out of the role assigned him if he doesn't like it or if he finds himself too deeply destroyed by it. But he may find that for his own benefit or because the inner forces are such that he cannot help himself, he is unable to get out of the role the group has selected for him without special help either from within or outside the group. In that case, because something inside him fits it, he will take the role the group assigns him. Free will, the concept of being master of one's own fate, turns out to be mythological as related to groups. (As it probably is also in individual life.) Yet, with careful work on the problem of achieving awareness of *why* an individual should be the one selected to be the group hatchet man, let's say, or the group Pollyanna, he can ultimately be enabled not to respond to the group's lure but to let someone else take on the needed role. To this extent, one who has achieved sophisticated self-awareness has more free will than people in a group presume.

Paradox 9—Groups Are to Run from; Groups Are to Join

Considering all the personal dynamics (those outlined in Chapter II) that go interweaving and whirring in us and around us, like some internal engine that has cut loose and wrapped itself in the entrails of other engines to make a mess, a monster or a miracle; and considering also all the paradoxical elements that beset us at every turn in a group, why do we go through it? Why do we enter a group? The answer, perhaps, is akin to the answer of Sir Edmund Hillary, who, when asked why he climbed Mount Everest, said, "Becuse it is there." For us human beings, groups are always there.

So discouraged are people with institutional groups that now, this very year, in the flowering season of the group, certain educators, looking at what we've done with our schools and our school systems, throw up their hands and advise mothers to keep their children at home. "Go back to individual tutoring in the old European style," they say. "Let children get their group experiences in the streets and parks and playgrounds." To get the work done, they advise, do-it-yourself in your own back yard: if you are rich, get tutors; if you are poor, get an older brother or sister—your own or someone else's.

That's all well and good, but I have never heard a mother say "yes" to that. More often one hears them say, "Thank God they're all in school"; or "Now, what do I do? Summer is here and school is out—those long, long days!" Or they say, "My child won't listen to me or his dad on how to do arithmetic—only his teacher knows anything. I can't even help him. He tells his father that's not the way to do it, and he tells me he can't do it himself, and then he goes into a tantrum and so do I"; or "He drives me crazy just doing homework—it should be fun, but after ten minutes I'd like to kill him. And his father has even less patience than I." Let the teachers struggle—not us, think the parents.

From what any observer sees of mothers with their children at supermarkets or playgrounds, I doubt that anyone would think that educational facility flows as naturally as mothers' milk. There are in fact many first class teachers, counselors and therapists, who would be the very last persons their own children could learn from or listen to outside the group setting—where they reign. As to sibling love or kindness and the sharing of skill among children, one doesn't have to quote Freud—just look about on playgrounds. One knows that though children can indeed help one another, it takes careful supervision to get them to do so—left to nature, I wouldn't count on brotherly love for more than thirty minutes of one rare, rainy day when the moon and stars are in the right place.

Moreover, it is a normal urge for human beings, especially young ones, to get outside of their small worlds and become part of other people's worlds—with their peers surely, but also with adults other than family and neighbors. The world is not made up of people of one age group (even though we in this country like to act as if everyone were between eighteen and thirty-six). People need and want the experience of different groups. Their railing against any group they are in is part of the fun and the process; it is as expected and predictable as leaves turning in autumn.

Paradox 10—The Group in One's Head

Anyone would grant that it's easier to manage one-to-one relationships. I can talk to you and you to me, and we can "know" each other, Biblically or otherwise. This is the theme not only of ghetto people and of hippies (who may nevertheless live in communes) but also of politicians, educators and psychological types, who all huddle in vaguely incestuous societies, and for recreation see each other for fishing or bridge or a comfortable hair-down, slipper-wearing evening. Solitariness is for the most part a myth. Even if one sees no one but his own wife, his and her parents are there, in fact or in spirit. Like it or not, you are in a group. The minute one goes out of the house to work, the group expands to include not only those present who affect one directly, but also all the invisible groups who determine how everyone will react. Each person brings other groups into the office or classroom with him, just as children bring family and friends and enemies into the classroom with them.

It is often just this factor of the group-in-one's-head that makes for difficulties among students and staff when they deal with the issue of race, with black-white or Indian-white relationships, etc. Our internalized groups demand a kind of loyalty without thought. If one is a white liberal, one must think such-and-such; if one is a black, one must act so-and-so; if one is young, this way; if old, that. Attitudes sometimes are quite unmatched with the way one really would think or feel if one were allowed to think or feel for oneself, rather than for the group-in-one's-head.

I have been amazed time and time again to see people change personality with a change of role or of status. I have seen a remarkably talented, humane, inspired teacher, when promoted to an Assistant Principalship, change within one year in such a way that her concept of doing her job was to be strict, rigid, disciplinary—to treat the children she had once enjoyed as guilty until proved innocent. I have seen crooked lawyers when made judges become not only exemplary in their fairness, but wise as well. I have seen a brilliant child put into a group for the retarded act as if he were indeed retarded, and to some extent also vice versa. The group-in-one's-head determines what one's stance will be. Which self is the real one: The self that acts in a particular way in a group, or the one that acts differently when all alone? Isolation cannot tell us how we will behave in this or that group. One is defined by the groups that have borne and reared one, by the groups that educate one—by all the groups with which one negotiates and in which one participates.

To gauge a child's reactions and potential, one needs to look at not one but a minimum of three groups. One must look horizontally at the group surrounding the child at the moment, and then at the vertical group he carries on his shoulders into the classroom—his parents and grandparents, his culture and his social class. Third, one must consider the internalized group made out of the first two elements: his family, his friends, the economic and cultural societies he experiences, the mode of communication he lives with. A teacher may think he has (if he is unusually lucky) a group of twenty-five children in his room. He is in fact dealing with a minimum group of one hundred twenty-five, and maybe more. No wonder teachers are weary at the end of the day, especially since they themselves also carry a carload of people with them into the same room. In our present state of knowledge, no one can hope to assess that mass. We are still at the Linnean or classifying stage of assessment, where introspective reporting or video tape are the best investigative tools we have.

Paradox 11—Assessment of Groups Is Made Individually

The measures we have to gauge people in groups are far less sophisticated than those we use in individual assessment, and thus we are inclined to prefer the more customary individual interview or test to guide our judgments. But reality would be better served if we could come up with more accurate group measures. What forces are there for instance behind a socio-gram? What does it *mean* in time and in environment that one child is selected by more people to be popular, to be feared, to be followed, to be hated or ignored? How many invisible groups affect the choices? How much do the space and the teacher or leader have to do with the situation?

Our group measures are roughly stated and defined because it usually appears to us so much easier to gauge singly—one by one. But the ark that was supposed to save us held all kinds, met all needs, together. There is no account in the Bible to tell us how many of each species survived, and who devoured whom, and what forces made it possible for some species to develop the group skills to survive, while others died out.

So, however much a group is our milieu for living and learning, we are for the most part too bewildered by it to evaluate it except additively. The whole, the *Gestalt*, is often avoided even by those who claim to think in *Gestalt* terms, for usually they handle groups by dealing with an individual on a one-to-one basis, with the rest of the group as audience, not participants. This procedure often is justified on the basis of the concept of "figure-ground" the group serving as "ground," the individual as "figure"; in such a case, only the figure is focused upon. All in all it seems that whether we speak of theory, or practice or evaluation, groups are to run from, even now at the very moment when they are being lauded as remedies for all our social and personal ills.

Teachers are of all people the most conversant with groups as an operational base, but in consultation one finds that nearly every teacher assesses the children and their behavior as if the group existed only as a two-dimensional stage set, rather than as the mini-world it much more resembles. We cannot say teachers ought to use this or that tool to evaluate. For depth tools for groups do not yet exist. In the development of such tools teachers could be a great resource; they could help to make group assessment meaningful. Anyone may know certain important things about the individual child, but until one sees a child function in a daily group, he has only a limited index as to what goes on in the child's mind, and where help is needed.

Yes, we have groups to shelter us from loneliness, and within them we often feel lonelier than we would on any mountain top or lighthouse. We have groups to get tasks done—learning in classrooms, administrative tasks in meeting rooms, defining and working out of job roles, competencies, rivalries, in staff rooms—yet we often do everything but the task we come together to do. It is only when our leadership fits our needs sufficiently so we can hear the voice calling us to work above or below the din of distraction that we are, as a group, led away from our struggles within ourselves and find that we can do our task. The experience makes us feel good. We feel more competent and perhaps less lonely, and indeed we may be so.

No wonder leading groups is sometimes exhilarating, sometimes frustrating and exhausting. No wonder some teachers and many therapists prefer to tutor or to work with individual children. No wonder some leaders choose either to lead with a single tight rein, letting no distraction occur, or to hand over the leadership to the led when they clamor for it. That last situation is what gives rise to our final paradox.

Paradox 12—The Halt Leading the Blind

The grabbers of leadership often regret it when leadership comes their way. For them there is a further paradox: How can one lead a given group in a given period of time to do a given task, when one is, inside oneself, experiencing all the fears and doubts, angers and frustrations, that one's group is feeling, and when one knows that every leader is always open to attack? How let go, how keep hold? How cater to basic needs and still expand those needs enough to get a job done? These are the tasks of leadership and self-discipline. How can one take on the leadership thrust on one, knowing that leadership often engenders hostility and anger? That is a task that calls for courage and self-acceptance. And on the other side of the coin, there is the problem of how to follow, not like a sheep but like a human being with responsibility for decision-making. That too is a particularly difficult task for school groups, since school systems tend to demand sheeplike followership.

Now that I have indicated a dozen paradoxes of group life, let me summarize with the paradox that most lures and most terrifies us all, from child to adult to aged person: the desire to enter the group fully, and the simultaneous, paradoxical fear of "being swallowed up" in the group. One is afraid one will lose one's identity in the oceanic morass of the group, and yet, at the same time, one of the greatest dreads in being in a group is that one will *not* lose oneself, that the group will never be a real group, never jell, never coalesce into oneness. This yearning and terror are akin to the experience of love, to fascination with death, or to participation in a mystical religious experience. Such experiences are usually dealt with alone, or by a pair. But any meaningful group has as a substratum the question: How am I to be *I* and *us* at the same time? This is the most sophisticated problem of human social life, as any aware married couple can testify. Any self-aware teacher too can give many examples bearing on it, including many from his own experience. If the problem is so difficult with two or three people, how can it be dealt with among ten or twenty?

There is nothing that says one cannot be a part of a group some of the time for a given purpose without being swallowed up in it like an amoeba in a mass of amoebae. The prestidigitation involved in moving into and out of a group is a matter of point of view. It involves learning that *being a part of* means that one is there as a whole, unswallowed, unincorporated individual, and also at the same time that by being oneself in the group one cannot but be part of the group. The group is not the same group it would have been were any of its members not there.

V

Group Games and Teacher Traps

Here are some typical games played in classrooms or play-grounds, in the waiting room of the office of the principal or the assistant principal, or within counseling or therapeutic groups. Feel free to translate them into adult group activities in or related to the school, or, for that matter, any place where groups meet in order, presumably, to get a job under way.

TRAP 1—THE "WHO DID IT FIRST" SYNDROME

Called out by a parent, a seventh grade teacher leaves her room unattended save by a monitor.

"Hey, Dick," says Sam, "you got that picture from *Playboy* in your desk. Show it here."

"Nah," says Dick, "you guys'll tear it. It belongs to my brother, I ripped it off of him."

"Come on, Dick," plead a few voices.

The monitor makes initial threatening sounds, writes names on a list, is glared at, and subsides for good!

"I bet you're hiding it 'cause you don't want Kathy to be jealous," taunts Fay. (Giggles from the girls.)

By this time Henry has jumped over to Dick's desk and opened it; he gets out the picture and holds it high.

"Wow," he says. "Wow, what boobs! Bet none of you'll ever have boobs like that!"

He waves the picture so no one can see anything and dances about the room, mimicking a sexy walk and making lewd gestures.

"They just get shots to make 'em big. That's all, it's not real," shouts Willa.

"You gonna get those shots, Willa baby?" Jimmy taunts. "You can be my gal if you get those shots."

Leo is now fighting with Henry to get hold of the picture and Dick is shouting: "Don't tear it. Jeez, it's my brother's. Look out, you'll ruin it."

The girls are either pretending to be shocked or showing off, and the boys are so high they've lost all sense of where they are. The teacher walks in. At first no one notices her angry, cold face and stiff presence. A curtain of silence descends. Miraculously the somewhat torn picture disappears.

"What exactly is going on here?" the teacher asks. (Silence.) "Leo, Sam, Dick, Mary, Sue, what were you doing?"

Sam invokes the magic. "*Henry started it*, Miss Richard," he says, waving the invisible wand.

"I did not. Dick had the picture," says Henry, trying to avoid the victim role.

"Can't a guy have a picture?" says Dick. "I didn't start anything."

"You did, you creep," says Henry.

"That's enough," says Miss Richard. "Henry, I don't want to hear a word."

This may be because she herself, despite sophisticated awareness of children's sexuality, is uncomfortable with sexual material, or it may be simply because the excitement caused by sexual discussion among pre-adolescents and early adolescents has made the children too high to settle down to work.

"Henry, you will go to Mr. Davis's office and you will go to Detention Hall after school. I can't trust you to behave when I leave you for fifteen minutes. The class will take out geography books."

Henry walks out, giving a finger sign to the other boys and muttering, but not too unhappy at the prospect of getting some free time in the principal's office to indulge in sexy daydreams.

That's the short form of the game. The scene could last hours, with each one blaming the others, and each one passing the buck. So long as the teacher colludes and accepts her role in dealing with the perpetrator of the initiatory act as an individual, and not as speaking for the group and their sexual interests and concerns, the underlying dynamics will be buried. One class member will be selected to be the sacrificial lamb; the game will be played and no one will need to learn anything about why what happened did happen, and how the whole group was involved, and what different things the incident meant to each member.

Let us consider the specifics of this example:

Dick often had sexy pictures in his desk. Dick was worried about his body in comparison to those of other boys of his age, and dreaded the shower room after gym that was coming next class period. He wanted to talk about his worries, but could not do so, fearing ridicule from others, fearing ignorance and fearing his fears. The other boys were also preoccupied in one way or another with their changing bodies, particularly the genital areas, and were mightily relieved to find Dick's picture an outlet for being pre-adolescently sexy in a group, in a schoolroom, where clearly no one was going to have to go too far, or have to reveal his own doubts, fears, and wishes. It was a tax-free safe activity.

The girls, who were of course more developed than the boys, were enjoying the titillations and the fantasies as much as the boys. Each of them used the attitudes of all the others—Sue's giggles, Fay's guffaws, Mary's prudish disgust, Linda's pretense of being shocked, Judy's honest bewilderment. They also used the boys' hilarity for their own needs to talk about sex, to imagine, to learn.

The excitement that the subject of sex had aroused might have been a cue for the teacher. If she were more comfortable, she might have commented on the preoccupying interest in sex and the probable factual confusion of the group. She might have taken note of it, and at a later date—perhaps the next day—she might have brought about a class discussion at a time when the class could handle it more coolly. Or, she might have scrapped her lesson plan and at once brought the discussion up in an orderly fashion. Instead, especially since she wanted to avoid seeing the provocative picture and having to deal with it, she fell smack into the "Henry-did-it-first" trap. If the class was then in fact able to calm down and get back to work, maybe that was for the best. A lot of needs were taken care of. But the probability that they got much from their work right then is small. Another possible handling might have been a couple of moments of silence brought about by Miss Richard, then a comment: "You people certainly got carried away. If sexy pictures go to your head like that, I guess all of you have a lot of feelings and questions about sex. Maybe we can talk about it tomorrow. Now do you think we are ready to travel to South America by way of our geography books? Henry, why don't you tell us something you found out about the Andes?" It might or might not have worked.

What is it that makes the youngster feel better when someone else "does it first"? A partial answer is, as Redl points out in *When We Deal With Children*, that the one who "does it first" often reflects the acting-out of impulses others in the class were wishing or thinking or repressing so hard they didn't even dare to wish or think them. When someone "does it first," the others can keep a picture of themselves as noble, clean-thinking, courteous, peaceful beings and pile all the evil on the First Doer. The fact that they did not hesitate to follow does not seem to besmirch their self-image too much or too long. And since one dynamic of punishment is that it underlines the misdeed, it becomes absolutely necessary, in order to keep the self-image relatively clean, that not "*I*" but "*he*" should get punished or scolded. His getting punished is confirmation that "I" wasn't guilty.

In the typical case above, it is hard to say whether Dick or Henry or Sam was the prime doer, since any one of the three would have served the group's need. But since it was Henry who made active Dick's more passive holder-of-the-picture role, it was he who represented the needs of most of the boys and girls in the group to express sexual preoccupation. As for the teacher, abdication of leadership in that instance to "Henry did it first" satisfied her need to deny sexual issues. All then colluded in letting Henry be the bad one so they could deny their own impulses. All could hang the unacceptable unconscious on Henry.

There is nothing wrong in using such an economical method of taking care of inside dynamics that are indeed group dynamics— so long as Henry doesn't *always* get himself victimized—so long, that is, as the sacrificial-lamb role gets passed around, and the "bad" feelings don't all get dumped on one person all the time in order that no one may have to claim his own inner self. It is just this sort of election to the role of the one who will act upon the unconscious needs of a group that is seen in family structure. The Black Sheep of the Family (no matter how defined) is kept very black so that the others can think of themselves as very white. If he reforms, the whole family goes into a tailspin until they either take some of the "sinfulness" into themselves or elect another member of the family—wife, husband, youngest brother—to be a new Family Black Sheep. The same event gets acted out in non-family groups, as we have seen here.

TRAP 2—THE FAIRNESS SYNDROME

The obvious is often overlooked, especially when it parades in group clothing. No one would have any question, when dealing with individuals, that all our fuss about fairness originally derives from struggles in childhood to get as much attention as one can from mother or father, and that as soon as brother or sister enters the scene, the struggle to get one's share—or the lion's share—is intensified. One can predict the struggle among siblings. A little less obvious is the struggle between the adults of the family, or between adult and child for the most attention (usually from Mama, but often from Papa, too).

Papa: "You always are busy with that child. You never have time to sit and talk with me."

Mama: "As soon as you come home, you're reading the comics with that child. You never ask about my day."

Both: "It isn't fair."

What usually goes unstated here is that while the rivalries among children are par for the course, and even rivalries between child and parent are known to any wife or husband who has been the subject or object of envy, the dealer out of goods and manna is often more caught up in being meticulously fair than the rivals themselves demand. This fact lurks behind the scenes prompting the Fairness Game; it has to be played out as "haute" drama, simply because it does so often stay beneath the level of awareness. The Fairness Game derives, of course, from the same source as sibling rivalries; it is living proof of unresolved, unworked-out feelings about being treated fairly and about one's own sibling or parental rivalries. It comes as often to those who secretly recognize they have been the favorite ones, have been given the preferential share, as it does to those who have suffered from being the non-getters of preference, the ones thought to be able to go without, the neglected ones. The former group—the favored—are burdened by guilt from the past and are fearfully waiting to get their "punishment" for having been favored. The latter, of course, suffer from resentment, bitterness, and injustice-collecting. People in both categories find it nearly impossible to deal out decisions for fear of being unfair. Thus they are sometimes immobilized—trapped, that is, into playing the fairness game. It is a sure sign that the players have never resolved their own problems about having "gotten" or "not gotten" and about the revenge or retribution they fear must follow.

For a teacher (or for that matter, for a parent, therapist or administrator) to be so trapped can bring to a halt any work on the primary goal. If the disease is a severe one, it can also ensure that few individual needs will be cared for—all will be sacrificed on the altar of utter fairness and equivalent favors, turns, attentions, helps, praise—whatever may be required. A group can get a leader to play the Fairness Game any time it wants to see a little excitement, or any time it wants to avoid the task, or any time it wants to see the teacher or leader squirm.

A rule set before a teacher which has much truth behind it is that every child wants the teacher to be fair; a class will jump on any favoritism before the teacher even knows he is feeling it. Usually the child picked as favorite will be picked out by the group to be disliked or even ostracized. The question then becomes: what's fair? Is fairness a question of each child's getting the same amount and kind of time, help, material, reward or punishment? Or is fairness a question of giving each child what he needs—that is to say, as far as that is feasible? Can a child understand this difference? Answer: he can, if the adult can. Any hole in the adult's understanding lets the whole flood of injustice pour in.

Example 1

The Open Trap Lucy: Mr. Trent, Karen always gets to sit next to you in reading class. That's not fair.

The Fall-in Mr. Trent: Why, Lucy, Karen didn't sit next to me yesterday or the day before.

Lucy: But she did three times last week. Karen's your pet.

The False Solution Mr. Trent: No, she isn't, Lucy, and I thing you've counted wrong. I like all of you just the same. (This is a grievous lie, unless Mr. Trent is a computer in disguise.) We'll take turns and everyone in the class will sit next to me by alphabetical order.

Now in all probability at least fifteen children in the class would much prefer to be as far as possible from Mr. Trent so they can daydream, write notes, wriggle without criticism, doodle without seeming to be rude. Lucy is simply testing. Presumably, Mr. Trent has two sides, and if he moves, it is possible for him, without going into numerical counts, to move in such a way as to be able to say, "Lucy, if you need to sit next to me today, why don't you sit on the other side of me?" This maneuver, however, won't solve anything if what Lucy wants is to get Karen out and herself in, or if the idea is really just to put Mr. Trent on the spot. A more realistic solution might be for Mr. Trent to say: "It's fair, Lucy. Karen needs to sit next to me today because she's having a hard time concentrating. You need a chance to read out loud, so why don't you begin today's story?"

This answer implies that there are different needs in the group, and that Mr. Trent is aware of many of these needs and will try to attend to those he sees. He doesn't fall into the trap of defending himself against an accusation of favoritism; he doesn't take on responsibility for dealing omnipotently with all the needs he imagines.

Example 2

Mike is the class mess. He wanders about disconsolate or scared, disrupting every activity because he can't get started on anything. Once started, he can't stop. Transitions from one activity to another are hell for him (as they are for most people) but in Mike's case response to transition tension makes life harder for the rest of the class.

Mrs. Kern's supervisor has told her to stick close to Mike in transition times and help him get started. But Mrs. Kern has not been able to carry out this advice successfully because she believes that it is unfair to the rest of the children to spend so much of her time with one individual. In addition to being annoyed by Mike, she is getting to dislike him, because to her mind, he is putting her in the unholy position of discriminating and being unfair.

She herself introduces the "that's not fair" game: "Mike," she says, after two or three minutes of helping him, as she sees the hands of two other children aloft calling for her help, "I can't spend all my time with you. It's not fair. The others have as much right to my help as you. Just go on and do the best you can."

"Yeah," says Dave, "he's always first getting help. It's not fair."

"You never help me," whines Rosie. "You always help Mike."

By then, between Mrs. Kern's statement and the gathering

cloud of group resentment, Mike is embarrassed. He feels even more inadequate and anxious than usual, and is about as able to do his short division as if he were asked to do calculus. He begins to chant to himself and roams over to the aquarium, wishing he were a tadpole instead of a boy. As he stands near the tank, he drops the fishfood and knocks over a bowl of water. Now, Mrs. Kern is really angry, and the class is divided between giggling and glaring at Mike. No one is doing his work.

"Get out of this room," Mrs. Kern says between her teeth, "and don't come back until you can take care of yourself." (This is patently impossible for Mike at this moment.) "It's not fair." This time she's more honest, for she means it's not fair to *her*.

Instead of announcing to the class, as she had, "It's time to play the fairness game," thus putting both Mike and herself on the spot, she might have said, if challenged by the class, "Yes, I know it seems as if I help Mike a lot, but Mike needs help getting started, and as soon as I have got him settled, I'll try to help you others. In the meantime, why don't you try to help each other quietly? We've got a lot of good dividers in the class who can help those who get stuck. Jim, Jeff, Bert and Louise, why don't you be the helpers while I'm busy?" No one would have minded; and while Mike would indeed have been singled out, as indeed he needed to be, the group would not have been disturbed by the symptoms of his misery—his roaming, breaking things, etc. In that situation Mike would not have been elected The Stupid One—he would have been seen as simply needy at the beginning of things which might have allowed him to do his job—and so to feel more adequate—and the group to do theirs. It was Mrs. Kern's own fear of being unfair, and her own resentment of Mike's inept way of *getting attention* that created the situation.

To complete the discussion of the fairness syndrome it need only be said that this syndrome is one of the major reasons why people are fearful of leading groups. What they are afraid of is being immobilized by their old unresolved personal problems of who gets what, when, and how much. Fairness becomes so mixed up with doling out equal portions of love that leaders begin to feel they are "undemocratic" when they treat people as individuals, each with his own special requirements at special times. "Why, it nearly seems anti-American, anti-democratic, not to treat everyone *the same*," one hears. Yet it is precisely in the realm of caring for individual differences while living in a group that actual democracy, not its self-destructive facsimile, can be practiced. Jefferson had no such nonsensical thought as that each person needed *the same thing*. What he and Lincoln and John Dewey— to name only three proponents of true democracy—cared about was that a society be formed where individuals with *different* needs and talents could be served *differently*, and still find room for one another while working together in groups. The Fairness Syndrome, while pretending to be "democratic," in fact neglects individual differences, condescends to the un-needy in certain areas, and fails to care adequately for the needy. Since groups are made up of individuals who, if they lose their individualness, lose their ability to be self-determining within the group, the Fairness Syndrome in reality caters to unresolved emotional problems appropriate to the first years of group life but not afterward. It can become dangerous to democratic ideas rather than supportive of them, as our societal myths would have it. Like so many of the group games we play, the Fairness Game can and does contribute to the infantilizing of everyone, especially in schools—not only the children in our schools, but the staff as well—of which more later.

TRAP 3—THE DO-GOODER SYNDROME

Miss Manning is a good young teacher. She is imbued with many ideas about how she is going to use the group to help her with class management. Indeed, by dint of her efforts, her third grade is already far more of a group than any of the other sections in the school. She has brought them far enough to be able to deal with Frank's noisy fidgets by letting him be mobile during a class while the others sit still; thus, she and they have overcome the "fairness syndrome." A subgroup has managed to take care of

Beth's tears and timidity so that Beth, now sitting between Amy and Lois, is comparatively dry-eyed and can now speak a bit above a whisper without the boys' yelling "Louder in front." Miss Manning has indeed mobilized her group to take care of some disturbing symptoms in her class.

But there is Arnold. Arnold has titanic tantrums in which he tears up other people's work, kicks, bites, turns red easily and holds his breath or roars. Arnold goes into these tantrums any time he's not first or best in nearly anything, and any time something new comes up. Moreover, Miss Manning herself can hardly abide Arnold. His tantrums are bad enough, but his whine goes right through her nervous system, and when he isn't roaring, he's whining. She has, conscientiously, gotten in touch with his mother. (His father is living in another city.) The mother was rude and irritated by the teacher's calls. For a while Miss Manning had sympathized with Arnold, recognizing that he too must find his mother's unpleasant too-busy-to-be-bothered attitude hard to take, and that the fact that papa wasn't around must make it worse. But with the best good will in the world, one can "understand" just so long. Understanding does not mitigate the tantrums or the antics or the whine, and the class was constantly being disrupted by Arnold.

She thought, "I'll get the group to help." A very good idea that was, too, except that, like so many of us, she went to the group unaware that she had not worked out her own feelings about Arnold, so that she was in fact dumping the problem of the feeling of helplessness that Arnold aroused in her on the group. Because of this, she couldn't be as honest as she would have been had she sufficiently understood what Arnold did to her to be able to take responsibility for her own role as teacher, and let the children take theirs as students.

On a day when Arnold was absent (she couldn't face the problem with him there), she took the group into her confidence. Without Arnold it had been one of those days teachers dream of, days which happen only once in a rare while. Everything from arithmetic to zoo study had gone beautifully.

"Arnold," she began her group meeting, "is absent." The class

giggled in relieved fashion, showing they felt as she did. Arnold
was a pain. "I wonder if we could help Arnold. Can anyone in
the group think of some way we could help Arnold be happier so
he wouldn't have these tantrums?"

The courtesy and restraint of children are amazing when you
think of it, and no one, not even verbal Billy said, "We could gag
him and tie him to the chair," or "We could take up a collection
and send him to Turkey by tugboat." They liked Miss Manning
and caught her solemn tone; they got the cue that what was
wanted was a good-deed-and-sympathy session.

But wise little Sylvia did say, "Miss Manning, I don't think I
feel like doing anything for Arnold; he just turns me off. Maybe
the best thing is to ignore him."

And Larry said, "I kind of feel funny talking about Arnold
when he's not here." Miss Manning managed not to hear this.

Then the group came up with noble thoughts, like: "He could
sit next to David" (the most popular boy, who muttered, "Oh,
Lord") and "We could invite him to be in charge of the food at
the Halloween party. It might make him feel good," and "When
he gets into a tizzy, we can each of us talk to him and no one
should be mean to him." All of which of course was not only
futile—it could last no longer than a day—but also presented a
good lesson in group dishonesty. And while an individual can be
dishonest and mask it, the true feelings of a group will out: in
the next week, in spite of or because of all the honeyed attention
from the class, Arnold got even more demanding and obnoxious.

One evening, Miss Manning went home and said aloud to her
roommates, "I didn't know I could hate a kid, but that whiney,
nose-drippy, red-faced monster, Arnold—I hate him. I could
cheerfully kick him." It dawned on her then that maybe the class
felt like that too, and that maybe the sweetness-and-light approach was not only phoney, but unworkable. She was honest
enough to blush, recollecting that she had induced group hypocrisy by invoking the sympathetic aid of the group when all they
would have liked to do was to dismiss Arnold from their minds.
She came to school the next day and, sure as Satan, during the
second hour of the morning, Arnold got into one of his red-faced,

breath-holding fits, ending up in screams. He was packed off to
the nurse's office to be cooled down, and when he returned, Miss
Manning was forced to turn from the class project on the Indians
to Arnold.

"O.K., Arnold," she said. "We did you a great disservice when
you were sick one day in October. The group decided to help
you. We had no right to do that without you being here to hear
what we said, and of course it didn't work, because the kids and
I [note her skillful differentiation] can't do anything for you
without your help. I for one have had enough of your carry-
ings-on. I think the class has, too. We can't have fun or get our
work done, and what we're doing sure isn't helping you. So you
go ahead if you want to and have your tantrums, but when you
do, do it in the closet room. I'll help you get in there if need be.
The rest of us are going on with our work, and I'm not going to
attend to you while you're carrying on. I'm going to ask the class
to help by doing the same thing. If you can go a whole hour without a tantrum, I'll put a penny in a jar, and at the end of each
month, we'll count the pennies, and by May you can choose any
game you want me to buy for the class with the money collected."

The class clapped. Arnold sat sourly and then began to whine.
Miss Manning quickly started the class's favorite spelling game.
Though the combination of insight and behavior modification
techniques didn't cure all of Arnold's ills, it did help him get on
in school, and the class too was able to get on with its own tasks
and not focus on Arnold.

The new set-up helped because now Miss Manning was taking
her leadership role back into her own hands, because the group
now knew what was wanted and could do their part, and because,
working on behavior modification principles, Miss Manning was
rewarding acceptable nondisruptive behavior, rather than disrup-
tive behavior. She did it with a group reward in which Arnold
could share, not an individual one. True, by May there weren't
enough pennies to buy the volley ball they all wanted, but there
were enough to get a ring-toss game, and Miss Manning had
learned, first, that to lead a group you don't elicit phoney responses you yourself don't feel; and, secondly, that you get a

group to help only when you take your own role in the group. For her the role was to be the adult leader, not the instigator of good deeds. The group had learned that they were there to learn and live together, not to minister to Arnold. As for Arnold—he learned he was there to learn about living in a group, not either to lead or mislead it.

TRAP 4—THE "WILLING SUCKER" SYNDROME

Dr. Fritz Redl has called one familiar group maneuver "The Case of the Willing Sucker." The idea of master-sleuthing suggested by the title is fitting, for it takes some fast eye- ear- and foot-work to determine who is in fact the originator or director of the play, and why Bob or Kit or Mary has been selected for the role of star actor or actress in it.

The drama according to Dr. Redl's script goes this way:

There are twelve to fifteen kids sitting around a table at lunchtime. Barry is bored or would simply like to maneuver some excitement. Containers of milk and spoons are convenient props. Barry is fully aware that the adult—teacher or paraprofessional or whoever it is—sitting at the table is involved in a conversation with Tony and Jill. By merely picking up his spoon and flicking the spoon-end down and up, down and up, he catches Bob's eye. He says nothing, and in fact does nothing except flick the spoon with one hand and move his milk nearer. He is absolutely pure of overt ill doing, but Bob, rising to the bait as soon as it is offered, connects the spoon flicking and the milk—just as he is meant to do. Bob nudges Patty and flicks some milk first at Lucy, then at Mark, and is becoming quite skilled when, of course, Mark avenges himself in like manner; Patty whirls round and wipes her dress, Lucy swears, and the table is in pandemonium. Milk is flying, containers are being thrown, and spoons are banging. The adult sees Bob as the central figure—as indeed, in a way, he is—and it is Bob who gets punished. Either Barry is completely ignored, or, if the teacher, experienced with the Barrys of this world, turns to him asking, "Barry, what are you doing?" his answer is, with injured innocence: "Nothing. I'm not doing nothing. Jeez, can't a guy touch his spoon?" The adult is left feeling helpless. If he is a wise teacher, he knows full well that it's Barry again, with Bob in the role of Barry's puppet. How is he to make Bobby and his multitudinous ilk immune from taking on such willing suckerdom time after time?

If the drama were translated to adult groups, it might well give off an odor more of hostility and less of mischief, but it would still be recognizable. It might go like this:

Setting: A board meeting. Because of urgent phone calls the night before Mr. Jay is aware that Mr. Beal is determined to put through a wage raise for the Pupil Personnel staff. Knowing how limited the funds available for raises are, and being committed to getting more slots for a Remedial Reading Program, Mr. Jay makes use of something else he happens also to know: the chief superintendent has to leave the meeting promptly because his wife's sister is to be married that very day. The superintendent's subliminal agenda will be to get essential business under way at once; he will brook no diversions. Mr. Jay reasons that anyone who tries to take the group afield today will be a dead duck. He knows also that Mr. Beal is one of the world's easiest people to seduce into rambling, especially when led into discussion of his present favorite topic, Behavior Modification. He knows that today's agenda will be read alphabetically, and that Pupil Personnel comes directly before Remedial Reading and that both come late in the day after Language Arts, Mathematics, etc.

Being a good politician, he would rather be the first on the agenda for tomorrow's meeting than last for today's. All he has to do is to see to it that Mr. Beal gets involved in his favorite topic. At the meeting, Mr. Jay sits back, lighting a pipe or two, gallantly getting Mr. Beal a cup of coffee when he starts to get himself one. Just as Mrs. Stillman's discussion of the needs of Mathematics is drawing to a close, Mr. Jay slips a clipping headlined "New Methods of Behavior Modification in Psychological Assessment" beneath Mr. Beal's eyes. It has a friendly note on top: "Jake, thought this would interest you."

Mr. Beal, who is always bored by Mrs. Stillman's reports,

smiles gratefully; innocent Isaac that he is, he does not know he is being led to the sacrificial altar, and surreptitiously reads the clipping.

So engrossed is he that when the superintendent turns to him with "Well, now, Beal, Pupil Personnel is next and we have just twenty minutes. I have to leave at four today, remember," Mr. Beal jumps and rouses from dreams of professional glory.

"Sir, I simply must share with you the importance of bringing more Behavior Modification techniques into our system. I have been reading how an entire system was rejuvenated by its use"— and off he goes down his favorite road. Mr. Jay looks on with seeming fascination.

The superintendent shuffles his papers nervously, packs them away in his brief case. Twice he intervenes in polite fashion— "But, Mr. Beal . . ."—"Mr. Beal, please, the clock . . ." After ten minutes he angrily insists that Mr. Beal get to his specific budget requests. Seeing his irritated face, Mr. Beal flushes and gets to work, but it is too late. He cannot get through on time to give his justifications. The superintendent says irritably, "Well, Beal, time's up. We'll get back to Pupil Personnel Budget at the end of tomorrow's meeting after the Remedial Reading, Social Science and Social Work Programs. I advise you to confine yourself to figures, not theories, at that time. Mr. Jay, please prepare to begin with purely budgetary reading needs in the morning." Quietly Mr. Jay nods his assent; he is careful to conceal his inner triumph.

The dynamics of this game is a sophisticated sense of the meaning behind power, a kind of Svengali knowledge of how to manipulate those more vulnerable than yourself to your own ends. The attempt is to conceal one's maneuvers by protecting oneself from open hostility or open attack, but still to get one's desires acted upon by others. The power implicit here is heady liquor, and for the skillful next to irresistible, if one gets away with it. The best technique a teacher and leader can use to prevent such manipulation in the classroom is to try (often a losing battle!) to catch the manipulator in the act and bring the matter out in the open. This will not only give the teacher or leader satisfaction, but help the child or adult manipulator grow to be able to risk himself and his own feelings *out front*—to develop his acuteness in using leadership directly, instead of hiding his feelings and wishes and needs behind someone else. "Getting away with it" is often a Pyrrhic victory.

TRAP 5—THE DARE

We are told that, notwithstanding Cecil B. De Mille and our TV spectaculars, nothing has ever offered a more dramatic spectacle than the Duel, that hangover from the Days of Chivalry. (Undoubtedly the Romans, Greeks, and Early Egyptians had their own forms of this game.) As time went on, the duel became more and more formalized, more and more rigid in structure. The result could still be, and often was, a corpse. In Europe and in America, dueling went on through the nineteenth century, killing one of our newborn nation's brightest luminaries, Hamilton, and indirectly ruining the career of his opponent, Aaron Burr.

Today's version is not half so glamorous and choreographic as the ancient duel, but we still have our feuding mountaineers, our street gangs, our fights in the alley, our revengers in the night. In cases where gangs and their leaders are involved, the dare and its conclusion are nearly as much a way of life as dueling used to be, and often as lethal. A common and dangerous form of the modern Dare-and-Die Game is the game of "Chicken," played with cars, racers, or motorcycles. There we have the old challenge, the appointed place, the encounter, and again some people in the group may not come out alive. However, being more groupy than the duelists of old, we tend, like Samson Agonistes, to take others with us when we act on our personal or group gripes.

Those who participate by watching are often present at the moment of decision as audience, just as in the duels of the Middle Ages. Spectator participation—in actuality or imagination—has much to do with the outcome, with the need to carry through the dare without negotiation. No matter how much the elected opponents may want to forget the whole thing or have done with it peaceably, they have become representatives of their groups; they are onstage and the show must go on. Neither representative feels he can go back to his own peer group without proving his "honor," no matter how inane the definition of honor may be, and no matter how great his reluctance to proceed. It is as if he could not live without that image of himself, which is, or which he thinks is, the only acceptable one. If that effort fails, a man (this is as a rule a syndrome of males) feels he has lost his identity or his manhood and therefore has no right to live. The Japanese samurai with their hara-kiri stabbing of themselves in defeat have exactly the same formulation of values, except that they only do themselves in—they do not shoot it out with their opponents or race it out with 180-horsepower engines.

One has to say "opponent" rather than "enemy" in these circumstances, for in fact the participants in a duel or even in a rumble or roadway confrontation, may not be enemies at all. It is all a matter of "honor" and has little to do with intrinsic relationships or points of view.

The dynamics in such group games center upon identity, including sexuality—upon the concept of machismo and honor as a man or boy—and upon the question of how one can live with oneself if one has failed to live up to the ideals and attitudes of one's peer-society. Failure comes not from losing, as in a war, but from not being willing to play the game. It is for this reason indeed that we call this activity a "group game"; though dead is dead, a "game" does not have the same motivation as a fight to the finish or a war. It comes less from hatred than from vanity. Girls have their own form of dare-and-double-dare and their own feuds, but their feuds have tended in our culture to be less lethal—except as they become the focus of many of the boys' duels or feuds. Women are traditionally assigned the role of raison d'être for many of the duels: If you want to start a fight, just take the simple expedient of calling a seventh-grader a mother-fucker.

A teacher may get caught in the acting out of the "dare" phenomenon. In or just before adolescence, there is often an identity crisis—a crisis that involves a shifting ego-stability. The more shifting there is, the more frequently dare-battles are likely to occur. For instance, a familiar form of that potentially dangerous game is this: A teacher is marking papers, unaware of certain millings-about in the classroom. The children's talk may have to do with a subgroup that is insisting that Cal has a crush on the teacher. There is hot denial.

The dialogue might then go: "Cal wouldn't say nothing fresh to her—his lovey-dovey pussycat. It's all 'Yes, Miss Keller; no, ma'am; sure, Miss Keller,' with him."

The accusations mount, taunting Cal, who considers himself tough. Then someone drops the gauntlet: "You call other people plenty names, but betcha wouldn't call her a name."

"What kinda name?"

"Well, a name."

Now everyone has suggestions: "Betcha wouldn't call her a mother . . ." "Betcha wouldn't say you're a no-good pussy" or "You wiggle-ass."

Roars of laughter greet each suggestion till they diminish to more real possibilities.

"Betcha wouldn't dare even say when she calls on you, 'Miss Keller, I just don't want to say, and I ain't going to tell you.' " Since this is in the realm of possibility, they all dare him to say this.

When it is time for seventh-grade English class, Cal looks frantically at Miss Keller, pleading with her not to call on him. Miss Keller sees a strange look, but she doesn't get the message.

"Cal, will you tell us about what John Steinbeck was saying in *Of Mice and Men*?"

He shakes his head no.

She pushes, with a "But Cal, you gave the book back yesterday and you said you liked it. What did . . ."

He catches the eye of one of his dare-tormentors. Dilemma. Which should he obey? She's here now—but they're here too, and they'll be outside at 3 P.M., and he can't risk their jeering— he can't risk seeming a sissy. A dare is a dare. So—he says the words.

She is startled. "Cal, that's impudent. What's going on with you?" Cal glares and sulks. "Answer me, Cal." Cal is silent. She is amazed. "Cal, you will stay in an hour after school in detention hall today and write fifty times 'I'm impertinent and I'm sorry.' Do you hear me?" Cal, in misery, nods his head yes. She makes it worse. "Cal, speak up." Cal refuses, and is sent to the assistant principal.

Now it is a fact that Cal likes Miss Keller, not passionately, as the boys have said, goading him, but he just likes her. He doesn't want to be rude. He doesn't want to be punished. But where honor beckons, and where loyalty and pressure weigh most heavily, he has had to choose. Peers are more important to him. He has been challenged and he has accepted. His social identity is preserved. Punishment and a "Bad Deportment" mark on his record cannot really compete with the approval of his peers.

When I was a child, we would dare people, then double-dare them, and then "D-double-dare" them. While the first you might refuse, the second would be pretty hard to withstand, but the "D-Double-Dare"—that was sacred. Once D-double-dared in follow-the-leader, you'd jump off stone stoops far too high for you, you'd bruise your knees, cut your hands, but jump you did, even if it meant the next stop was the hospital emergency room, as it sometimes was—and sometimes still is.

A teacher's best hope of handling this sort of activity is in his sensitivity in differentiating behavior, his ability to recognize when someone is being impudent and challenging, let's say, because of forces within himself, or in relationship to the task or the adult authority, and when it is a case of responding to an explicit or implicit dare, in which the child is being put into jeopardy with his group by a given demand or task. If the latter is the case, it is a wise teacher who can let it go and not get trapped. The dare has virtually nothing to do with him; he is only a *deus ex machina* who exists to make it all happen. To become entangled at such a moment with one's own personal hurt or one's specific teaching mission is only to complicate and obfuscate. Moreover, it may be an entire neighborhood that one is dealing with rather than the particular youngster in question. The rest of the daring, tormenting gang may not even be in the schoolroom. The reason the boy before the teacher is behaving as he is may derive from a week-

end confab among his neighborhood group, a defeat at the hands
of his taunters, a need to establish or re-establish himself in his
own eyes as well as in theirs. Such behavior becomes nearly
doubly obnoxious to the adult, but a sensitive teacher can sense a
more powerful group in the wings of the child's life and avoid a
futile and sometimes destructive confrontation.

How can the teacher sense what the situation really is? A
teacher can tell by being his own barometer and trusting his own
perceptions. If Cal, for instance, has generally been pretty easy
to work with, if one has information that this child does not dislike one, if his customary demeanor is not usually rude or provok-
ing, one may guess that it is inner turmoil of some sort that makes
him act in this atypical way. Though he may play his part to the
hilt, there is often something that is a giveaway of the fact that
this is rather a necessary act than a natural expression. It is more
useful to listen to one's own inner messages and dismiss the behavior with a firm comment that such language or actions don't
go in here—the setting of a limit—than to go into the counter-
productive "I am the Authority, and I will show you my power
group." A talk alone outside of class often may get things back in
focus if the youngster is not too intimidated by his group. If the
talk works, it may confirm one's hunch that this is a case of
Honor-at-Stake, not one of hatred or malice.

VI

Group Viruses—
the Nature of Contagion

CLOSELY RELATED to the games and traps discussed in the last chapter are certain underlying, pervasive phenomena that may beset any group but that particularly affect the teacher. These phenomena have something of the character of viruses in that they are difficult to isolate and deal with. They also, like viruses, involve the danger of group contamination and contagion.

The Giggles

Commonest among group contagions is the well-known "fit of giggles." Dotty looks at Laurie, puts her hands over her mouth and begins to shake, emitting sporadic squeals. Laurie joins in. Max says, "Hey, Teach, what are them dopey girls laughing at?" Before anyone has a chance to say or do anything, Peg and Judy and Ann join in, and then Arthur and Bob and Peewee. The teacher might just as well put away the homework assignments, for until the giggles have been giggled out no work will be done. She can, of course, send everyone involved (a good half of the class!) to the principal's office, but then she'd look foolish. So whether she greets them pleasantly, indulgently, humorously, or with rage, the giggles eat away seven minutes of the lesson time. They may take care of a number of needs. To guess at a few: Tensions or tiredness have mounted in the group, too much time has been spent in sedentary, concentrated activity, and it is normal release time; the giggles may take care of anxiety, for they often act as a calm following a storm. If someone—the teacher, let's say—has been very angry at a child, if something genuinely solemn or sad or even tragic has happened, the giggles are a common phenomenon and one of the most contagious diseases in the world.

Awkward, indeed miserable and shocking to everyone, is the contagious burst of giggles that comes after the announcement of a tragedy, a sickness or a death. There are many grown-ups who dread being caught in such an act. Children hate it, too. "I laughed when I heard my favorite aunt died; my God, I laughed. I was so afraid I would laugh at the funeral. How could I do anything so awful? I liked her. Yet I laughed." "I am terrified of hearing of anything really bad happening to anyone. I am so afraid I'll smile or laugh when I ought to cry." Why do we do things like that? The cause is surely anxiety in the face of help-lessness. It comes from inability to handle what one fears. It is a way to cover over fright. We have been told time and time again as children that it is better to laugh than cry, to smile than look sad, so we translate tears to laughter, sorrow to smiles. To please relatives and teachers, we have learned to hide genuine feelings so well that when real emotion is evoked, the wrong one may often come out. Such phenomena are far more likely to occur in public—in a group—than when alone. The group forces the inappropriate reaction rather than helping individuals come to terms with the painful feelings that most people would prefer those around them to conceal.

Similar to the giggle are the yawn, the burp, the stomach rum-ble, and the fart. Skillful performers can use them to express hostility. Each may come as relief, as activity versus passivity, as the satisfaction of a genuine physiologic need or as reaction to stress and anxiety.

How do these phenomena perform these functions? Here is an example: Mr. Zell has just launched forth on a description of medieval battles. He likes the subject and is soon lost in a verbal description of the colorful costumes of the participants. Larry yawns or burps or does both. Billy picks it up and produces some louder yawns; Jim then comes up with a prize yawn. Now the general oxygen intake and output cannot be ignored. Mr. Zell might react by getting insulted and sending Larry or the whole yawning subgroup out; if he feels his vanity particularly attacked, he might keep the whole class in from recess. But wouldn't it be better to recognize that though he may be entranced by the subject he is discussing, the class is not? He's gone on too long and it's too soon after lunch. If at this sleepy post-lunch hour, he had the class act out a battle or improvise the costumes he is describing, the yawning disease might be cured. Instead it is likely to become a favorite part of the class repertoire, used to get Mr. Zell's goat, and to put him down from his ego trip—not too roughly after all—rude but not too bad. Such noises may be heard as signals to the teacher that whatever he's doing is unlikely to work. One yawn or burp is physiological, two may be, but when yawning or burping gets to be a group activity, it's as clear a signal as a stop sign to do just that.

The Inner Circle Language (The Lingo)

Another not too serious contagious group disease is *The Inner Circle Language* or *The Lingo*. This phenomenon is as common in groups as inventing a password, a handshake, an oath of allegiance; all express group in-ness. We adults too have a Lingo in the jargon of our trades, one trade as clubby and exclusive as another. In Washington, for instance, it is possible to go to a cocktail party and hear a whole dialogue little more than initials, pronouns, and simple verbs: "Did you know he was riffed from the OAD after FTC lost part of its budget to the BLS?" This statement is seriously answered by: "Why, no, I thought his wife had got a job with HEW, and that he had transferred to the AIS until the assistant secretary reestablished ONI."

A phrase comes in and is used again and again until it means everything and nothing, and then it disappears. But while it is in use, it delimits and bounds a group as strongly as a national border. It is as contagious to aspirants and ins as the common cold. If, as an adult, you don't understand the Lingo, you're out of it; but if you overuse it, you're thought, often accurately, to be regressively juvenile, or to be trying to con the young by seduction. For the Lingo is an age-group language; it catches on like fire in dry timber. Anyone who doesn't talk that way—whatever the way is for the moment—is considered queer. There are groups who as part of their unity against the outside world have developed a private, often graphic, group language all their own: the homosexual group, for instance, has idioms and phrases of its own. Sometimes a word, such as "gay," becomes public property, but often other words—"fag-hag," for example—are kept mostly within the inner circle. Likewise, there is the language of the drug group: they push or deal, trip down or out, shoot up and freak in or out. Their names for the different drugs make up a dictionary in themselves. The Lingo is as transient as age itself, and changes year to year. Since the lingo of special groups, including adolescents, is both contagious and exclusive, it is inclined to be ambiguous. A non-in adult who deals with the group using it, first has to know which group is using which words and how, and how much of the lingo he as an outsider can be permitted to use before being seen as intrusive, as a group-language gate-crasher. The sin of knowing too much is held nearly as bad as the sin of knowing too little. Both extremes keep the outsider out—which is precisely what a special language is meant to do for the group it represents.

The strength of the lingo virus is explained by the needs it seeks to care for. It is part of the identity struggle and attempts to define who one's contemporary group is, as apart from the adults one is struggling to become independent of. For this reason, it is especially appropriate to adolescents, and particularly virulent during adolescence, since both identity and separation problems are being worked out by its use. The struggle is now to be a whole individual, on one's own, incorporating what one has learned from one's parents but no longer dependent on their approval or

disapproval, their economic or emotional nurture, for one's course
in life or one's decisions. Moreover, an even more primitive problem than identity is also alleviated by use of the Lingo—that of
loneliness: Use of the Lingo mitigates loneliness; and makes one
feel less isolated and more belonging. These three areas of need,
then—identity, separation, and loneliness—are all partially cared
for by the use of Lingo and account for the contagion it presents.

We have just discussed what may be seen as the more or less
benign aspects of group contagion, and have indicated some of
the needs these phenomena seek to take care of. But there are
also more virulent forms of contagion, often malignant and sometimes lethal. Among these are scapegoating, bullying, gang attacks, gangbangs and even murders. There is ostracism and there
are lynch mobs; there are Let's-Get-A-Victim Games, and Cruci-
fixion Rites. In fact, much of the terror arising out of joining a
group, especially a large group, where it is hard to hear and
attend to an individual voice, comes from terror of (a) being oneself the victim; (b) not being able to stop a group from making a
victim of someone else; and (c) finding oneself playing an active
role in the game of Getting the Victim.
A teacher is quite justified in becoming fearful when his group
is beset by a plague of sadism or action that is bound to lead to
destructiveness in one or some or even in many. Such a plague is
damaging not only to the victim, but also to the whole group of
participants. There comes a point in such mass action when the
course is irreversible, when the group can no longer be stopped.
This is a point where, though we know disaster is inevitable, it
seems the plot, as in a Greek tragedy, has to be acted out to its
bitter end. The contagion is no longer controllable; it seems to have
gone beyond the power of any member or leader to halt it. Where
that point is, and how to intervene before it is too late, is as
puzzling as it is crucial. When a teacher or leader has let matters
go beyond that point—as can happen sooner or later to all of us
who are in charge of groups—can we ever call a halt? How? If we
cannot, how can we live with ourselves and the consequences?
How can we accept the group that (along with ourselves) has

made, or let, the disaster happen? How can we help the group to live with the individual responsibility that each member, including the leader, has to bear, without wallowing in guilt to such an extent that nothing is learned from even the worst experiences but self-hate or more guilt? Overindulgence in these emotions—self-hate and guilt—often guarantees a repeat performance. How can we help the group—and ourselves as well—deal with the realities of the situation, and learn from them? And how, if we are particularly self-aware leaders or teachers, can we determine how much our own unconscious, our own undealt-with feelings have caused us to be blind or deaf, and so to miss the moment when intervention was still possible?

We do not use these solemn words here to refer to such situations as a group's going on a rampage or roughhousing a bit, destroying property or ending with a bloody nose here or there, a bruised shin, or even a sprained ankle or a two-stitch gash—although the dynamics that enter into those events may well be similar enough to the actual tragedies to serve to train us and the group to be aware of potential dangers. By giving us practice in timing interventions, such events may indeed prevent more serious ones. No, our solemn words refer to other events: to the roughhouse carried as far as murder or grave physical injury; the game of "Chicken" that ends in the hospital emergency room or even in the morgue; the "Let's make you the victim" game that ends in the ward of a mental hospital or even in suicide; or the "Let's get that bastard" game that ends in those great American sports the lynch mob and the posse. It is the sport of the "If it weren't for those devils—they're smarter, dirtier, sexier, lower, richer, lazier than we are—" that makes possible pogroms, concentration camps, Atticas, Selmas, Ku Klux Klans, whether of racial or religious flavor. That is the game that makes for action in the back alley, behind the school, for on-the-way-home trompings, muggings and other brutalities.

There are some good examples of this kind of tragic group contagion in literature, in many cases based on autobiographical experience. To name but a few: The short story "The Day of the Last Rock Fight" (in *Able Baker and Others* by Joseph White-hill. Boston: Little, Brown and Company, 1957) is an example of group contagion and consequent disasters in murder and guilt. In Lillian Hellman's play *The Children's Hour*, a child by group contagion ruins two women and a school. *The Chosen*, a short novel by Chaim Potok, begins with a boys' baseball game in which the contamination of combined religious fervor and violence nearly causes a boy's blindness. In *The Last of the Just* by André Schwarz-Bart, we see group contagion over centuries at last result in the destruction of six million Jews in the gas chambers of Germany. Another example is George Orwell's "Shooting an Elephant," as interpreted in *Interpersonal Dynamics*, edited by Bennis, Benne, Benler and Steele.

Many parents become very upset when their children are placed in a group for the "emotionally immature," "the disturbed," the "socially maladjusted," the "ungraded classroom" or a "class for the slow learner." Aside from problems of social status and fears—primitive, social and also realistic—that the placement reflects on the success of the parents themselves as parents (as indeed it sometimes does), the fear most often expressed is that: If you place my Johnnie with that bunch of crazy, wayout kids, he'll go crazy too. If you place my Mary with those dummies, she'll become dumb. If you place Tom with that gang of vandals, he'll become a vandal.

There is truth in the idea that people take on the coloration of their environment. To adapt to a group, one must become somewhat like it, even if only for a while or only superficially. Otherwise one suffers in the role of fringe figure or outcast. Yet, in many, many cases, parents are upset because they delude themselves into believing that their child, at whom the school's finger points, is free of the disease diagnosed, whether misbehavior, low IQ or lack of achievement. Parents tend to think of their child as if he were what they wish he were, and therefore they use the phenomenon of contagion to deny the aching facts. The child in question may be the ringleader of the vandals or a true delinquent rather than a mere lost lamb following a pack of black sheep. Parental denial of existing problems, because of the pain they bring, often lays blame at the door of contagion and creates a problem of resistance to facts already hard enough for the school to handle, and so makes them even harder for the school to treat.

Because people do indeed catch each other's modes of perception and behavior, there has been increasing desire on the part of educators, parents and all those interested in social change through the schools to arrange for more mixing of people. The hope in each subgroup of course is that the beneficial qualities of each will rub off on the other. The fear in each group is that destructive elements may do so, or that the subgroup's distinguishing differences will be so melted down by overexposure to other groups that the subgroup will lose its identity.

In the earlier part of the twentieth century, even within the public school systems, it was considered the best educational practice to have special schools, or at least special classes, for the intellectually gifted, for the slow learners, for those with particular scientific talent, for those talented in the arts. In many places special schools were provided (or came, de facto, to exist) for blacks, whites, Indians, Catholics, Jews, and so on. We need not discuss here the motivations that made this type of segregation an acceptable way of moving toward elitism or the racism implied in it. Nor need we discuss the results of that practice, which certainly intensified stratification not only by brains and race, but also by economic opportunity. Here it is appropriate to mention only that when a group becomes exclusive, it "excludes" the possibility of exposure to other perceptions, other ways of life, thought, and expression, and so by the quarantine it sets up limits experience and understanding for all. As this century has brought large masses of people closer together, we have developed a greater awareness of the need for communication and interchange at the source—in childhood and youth. Pressure for more and more heterogeneous grouping within the school grew—though often such grouping came about only by legislating it into the system. Thus, the dam was opened, and the force of "contagion" became free to do its work.

It has been established by many studies that when blacks and whites are exposed to each other under the leadership of suitably oriented teachers, in schools where variety of subjects and attitudes are appreciated and taught, both groups, black and white, do much better than they did when segregated. Likewise, it has been found that, barring extreme cases, where dull and bright are mixed, each learns from the other; the depth and breadth of learning increases for the total group when the needs of subgroups are cared for. Thus exposure to variety of experience and the consequent contagion is seen as a positive value to be pursued heartily.

Yet, however valid the basic idea, we have seen that its practical application lacks a sophisticated understanding of what happens in large groups in which subgroups have room for expression of their own characteristics, and in which the various tasks at hand determine kaleidoscopic changes in the membership of subgroups from task to task. Moreover, the task is not always what it seems: e.g., while the hour may be scheduled as geography time, the real task may be the integration of the bused-in students into the group. It takes an extraordinarily group-gifted teacher to sort out the real task from what the school board tells her should be her task. Unless she does this, however, the good effects of contagion get swamped, and the result is a homogenized product where no subgroup needs or characteristics are respected. When this happens all subgroups lose out and object; often they become so panicky that rather than work the problem out they retreat to ironclad small subgroups where none may join but the elect—the black, the white, the rich, the poor, the achievers, the troublemakers—whatever the subgroup specifies.

Retreat from contact is not unlike the medieval flight from the plague. People run to suburbs, to private schools, to their own ethnic groups. The fear that motivates them is a common one in group life: the fear of loss of identity, loss of the boundaries of the self, loss of those characteristics, attitudes, ways of speech and thought of one's subgroup in which one sees and knows oneself. The fear is that no one will remain himself, that all will be made uniform. Where differences are not accounted for and subgroup boundaries not respected within the heterogeneous group, this panic reaction and enmity or withdrawal—the familiar Fight-or-Flight phenomena—are bound to worsen, the more one fails to acknowledge the underlying emotions. But variety within a large group can in fact work well if subgroup boundaries are recognized, and if the "contagion" flows naturally from the task. The six members of a class, for instance, who are gifted in carpentry will become more available to each other when the task of making something together allows them to respect each other's skills and to help those less adept with tools. Those who are fond of science experiments or acting in a play or group discussion of current issues, can be open to the contagion of each other's ideas if in other areas their identity as subgroups is realized and accounted for, and the differences within the group accepted as assets, not threats.

With a great deal of work and with training in observation and analysis of the differences within a large group—a class or even a school—so that both subgroups and primary tasks can be identified, it is possible to use contagion as an enricher of education instead of fleeing it as a dread disease.

VII

The Staff

THERE IS overwhelming evidence that what a leader of a group really thinks and does, or how he really feels, gets itself communicated to his group whether or not he wishes this to be so, and regardless of what he may believe himself to be communicating. The teacher who in response to a child who has had a fight with another child glares at him red-faced and tells him: "In this classroom no one gets mad at anyone, and no one hates anyone" gets his real message across. Similarly, the principal who thinks of himself as democratic and open to ideas, but in fact likes to keep tight control and feels threatened by any move he sees as undermining his power, may, after making a statement of policy, ask for suggestions, but his "I'd like to hear what you all think about the change in schedule. Any suggestions?" will be greeted by silence, or at best by a polite extension of what has already been said.

As a matter of fact, an acute group leader or teacher can find cues in the group's response or behavior as to what those attitudes are that he has concealed from himself, or at least what his own attitudes have conveyed to his group. The group can thus become his teacher, helping him by their action to get in touch with his own feelings and attitudes.

Here is a story that shows how the group teaches the teacher: Mr. Stone, a fourth grade teacher, finds that one or another member of his class is continually getting into the kind of trouble in which the principal, Mrs. Johnson, has to be involved. Mr. Stone is embarrassed by the number of times this has happened. He has apologized to the principal and made a number of reasonable-sounding excuses for his students. He has scolded the class, deprived the group or at least the group-elected culprit of recess play, or sent naughty children to after-school study hall for expiation of their misdeeds. Still the misbehavior goes on—this day, John, that day, Lucy; last week, Susan, Greg and Tom; next week, Mark, Ellen and Bert. Mr. Stone goes home raging at his impossible class, worrying about his bid for tenure in the light of what the principal must be thinking of his management techniques.

Having calmed himself with a drink and a pipe, he now begins to ask himself what the group can be telling him about himself that he has not faced squarely. He unearths the concealed fact that he has since September been holding a grudge against Mrs. Johnson for assigning him a fourth grade class when he felt better equipped to teach the sixth grade. He had not believed her when she said he needed experience with the early development of cognitive and relationship learning. He thought she was discriminating against him and felt his assignment to the fourth grade to be a demotion. He thought he had handled his resentment and had adjusted to the change. He had even told himself and others he was glad about the change—the fourth grade was easier to handle. Now he found in his self-assessment that he was also angry with Mrs. Johnson for never coming in to see his class's exciting science project of which he and the children were both so proud; he wanted the praise that he felt he had earned. He had invited Mrs. Johnson several times, but though he had seen her visiting other classes, she had not come to his room for a class observation visit since early fall; it was now January.

Musing thus at home over the injustice of it all, he pounded his pipe on his hand and said aloud, "Yes, I am still mad—damn it, I think she has it in for me. She's a belittling, man-hating bitch." Having said that, he saw that he had somehow conveyed his resentment to her via his group, and that though he had scolded and protested, there had been a part of him which enjoyed irritating the principal—and this the children had responded to. They were acting in a way that answered his covert needs, even though these were contrary to his spoken desires. He now began to be amused at the recognition that, though she had not come to his class when he wanted her to, the children had seen to it that she nevertheless came often for momentary scolding visits, and he recalled how, after her departure, he had neither immediately silenced their mimicking of her flouncing exits nor tried very hard to stop their grumbling. He remembered that he had actually sometimes smiled at their antics before bringing them to order. Realizing that this resentment of his was calculated to do both him and the children harm, he could now think about whether he ought to approach Mrs. Johnson directly about his complaint, or deal with his resentments himself and not have to transmit them through his class. Having thus learned from his class about his unresolved feelings, he found now that the misbehavior that went on in his class miraculously no longer involved the principal but was contained within the class itself.

This kind of learning takes place among adults as well as among children. The difference is simply that children look to adults as guides for their future behavior and so integrate unspoken messages more thoroughly and more quickly. They may be thus more clear than adults about the discrepancy between what is said and what is so.

To illustrate how both adults and children model themselves more on leadership behavior than on words, consider an experiment tried by the director of a secondary school where there was a higher than usual incidence of lateness. Not only were students late for the beginning of school at 9 A.M.—they also reported late during the day for class after class, for interviews with the counselor, and even for their own student meetings and activities. The effect of exhortations addressed to school assemblies and even to separate classes lasted no longer than a day or two. Punishments and deprivations had even less lasting effect. The director recalled a story the late A. K. Rice of the Tavistock Group Relations Institute had told about his experience as consultant to a small family steel factory in England, where lateness and absenteeism had risen to an alarming degree and where even bribes of bonus-pay, extra snacks, and coffee and tea breaks had failed. Dr. Rice had suggested that every one of the people in management positions make it a point to be punctual and careful about their own times of arrival and departure. This was done, though with skeptical acceptance—but it was done. Within a surprisingly short time promptness of arrival as well as a marked decrease in absenteeism occurred. The school director decided to try the same device.

First, without saying anything, she wandered about the halls and noted that many teachers either came a little late to classes or rushed in breathlessly at the last moment, and that many others were in the staff room when the class bells rang. She found that at the starting time for teachers, 8:45, few were at their desks. Many came hurrying in just before the final bell at 9:00, but a few straggled in just after. She also noted that staff meetings which were scheduled for 4 P.M. actually began nearer 4:30 and that instead of ending at 5:30, meetings went on closer to 6:00, with some people drifting out while business was still going on.

Without scolding, she waited at the next meeting until 4:45 when everyone was there who was coming. She told the staff of her observations and passed out sheets with lateness statistics for students and staff. She asked them to help her in an experiment requiring that for at least one month, every one of the staff be rigidly prompt—that is to say, that the teachers come *not one minute early* and *not one minute late*; using good watches and checking them with the clock in the school entrance hall, and teachers were to follow the schedule to the second. She asked them to be very careful *not* to say one word to the students about any latenesses, but simply to be on the dot themselves and to note latenesses (without comment or disapproving looks) on a sheet

which they must without fail send to the school secretary at the
end of each class. "Remember," she said. "No comment, no looks;
just be there yourselves at the exact time, and, just as important,
close the class, or meeting, or whatever, at exactly the moment it
is scheduled to end, so there will be no pile-up of possibility for
lateness at the other end. If anyone wants to speak to you after
class or to get special help, schedule such interviews in study-hall
time or in the interval between school closing at 3:00 and the
time you are supposed to go off duty at 4:00. Leave at 4:00,
even if you only go to the staff room until the building is cleared
of children. Then of course, if there is work you wish to do in
your classrooms, the building is open until 5:00 and you are free
to stay here to do it. At 6:00 promptly, I will see that the building
is closed except for PTA meetings and special scheduled events."

She got the staff to promise to cooperate for one month, although they looked at her as if she had lost her senses, and she
heard expected grumblings and jokes about her naïveté and her
secret desire to be the countdown person for takeoffs to the
moon. She heard the teachers laughing at her idiocy as she went
down the hall for her coat and bag.

Her staff of twenty, however, except for one habitual latecomer,
did as she asked, and even that one, because of peer-group pressure, was able to be far more prompt than ever before. She collected all the late slips, and within one month—in fact within
three 5-day school weeks—was able to announce that the lateness
of the students had been cut from 46 per cent to 6 per cent. The
staff was amazed. Almost all of them voted to keep up the system
including punctuality at staff meetings for three more months.
They commented on the degree to which they found themselves
less frantic and less tired when they could be sure that the
boundaries of each class and each meeting were firmly set. And
all that had been accomplished without wasting time on futile
lectures on tardiness! They commented too on how much more,
rather than less as they had anticipated, the youngsters were using
the extra talk- and help-time in study hall period and in the hour
after school. And what a relief it was not to have to repeat everything for the benefit of latecomers! Their own meetings too

seemed to get more done in less time now that there was no need
for repetition. They recognized that the director herself in her
own behavior had done with them just what she had asked them
to do with their students.

Then the director surprised them all again by asking them to
see if they could reverse the process. They were shocked and
were now sure she was out of her mind. She had got what she
wanted, and everyone was happy. She laughed and agreed, but
reminded them that this was an experiment: she wanted to see
just how much influence staff-group leadership behavior in itself,
without words, had on the students. She reminded them it was
now May first and that school would end in late June, so that
not too much damage would be done if they went back to their
old habits. If, indeed, staff behavior was as significant as she
believed it to be in affecting group behavior, they would return
to the rigid-promptness regime in September when school began
again. With much reluctance the staff agreed to do as the director
asked, keeping equally careful track of tardiness. However, they
balked at going back to their old staff-meeting time habits. They
refused to return to the late beginnings and overtime they had
been relieved of. This amendment the director happily accepted.
The reverse procedure took a bit longer to do its work, since a
habit of promptness had been set in motion—which says something about learning and unlearning patterns for groups. Now the
director reported that within five weeks of the staff's retreat from
its rigid time schedule, lateness had risen from 6 per cent to 21 per
cent; by the time school ended two weeks later, lateness had
risen to 28 per cent.

The staff of this school never got over the lesson of the director's experiment, which was, indeed, a lesson in more than
promptness: that it was what was done by those in leadership
roles, not what was said, that furnished the barometer of what
would in the majority of cases be picked up by both staff and the
students. The director made no bones about the fact that she
hoped the lesson from this event would be translated to other
areas. As for promptness, the staff, that fall, except for new members who had not been in the original experiment, voted unani-
mously for a rigid staff-promptness schedule. The new members,

she reports, thought when they entered the school that they had come into a colony of military rule. All this setting of watches by the hall clock, this looking at the second hand before entering or leaving a class! They thought such behavior more appropriate to a spy mission than a school. They were, however, soon won over by pragmatic proof. It should be added that the director was aware from the start that the experiment would not have worked if she herself had not been punctilious about her own schedule, and if the great majority of staff had not only agreed to but acted upon the plan. It is the total ambiance of management's attitude that is relayed: without joint action, any plan is bound to be ineffective. By the same token, a leader may have marvelous ideas, but if his group is not willing and able to follow them out, they cannot, no matter how gemlike, be put into action.

To a very large extent, a school is only as effective as its staff will permit, and a staff is only as effective as the principal's or director's leadership permits. When a school's autonomy is circumscribed by its place within a system, the leadership of the controlling system can seriously hamper or brilliantly further the effectiveness of the principal and his staff and so directly affect the experience of the children.

Up to a point, a principal who is particularly adept in human relations, negotiations and clear thinking can operate in such a way that he gets more autonomy for his school, sometimes by direct confrontation, sometimes by persuasion and compromise on unessentials, sometimes by taking considered responsibility for controversial decisions and their consequences.

Likewise, though to a lesser extent, there are certain teachers (and these are not always the best as far as teaching skills are concerned) who are able, by charm or wiles, by obsequiousness, or favor-doing, or even by force and well-directed aggressiveness, to circumvent a principal's edicts and desires or even some of the orders received from above. This fact is not one that makes a school a happier place to work in, either for the children or the other staff members. There is bound in such cases to be some envy of the manipulator and some divisiveness in the staff. On the principal's part, even if he is blind to the maneuvering, at some level some guilt or resentment does exist, some awareness he is being "had."

Getting one's way by manipulation, even to promote good causes—such as the welfare of the children—may be a realistic lesson for children to learn from their teachers, but it is an uncomfortable one. It means that they are learning that to get a task done one must work people before one can work at the work. It is confusing for many children to deal with the message this kind of operation conveys. Children hear adults say: "Be open and honest," "Speak up," "Don't try to get around me"—yet they are aware that their class is, let's say, the only class who has managed to go on six class trips when others were allowed only three per class; that they alone got to stage a play at night, when they know the other sections of the eighth grade were refused this privilege. They may revel in their teacher's powers and resolve to be like him, and they may well have profited from his manipulations. They may or may not know that their teacher chauffeurs the principal home daily and that it is because of this or some other personal hanky-panky that special privileges accrue to their class.

Some children become apt students of ways to get around people, for purposes more or less noble; some are embittered by the hypocrisy involved in getting one's way, and for themselves adopt an attitude of withdrawal or of outrage. If this is in fact the uncomfortable reality of everyday life, then they are certainly exposed to the lesson at school. Such a lesson does not jibe with our moral or mental-health tenets, and thus it is bound to be a double-edged tool—a lesson that the ends justify the means, however much we preach otherwise.

For certain children, indeed, there is no need for such lessons from the staff unless for refinement of techniques. They seem to bring with them to school a full blown talent for getting their own way by manipulation. There are children who can wheedle or worm nearly anything out of most teachers, children who are so adept at sizing up a teacher's soft spots or weaknesses that they know just where, when, and how to attack or ingratiate themselves. Some such children can infect a whole class if the teacher is unable to recognize their maneuvers and to set firm limits and deal with them promptly. Some successful manipulators will grow up having mastered at home and at school a full curriculum of techniques useful in the control of others. These are our inveterate swindlers, petty and grand, our exploiters of others in personal, business or political relations. They are our future Watergate operators. The premium on pleasing in schools has too often taught them well and reinforced their conviction that this is what life is all about.

Other young charm-boys or charm-girls tend to be more guilt-ridden behind their charming surface than their more purely opportunistic brothers and sisters. They grow up with the gnawing conviction underneath it all that they are fakes. Even the most brilliant of them often end by telling their wives or their husbands, their therapists or their ministers, that they live in dread that some day they will be exposed. They have been so good at conning others they have ended by not knowing if they have any of the talents or skills other attribute to them. In their hearts, and in their dreams, they are sure that they have little inside, that their facility in taking in others must be sheer fakery. Sometimes that is true and sometimes it is not. But such charmers have lost the ability to distinguish; they often denigrate their real talents because they have so often got away with covering up their lacks.

Teachers who get conned or who fail to call a child on his maneuvers, teachers who are flattered and thus blinded by the child's courtship, reinforce the child-manipulator in getting his own way, in "getting away with it." Such a teacher often uses the child to satisfy his own vanity needs: he grades the child more for charm than for work. He does not set limits or help the child see that a piece of real effort actually does bring more rewards than a piece done only to please, or to maneuver.

With its emphasis on achievement, on success, on rewards for high grades, the leadership of a school often acts as if its task were indeed to teach the children how to "make it" in the world, one way or another, rather than to deal with the process of learning, of mastering the skills needed to cope. It may well be that to succeed in our schools, all of us from student to administrator have to devote a major portion of our energy to manipulation and circumlocution.

Our large-group culture certainly subscribes, by its commercial values or by its counseling, to the hypothesis that everything is done for some ulterior purpose, that little is of value in itself except as it can be used to achieve our own goals, covert or overt. You get a degree in order that you may later have two cars and own some real estate. You take certain subjects in order to ascend the next step in your career ladder, or to get the authorities off your back, or to silence or please your parents. Whatever we may say, this is what the staff and the total large-group hierarchy of the schools are often teaching us, in one way or another, in messages without words.

It is impossible to go into the meaning of the word "leadership" without immediately finding people debating the virtues and errors of democratic versus autocratic behavior, as if this were, in fact, the only way of thinking about leadership. Now everyone in America knows democracy is "good" and autocracy "bad," so the question becomes: how can we rid ourselves or our leaders of all vestiges of autocracy? (At least as far as the eye can see; as to what's done sub rosa—well, if they're skilled enough to hide the iron fist within that velvet glove or to pull off a Watergate break-in and so eliminate competition, so much the better.) How can we be democratic and still get things done—that is, done our way? In attempting to achieve the accolade of being a democratic leader and at the same time operate effectively, people get themselves into all sorts of pretzel-like positions. They may abdicate decision-making altogether, leaving it up to those for whom the decisions are made to decide for themselves—a rough thing to do to children who are until adolescence supposed to be exempt from major decision-making. Or they may delegate decision-making to their assistants, and so have built-in scapegoats to blame if the decisions are unpopular or fail to work. Or they may resort to a fancy kind of footwork, pretending to leave the decisions up to others, either assistants or those for whom the decisions are made, but in actuality offering only a spurious choice: if the group does not decide the way the leader wants it to, it soon finds its decision vetoed and another decision being put into effect.

All these maneuvers are carried out in the name of democracy, on the dual assumption that, one, democratic leadership means simply not asserting one's responsibility for decisions made, and, two, that leadership is a question of style rather than of doing, in the best possible way, what is appropriate for accomplishing a given task. True, some tasks lend themselves to participatory procedures and are best done that way, even if "that way" means that more effort and thought and time are needed in the process. But some tasks are better delegated and supervised, while others require immediate one-man decision-making. If the process of choosing the one man in question is truly democratic, then the person chosen must be trusted to make the decision. Not to make the decisions is a betrayal of the trust. That the person in charge may err is certainly true. It is also true that he may have to take hostility for doing anything or nothing. In any case, if the trust proves to be misplaced, *presumably*, in a working democratic system, the decision-maker will be removed from his job.

No one who has lived any part of the twentieth century can possibly be blind to the dangers of autocratic decision-making. Not only are people often forced to do someone else's will, but in accepting the passive role of sheeplike followers, they lose the ability to think out for themselves what it is they do want. They become like dependent infants, unable to survive without someone to decide the course of their lives for them; the penalty for not accepting the decisions so made may well be death, or at least imprisonment. True, in an autocratic system roads may be built and trains may run on time, as Mussolini sympathizers used to boast, but the travelers on those trains and roads become unthinking automatons, who fall into disarray and are lost when their leader falls or when he dies. Only the short-sighted can believe that overall or underlying tasks can possibly be done better under autocratic rule. (See Bruno Bettelheim's *The Informed Heart*.)

Yes, there are times when tasks demand immediate decision and action, when there is no time for participating democracy of any sort. In a fire, the fireman's command is not to be argued with. In a ship casualty, the captain must be obeyed. In battle or skirmish, the commanding officer, appointed presumably because of his training and skill, must make the decisions, and though all must take the consequences, it is the leader who will get the credit or the blame. But we are not so naive that we cannot distinguish between emergency behavior and the more long-term decision requirements of everyday life.

Trust, as we have already indicated, is a basic element in group survival. But too much trust is as dangerous as too little. In the former case, a leader, perhaps for multiple reasons, abdicates his responsibility without a thorough thinking-out of the facts, and leaves the decisions to be made by the led. In the latter case, the leader is unable to delegate power to anyone: he trusts no one. In both cases, effective and representative functioning of the group in its tasks is lost. We may think of Hitler's Germany and post-World War II France as examples, or we may bring the problem closer to current American school history and see the Teachers Union control in the Newark strike of 1969 as an example of too much trust given the leader, and New York City's reaction to Brownsville's attempt at planned community control of schools as an example of too little trust. Out of the human dilemma about trust—too much? too little?—comes, on the one hand, reluctance to delegate responsibility and authority to get tasks done, and on the other, a too willing urge to abdicate responsibility and shift the blame, laying down one's own power at the altar of "They told me to."

Some skilled leaders have the ability to select assistants on the basis of competence and to share responsibility with these delegates, while keeping responsibility for the overall final decisions in their own hands. Robert Kennedy's *Thirteen Days* gives us a brilliant example of shared decision-making in a crisis; note how the final responsibility rests clearly in John Kennedy's hands.

STAFF GROUPS

The Faculty Meeting

"Oh, God, it's the first Wednesday of the month—faculty meeting!" is the customary groan with which most staffs in most schools greet their scheduled time together. They think of the faculty

meeting as a necessary evil, a requirement, a bore, an event
only a little higher up on the ladder of happily anticipated events
than a dentist's appointment. For this reason many administrators
call only one staff meeting a month; others suffer through weekly
or even bi-weekly meetings. The paradox here often is that the
less frequent an activity as deadly as most large staff meetings,
the more it tends, if nothing is done about it, to get even worse;
while the more frequent the meeting, the greater the chance it
may engender something less deadly. This is partly because if
there is only one meeting a month, the time is taken up with
announcements and regulations. If there are more meetings, there
is at least a chance, given an imaginative principal, that something
more stimulating may come up as people get to know each other
somewhat better.

The larger the school, the more unpopular the staff meeting.
This, of course, is only logical, since in large groups it is always
more difficult to get discussions or interchange of opinion going.
In a large group, moreover, even the simplest announcements are
likely to be heard and interpreted differently by various subgroups. Indeed, half a meeting can be—and sometimes is—taken
up by arguments about what an announcement really meant, and
whether the announcer really wants the staff to do this or that, or
something quite different. In a large group, it is often difficult or
impossible to hear correctly; even when an announcement is
heard, no matter how simple the statement, there is inevitably
someone who will question some detail of it, and someone who
will comment further. But many people in the room have not
heard at all, some because they weren't listening, some because
of an undercurrent of private conversations, and some simply
because they are not interested. After any announcement, one
is sure to hear among the mumbling: "What did she say?" "Was
that Monday's schedule she was talking about or Thursday's?" "Is
that because of the new superintendent?" or "Has he flipped?
We've just got the whatnot straightened out!" Even if the
announcement is repeated, too much is going on for the speaker
to be sure the group as a whole has heard.

Moreover, if announcements affecting the whole school are

sent out in written form after they have been announced in staff meeting, a reasonable complaint emerges: "Why didn't he simply send the notices out in the first place? Why do we have to have a meeting for that? As if we don't have better ways of spending our time!" Given the general run of faculty meetings, this is a perfectly valid comment. To have a meeting because the city or county requires it is hardly reason enough to take two or three hours of the time of task-weary people. Considering the content of many such meetings it would indeed be more useful to the staff to make announcements over the loud-speaker at closing hour and then send them out in writing, and to order the teachers on that day, on pain of a supervisor's frown, to get out in the fresh air, or go shopping, or rest or just chat with friends away from the school building.

This is not to say that there are no good reasons to hold staff meetings. There is often a genuine need for interchange of views on problems and methods, for getting to know one's colleagues—for people who work in the same institution do have common concerns, no matter how differently they interpret them. They need to get together to talk about the children, about the subject matter they teach, about staff welfare, community and parent involvement, innovative programs, and so on. It is when these purposes are not being met by staff meetings, when essentially nothing is gained but a lesson, already too well mastered, on how to handle boredom, that an administration must consider whether it would not be better to cancel the meetings rather than to have "negative input." But would it not be better to redesign the staff meetings so that some, if not all, of the purposes listed are fulfilled? Knowledge of group dynamics will help in this undertaking.

The very idea of redesigning the staff meetings to meet staff needs more aptly brings us back to the subject of the effect the behavior of the leadership has on the group—in this case, to the effect of the principal's behavior on the staff. A principal who has the wit and initiative to look at his staff meetings and recognize that they are on the whole an exercise in futility, contributing little to staff communication, staff growth, staff morale, or even to the process of getting necessary immediate tasks done effectively, has, by that recognition, begun a process which indicates he is serious about the enterprise in which he is engaged and can look at it critically. Further, if he looks at the goals he shares with his staff and, with their active participation, first by open meeting, then by committee, designs a program for staff meetings which will attempt to meet those goals, he demonstrates the kind of leadership that at least does not avoid the difficult. Even if the principal and the planning committee prove not entirely successful, the process of redesigning in itself will have given the staff an opportunity to grow, to think, to communicate. Though final decisions may remain in the hands of the principal, the morale of the staff is likely to be higher at once, in anticipation of the redesigned meetings in which they are to have a responsible part. This is especially so if the principal is lucid and flexible enough— again with the participation of a staff evaluation committee—to discard any elements of the new design that don't work and try alternative methods.

Some principals get stuck at just this point. In spite of living, as most of them do, in a rigid system that allows little margin for error (thus insuring more errors) and little time to try things out for size and fit (thus perpetuating errors), some principals do take the time to rethink their programs, to redesign the meetings with the help of selected staff representatives, and to inaugurate new systems. But it is as if the principal's quantum of energy were exhausted at this point, as if he were announcing: "That's done and now we'll stick to it, come hell or high water." Yet any principal worth his salt would at once admit that any innovation is likely to have kinks in it, and that these will need to be worked out before it can be evaluated, as it must be, by pragmatic results.

By sticking to the basic goal, that of achieving staff meetings which will be effective in getting necessary work done, and so improving and enriching communication, staff morale and the fulfillment of school needs, the principal demonstrates realistic and valid leadership: that is, he recognizes it will take time, effort, doing and redoing, frustration, and even some failure to put together a plan tailormade for that particular group working at the particular task he is concerned with.

Staff Communication and the Leadership

Somehow the members of a staff must come to know one another, and the principal must provide opportunity for this. Once he knows his staff by observation on the job in class and, more informally, in the teachers' lounge as well as in personal interviews and chats, a principal can plan intelligently for useful staff meetings. Redesign works best if meetings are planned for both large and small groups.

A common guideline for administration in redesigning staff meetings is to limit the meeting of the large group to as brief a time as possible and to use that time for general purposes only. Usually, a general faculty meeting of approximately half an hour can suffice as a combination brief friendly get-together and a time for clarification of overall purposes. Refreshments and a few minutes of joint relaxation can create an oasis, however short-lived, of pleasantness for a population who have for the most part little opportunity to meet informally as a unit. Large group meetings can at the same time be used to get basic information across. Written notices and memos can be handed out and then clarified, for no matter how concise and efficiently prepared, such materials are likely to be unread, misread, or distorted, unless the written word is confirmed by human contact.

On occasion, it works well to have a large group convene for a special lecture or film or demonstration on a subject of interest to most of the staff. A consultant may address the group on problems of mutual concern or the group may meet for a pooling of the findings of separate groups which have been working on separate projects. The large group structure is useful too for the special events at which, after everyone has heard a speaker or a panel of speakers, a question or discussion period follows. If this form of meeting occurs too frequently, however, people stop listening; they use the time to doze or daydream, or they surreptitiously write notes for tomorrow's lesson plans. In short, their behavior is much like the behavior of their students when over-lectured to in large-group passive-listening positions. Once a month or once every six weeks should be enough for this kind of activity.

Another way of using the large group is to have the staff come together at the end of the allotted conference time to review what separate small groups or committees have done, to discuss the decisions made and the questions that arise out of them, and to indicate the direction work will take the following week.

Staff meetings other than those of the lecture, demonstration, or panel-program types do better when they break up into small groups after general announcements have been reviewed and questions settled. Such small group meetings may last an hour to an hour and a half, and the groups should be organized to meet special interests and needs. For example, in a high school there may be departmental or interdepartment meetings on subject matter to be taught, or on new materials, techniques, or behavior management problems and case studies. A group or two may wish to engage in an experiential study of groups by studying their own behavior as a group, or a group may plan seminar discussions of relevant educational literature—something many teachers wish they had time for, but rarely do. Or a group may explore the problems of race and economic class differences as these affect the school population. There is no limit in the number of areas of genuine concern to the staff that may properly and profitably be dealt with by such groups. In addition, subgroups may seek to enhance their ability to use their own resources by arranging for consultation either with a person proficient in the particular subject under discussion or with one proficient in leading small groups.

If they work, staff meetings can be a genuine tool for in-service training. They can serve the purpose so sorely neglected in schools of emphasizing the human need to come together and to exchange experiences. They can help each member exert his own authority by offering opportunities to give the principal the information he needs to decide on policy. Without this information, a principal does not have the basic material for making decisions and changes, or for dealing with those higher in the hierarchy than he is to bring about the changes a staff needs in order to operate more successfully.

A questionnaire sent out to 87 schools within a city system asked the staffs to describe the kind of meeting that would do best in their schools. The answers were: More talk about the children; more knowledge of what other teachers are doing; more help with issues of immediate urgency, such as management of problems (or, to use the usual wording, "discipline problems"); presentation of innovative methods, such as the use of learning machines and behavior modification techniques; more help in learning to deal with parents, with the very slow, the very gifted and the very disturbed; suggestions about how to use the specialists who come in for a few hours each week—the remedial reading teachers, the art and science specialists, the gymnasium or dance specialists, the school psychologists, the social workers. A list compiled from these questionnaires pointed out problems that cried out for the attention of principals; it was sent to them with suggestions for implementation, and a meeting was called to discuss the matter. Out of the eighty-seven principals, only twelve came. Out of these twelve, only four made changes in their staff-meeting format. All four reported being happy with the changes made, and all were planning to maintain them. There was unfortunately no data in this study from the staffs as to their comparative evaluations.

Informal Staff Group Meetings

Before we move on to the question of the administration and its relations with higher administrative echelons referred to above, there is one other type of staff group we should consider, the multifarious informal group.

There are, within the school geography, certain places—the staff room, the teachers' lounge, a table or alcove in the cafeteria set aside for faculty, and sometimes, in those schools where smoking is prohibited, the custodian's den in the basement—where the staffs meets informally. It is here—most often in the staff room—that cliques are formed, and alignments made and broken. It is here that gossip and rumor are shared, along with exchange of laughter and indignation, and the discussion of possible methods of infringement on, or circumnavigation of, the regulations. It is here that the staff discusses the principal, as well as the children and their often-cursed parents (in staff rooms the parents brought up are nearly always cursed!). A clever and power-hungry teacher finds the staff room fertile ground for planting seeds of dissension and plotting coups to undermine the principal or a teacher-favorite. A suspicious and jealous type can use the room subtly or directly to vilify other teachers. Here too friendships are made and personal problems come to light. The staff, like its student counterpart, has its secrets, kept between elected members and away from others. If the secret is actually breeched, or even is only thought to be, feuds arise. Like the children in the classroom, the teacher group chooses its scapegoat, and the scapegoat participates, willingly or unwillingly, in being chosen. And here the leaders—the fighter, the rebel, the doer, the sniper—all are selected out, usually in relation to the principal. The mode of relationship to authority will depend on whether the principal is liked or disliked, respected or held in contempt, on whether he is deemed by the group to be competent to do his jobs of running the school and of negotiating for the school with the system and its administration.

To study a staff room as people come in and out is a fascinating way to see how power emerges in a group, where the morale, the tone, of the school comes from, and how the leader is and remains the delineating factor, even if he never comes into the room.

Although temper tantrums and tears do occasionally appear in the teachers' staff room, they are more often staged in the ladies' rest room and, for all I know, in the men's room as well. Though sojourns there may start as a solo retreat in which the rest room is chosen for privacy, usually, especially at the beginning or end of the school day and in the lunch periods, one staff member is joined there by two or more others, sometimes accidentally, sometimes because of signs and sympathy, sometimes simply out of curiosity, and often in the service of the gossip chain—a chain that links most staff members. But the usual gossip center of the school is the staff room—the place where teachers mark papers, play cards, have coffee and visit. The less open the legitimate route for communication among staff members, the stronger will be the chain of gossip. The staff room is the incubator for tea and sympathy, for fun and gossip and rumor.

A wise principal stays out of the staff room much of the time, knowing his presence will alter the tone and make more tense— no matter how friendly the principal may himself feel—an atmosphere that needs to be relaxed, considering the amount of tension teachers are burdened with by the demands of their work. But equally, a wise principal will not completely avoid the room. He may drop in for coffee once or twice a day for a few minutes. This dropping in without barging in indicates interest and a shared enterprise. It indicates a desire to give the staff an opportunity to tell their gripes before these mount and occasion a serious explosion, or get carried about without being communicated. Talks with or, better, listening to, the teachers, as they speak of this or that problem with a particular child, give the principal a comparatively non-threatening way to find out what's happening in a classroom. His support and interest will usually be perceived as just that, and staff respect and loyalty are enhanced.

ADMINISTRATION AND THE HIGHER ECHELONS

Many administrators keep people apart because they are afraid of dealing with groups. This maneuver invariably causes serious trouble. It adds to the depersonalizing of the staff, to the isolation of staff members and to the cog-in-a-machine-assembly-line psychology that is such an offensive, depressing, and dehumanizing feature of modern society. When a principal or leader succeeds in isolating one staff member from another, it is harder to get a joint program on the road, because no one trusts anyone else. Why should they trust each other when they know each other so little? Although soliciting individual opinions may masquerade as a democratic method of operating, it is anything but that. People who have only peripheral or ritualistic contact with one another in spurious staff meetings or private tête-à-têtes tend to give up trying to feed data into the group; they are likely to avoid giving information to the leadership, since that seems pointless or spiteful or mischief-making. Thus, no matter how insightful a leader may be, he is likely to have too little information to be able to make wise decisions. When that is the case, everyone, leader and staff alike, abdicates his part in decision-making, and the task is ill-served. It would appear from the frequency with which this situation occurs that groups are so frightening or bewildering to their leaders that many an administrator would covertly rather fail in his task than risk being part of a group. I have seen an extremely able man fail in his job simply because he was terrified of groups. He would conscientiously pick one person after another to confer with. Each person consulted thought the principal's attentive listening meant support of his ideas. Each in turn was disappointed. Each felt secret negotiations were going on behind his back. No decision could be made with confidence because no group as a whole was ever made the vehicle for communication or policy formulation. Until a reorganization was made under a more group-minded person, work was minimal and staff turnover sky-high.

The solution for the leadership lies, as it does in reference to any task-oriented group, in thoughtful, arduous, though often frustrating, labor. It involves first being sure what the task is and then knowing who is on the scene to perform it so that the various portions of the task may be appropriately delegated. Where a principal has inherited a staff he has not chosen and assigned to its task, the searching out of specific talents and general efficiency may take imagination and insightful, sensitive labor. Some of the inherited staff may be superannuated or otherwise not competent to teach at all; others may not be competent to teach the particular subject or grade assigned them. There may be some who have personality difficulties, and some whose life situations are for the moment affecting their work adversely. Teachers who are untrained or inexperienced in a particular situation may be helped, as may some of the others. Indeed, it is rarely understood that a person incompetent in one situation may be better, may even be outstanding in another.

It is, then, essential that the principal know and utilize the assets in his staff and find ways to circumvent or minimize its deficiencies. To do so, he must have the power to get rid of those whose incompetence is damaging to the task (of helping the students in their learning) and to the group. Very often getting rid of the incompetent is very difficult in a public school system. The current practice in this dilemma is to transfer the incompetent, and even those who carry extreme disturbance, from one school to another within the system. Sometimes such a teacher is "kicked upstairs" to an administration post, where "at least the children won't be hurt." Although commonly resorted to out of desperation, this last is a pseudo-solution which ignores the power of a group to select one of its members and dump all the "bad"—that is, the non-group-fitting—attributes onto that one person and so avoid taking into account the irrational, or defiant, or malfunctioning aspects of themselves or their leadership. But if, indeed, as sometimes happens, there is someone who really *is* incompetent, whether because of temporary or permanent personality difficulties, or because of insufficient or inappropriate training and skill, or because of attitudes dangerous to the job of teaching or staff participation, the leadership must have the power to get rid of that person. Both the leadership and the group must inquire into the question of the extent to which they have contributed to making the person ineffective or unacceptable, but in the end the leadership must have the right of dismissal and must have the data to negotiate with higher-level administration to see to it that the students, the staff and the overall task do not suffer to the point of destruction because of the ill-functioning of one member. True, effective leadership and good group task-oriented morale can surprisingly often bring the odd-man-out into the fold, can help him achieve at least a minimal level of functioning. But sometimes, even under the best circumstances, and even at a minimal level, this is not possible, and the teacher must go.

What has been said about the relations between staff and leadership of a single school, and about the effect of leadership radiating from staff to children, and indirectly even to parents, is equally basic to the relation of leadership to staff in higher echelon administrative jobs. The word "higher" here is not at all intended to imply any real level of importance; it simply indicates level of hierarchy in terms of range—it refers to people responsible for overall policy, materials and budget as these affect several schools or all schools of a system. Included in "higher echelons" here are the school departments concerned with mental health and physical health, with the management of building and equipment, with community relationship, adult education and vocational training, as well as the administration department or school board itself.

In each case, the quality of leadership will depend on the administrator's ability to define the major task and the subtasks and his skill in delegating authority. It will depend on the ability of the leader to communicate appropriately and to elicit communication in order to get necessary information. It will depend too on the leader's ability to use his time effectively, to arrange meetings to meet needs as they arise. Some meetings will involve the leader and one other person; these are the meetings where the working out of understandings or feelings can be handled best. Some tasks will require small groups or committees to get spadework done on separate aspects of the job. Some tasks will involve the presence of larger groups for more formal announcements and for the discussion of vital issues, or just for general enrichment and information.

The ability of administrative leadership to ferret out what is not immediately apparent—what remains unsaid—as well as to understand what is said is a matter of primary concern. The amount of well-founded trust between leadership and staff will depend on the leader's ability to be open with his staff without burdening them with woes not relevant to their concerns, and on his willingness to take criticism and blame without falling into frenzies of *mea culpa*. It will depend too on his receptivity to staff suggestion, though the leader must guard against reading every idea that is brought forward as an imperative because he fears the price of ignoring it may be destruction of his image as a good fellow. The accolade of leadership as a measure of popularity is a direct result of our educational system—how many people vote for Johnny or Jane is right out of sixth-grade culture. "The most popular girl or boy in the class" is the high school yearbook value which deludes many into thinking popularity rather than task-functioning is the sine qua non of leadership.

One of the major agonies of good leadership is the fact that one is often hated, overtly or covertly; overt hostility, however unpleasant, is far easier to handle than covert antagonism. A leader—principal, department head, superintendent, or board member—is often hated for a combination of reasons. He may in fact be detestable, or he may be doing things or deciding things in a way that no one likes. He may be trying to change things— always an unpopular course of action—and he may be doing it too fast, sometimes in the hope of becoming popular or famous. Or he may be unwilling to change things when change is essential, sometimes in the desperate hope of keeping his popularity, or for fear of revealing his own inadequacy in the face of change, or simply out of shortsightedness—he may not understand the need for change. He may be envied for his position, power, or higher income, or because of attractiveness or charisma, or because there is an even higher position in the offing for him. Or he may be hated because he is no good at his job.

But again the leader may be hated not for himself but because he represents authority, and very few, if any, among us are simple and clear in our relation to authority. The unresolved element in our relations with our parents, our siblings, our friends, our husbands, our wives, to say nothing of our relations with past authorities—teachers, ministers, doctors, bosses—makes relating to those who represent authority complicated, even distorted. We project our own dependency needs, our fight-and-flight needs, our ambitions and suspicions, our distrust and our basic greed onto the person who leads us. The leader thus becomes a target for complaints both well- and ill-founded. His behavior and words are distorted to reflect the myriad unresolved problems of those he leads. A leader—no matter how skilled—has a gigantic task in trying to differentiate real from unreal reasons for the hostility he suffers. There is a limit beyond which explaining oneself is futile, yet up to that point some explanation is needed. The fine line in question is often blurred.

Willingness to face hostility without asking for more than is necessary is one qualification for leadership. In our country particularly, where people want so much to be the good guy, the nice fellow, the role of leader is especially painful. Too often, as we have said, we think of the battle for leadership as a popularity contest, and fail to choose as leader the person who, popular or no, good fellow or curmudgeon, is the best man to do the job. A leader who bases his leadership on being liked is likely to be as much a prey to seduction and manipulation as to be a seducer or manipulator himself.

SOME ADMINISTRATIVE PITFALLS

There are many administrative pitfalls, among them some that seem to me particularly prevalent and pernicious. Here are some of them:

The Popularity Contest Philosophy of Leadership

Here the task, however valued in the abstract, is forgotten or discarded in haste each time an issue arises where the leader must make a decision which he thinks will inflict pain, cause trouble, or make him disliked. But the fact is that if the job has to be done, and if it is a job that most agree is worth doing, immediate pain and discomfort, great as they may be, and great as the show of hostility aroused may be, will bring far less basic distrust and disrespect than defeating or deserting the task.

The "minority patsy" is a special case of "Popularity Contest Philosophy." Hiring a person who is less competent for a particular job, and in so doing passing over an incumbent who is more capable on the ground that the favored person is a desirable political choice, or is black, or is of the right background, age or sex, may indeed make a leader popular for the moment. Nonetheless, the result is invariably misery for those with whom the favored incompetent has to work. They have to spend time and energy making up for his lacks, and as a result they build up resentment. Often undeserved disrespect is the lot of the person who is chosen for a job not because he was qualified but for unrelated attributes. There is also increasing disrespect and even anger toward the boss who has hired him with so little regard for the staff's work needs and so much for his own comfort or vanity. In many ways, the selection of a person for leadership on extraneous grounds makes him a "patsy"—a sacrifice—and causes loss of respect from the very group he has been selected to represent.

The Non-Job-Doer

The Non-job-doer is the administrator who agrees to do a job or part of it but does not really believe in the work, and so consciously or unconsciously resists the task. Invariably in such cases the meetings, the staffing, and the decisions stall and there are many delays. Schedules become tight, crises arise, the project gets stuck, and in the end the work doesn't get done. If one analyzes the picture, one can see in every aspect of it—from the way appointments are made, the way decisions are delegated, the way the task is organized—that a beautifully conscientious job has been done to bring about failure. The staff that works in this sort of organization is made up of some of the most frustrated employees to be found anywhere.

The Samson Agonistes Administrator

The phenomenon of bringing the temple down with one when one leaves is something to look out for when an organization begins not to get its work done, when it chooses the wrong people to do a job, at a time when the director or higher echelon people are planning to retire or are about to resign. The idea seems to be "If I can't be here to do it, I'll see to it that it fails." The motivation is often quite unconscious, but the damage done to the institution is sometimes lethal and unregenerable.

The Helpless Leaner

The administrator who is a helpless leaner cannot make a move without calling in everyone to moan, groan, sympathize, and advise. The curious thing is that although more and more people get called in (usually one at a time), and although all are made to feel their advice has been priceless, no one's advice is ever taken. Nothing gets done; doubts always intervene. Such administrators may be perfectionists who fear to take a risk. Another name for them is "yes-but-ers."

The Prima Donna

The prima donna has to do it his way and only his way. He puts old incumbents down, or even out, and by the second week after taking over, considering himself skill incarnate, he has walked over everyone's toes so that unless he is one of the rare ones who can get away with it, he is not only hated but makes collaboration in the work impossible.

Let it be said at once that any working soul can add twenty more such types to my list. These five, however, are prevalent in schools.

In this chapter we talked first about leadership in the staff of a single unit, the school. We indicated the power leadership has there, in influencing group behavior even in ways of which it is unaware, and shown how the influence of teachers on the children's group connects directly with the influence of the principal on the staff group. The principal and his assistants in the administrative jobs in the school reflect the covert influence as well as the overt power of the system's department chiefs and superintendent; these in turn bow not only to the temper and moods of the guardians of the budget, but also to the controlling currents and undertows of the political stream, as well as to cultural pressures from above, below and sideways.

And so the arrows of pressure change direction. For as we now see, group influence on the school is set by the parents and the community—at least that part of the community, that faction of the parents, that uses its influence through group meetings and group statements, and the press, and through demonstration and concerted action. The forces they command may be used to achieve change either forward or backward. In either case, the influence, when mobilized, is overwhelming. When the large group of the public realizes this truth and acts upon it, change occurs.

Often the welfare of the children, on whom education is supposed to focus, is forgotten in the interplay of special interests and influences, and the children, alas, cannot speak up for themselves. Sometimes, contrary to public conceptions, it is not the parents, and surely not the lawmakers, who have the children's real interest at heart—it is the teachers. But sometimes when the teachers' own self-interest is at stake, teachers may work against the interest of the children. The interrelatedness of all these group forces as they press upon each other and get pressed upon in return seems to call for vector analysis to disentangle and put to use the energy so available and so often wasted. I shall deal briefly with these forces in the next chapter, not because they are so unimportant as to deserve brevity, but on the contrary, because the task of discussing them is so gigantic that a discussion in full would be an encyclopedia of power and thus too much for us to tackle here.

VIII

The Powers That Be—
and Those That Could Be

HARD AS it is for any group within the school social system to deal with its own members (for children to relate to one another, for teachers to work together, for principals to communicate with department heads), it is at least twice as hard for members of one group to deal with groups other than themselves (teachers with children, administration with teachers or counselors, pupil personnel specialists with superintendents, and all of these with The Board). If managing this interrelationship is a herculean task, then for the subgroups of the school social system to deal fruitfully with groups outside—groups such as the parents and community—is a googolplex times as hard. (A googolplex is a finite number with a million zeros after it!) And yet to survive and to be of use, to accomplish its task, produce its product—namely, to turn children into adults educated in the skills and mores of the culture—a group must continually communicate and negotiate with groups outside itself.

These outside groups are inextricably bound each to its own purpose and its fate. They orbit around the school in overlapping circles of self-interest and involvement. Parents, the community, health agencies, political parties, social and religious movements, special interest groups and legislative and budget-awarding bodies come and go, until, as in some topological problem in rubber-sheet geometry, it is hard to tell which is outside and which is in.

At the simplest level, there are parents and there are teachers —and even that relationship, as representatives from either group will testify, is anything but simple. Consider the relationship of parents to the school groups with which they as individuals most frequently deal—teachers, counselors, principals, school psychologists, social workers, and attendance officers. That in itself is a complicated structure representing different points of view and different interests. "The child is the common concern that brings us together" is the cliché that opens or underlies most parent–teacher meetings. Like many clichés, it is partly true and partly half-true; since the interests of each of the half-dozen groups mentioned above may differ, and the child may be either the reason or the excuse that has brought them together, not necessarily the subject of unanimous concern. The child often is used as a tool by means of which each group can further its own interests. The phrase "We are all interested in the child" is thus often more ritual than fact.

At the most complicated power-politics level, one can see how readily the ballooning of incidents between and among groups may get out of hand. (Witness the White House Watergate group and its relations with Congress, the judiciary and the press!) Out of this kind of escalation of group pressure, tragedies often arise. Our history books and contemporary newspapers testify to this. Schools have not been immune from the disease—the Newark, New Jersey, teachers' strike in 1970 is one example; the New Orleans strike of 1971 is another. The Ocean Hill-Brownsville defeat of decentralized schools offers a horrifyingly good example. *Teachers and Power* by Robert J. Braun gives the story of the American Federation of Teachers. In doing so, it exposes the anatomy of one major group-power controlling the destiny of the schools and the children, who are all but forgotten as group vies with group to survive, negotiate or dominate, rather than sell out or go under. For this report of the episode, I am indebted to Mr. Braun's chapter on Ocean-Hill Brownsville.

The elements making for tragedy in the Ocean Hill-Brownsville episode were many. (1) Economically deprived, largely black and Puerto Rican children were deprived of consistent schooling for nearly a year—they, whose skills and future required intensified and imaginative education, were given no education except the negative teaching that power begets more power, and that power, unwisely used, can destroy the best laid plans. (2) A Ford-funded, legislatively supported community-participation program planned for the education of the children on the basis of what the community saw as their needs died. It had tried to avoid the irrelevancies and deficiencies apparent in the unwieldy bureaucracy of the education department of the City of New York. Despite money from a most respectable source—The Ford Foundation—and an urgent message from the City's mayor, John V. Lindsay, as well as a more grudging mandate from Albany, the state capital, all failed before the more efficiently organized, ruthlessly led power-group, the United Federation of Teachers A.F.L./ C.I.O. Teachers Union local (Local 2) of New York City. (3) A third tragedy, and one that too often occurs in the midst of and in the wake of such group turmoil, was not only the emergence, but also the exploitation of racism by all powers. Since a majority of the New York City school teachers in Local 2 were Jewish, anti-Semitism rose dangerously high; and equally unnecessary, on the other side, many teachers and their families and friends became anti-black and anti-Puerto Rican. There was of course some violence, which is always either a tragic expression of helplessness on everyone's part or a provocation calculated to produce further violence to exploit for one's own ends.

The conflict began with the complaints first of individual parents and then of the community as a group that certain teachers were discriminating against black children; that these teachers were unable to teach black children because of their racist attitudes and their contempt for or ignorance about blacks. The governing board of the Ocean-Hill Brownsville experimental schools transferred thirteen teachers and six supervisors out of the

district back to the central board for reassignment. Since transferred teachers supposedly have few rights to have their cases
heard so long as another job awaits them, while "fired" teachers
do have such rights, Albert Shanker, the U.F.T. leader, claimed
the teachers had been "illegally fired." Though they had not in
fact been fired, the teachers were ordered by Shanker to go
back to the schools of the district in opposition to the directions of
the school administration. The city school superintendent, Bernard
Donovan, and his group confused matters further by reinstating
the teachers and ordering hearings of their cases, though this is
not necessary under transfer proceedings. Immediately after this
event, U.F.T. lobbyists in Albany distributed literature in the
legislative chambers warning that decentralized schools would be
operated "on the basis of local prejudice based on color, race or
religion." When 350 teachers of the district refused to meet with
the local superintendent Rhody McCoy (an extremely talented
black educator), Shanker cried "lock-out," the pro-decentraliza-
tion forces in Albany collapsed and the bill was defeated.

The U.F.T. leadership and followership used fear of threats,
retaliation and media control well. Braun in his book states:

To summarize: From a wide-ranging variety of sources, the
concept of decentralizing the administration of the New York City
school system and the concomitant control over personnel, curriculum and budget in a small geographic area was offered as a
possible solution to the city's apparently impossible educational
problems. The idea received support from a variety of organized
community groups, such as anti-poverty agencies, which had had
some experience in local program and budget control. It also was
endorsed by Mayor Lindsay, who saw it not only as a means of
improving education but also as a means of reducing the power of
the city's educational bureaucracy and of wringing more money
from Albany. The New York State Board of Regents, by law the
technical overseer of all public education in the state, also supported the idea as a means of improving the notoriously poor
quality of instruction in the state's largest city. The Ford Foundation, which provided planning funds and technical assistance to
the experimental districts created to test the idea, endorsed it,

viewing it as a method of renewing the interest of local residents
in the successes or failures of public schools—and thereby providing a catalyst for improvement. Several members of the state
Legislature, some for fiscal reasons, others for political or educational, lent their support.

Arrayed against the concept were those institutions, organizations and people likely to lose the most from the implementation
of a radical restructuring of the educational bureaucracy—the
school board which controlled it, the educational administration
which ran it, and the two major trade-union organizations which
derived their power from it, the Council of Supervisory Associations and the United Federation of Teachers. They represented the
educational status quo. Of these the U.F.T. was by far the most
powerful, the least susceptible to public accounting and ideo-
logically the most prepared to fight against the concept. Once the
school board had had its collective mind changed for it through
the addition by Mayor Lindsay of prodecentralization members,
the U.F.T. stood virtually alone as the major opponent of reform.

Through a series of actions which included a general refusal
to accept the legitimacy of the decentralization idea and its experiments, four strikes, intensive lobbying efforts and the use of a
public-relations campaign, the U.F.T. was able to produce a
decentralization bill which absorbed, and therefore destroyed, the
apparently successful experiments. It was also able to make the
terms "decentralization" and "community control" synonymous
for many people with black racism, turmoil in the schools and
potential civil disorder, thus making it almost certain that such
reforms would not be tried again in New York or in any other
major urban center in which the U.F.T. holds bargaining rights.
(And the U.F.T. holds bargaining rights in nearly every urban
center.)

"Things have worked out fine," Shanker was to muse months
after his victory. "That entire board of education is gone. That
superintendent of schools is gone. We got a decentralization law
about 80 percent of which is consonant with what we wanted. We
exhibited enough strength so that the black and Puerto Rican
paraprofessionals voted for us rather than a rival group, because
they wanted a strong organization. We were able to get an excellent and unprecedented contract the following June because the
city was unwilling to face another shutdown. I think it would have

taken us ten years to get the benefits that we got in that one single contract."*

But why was the victim Ocean Hill-Brownsville, not P.S. 201 or the Two Bridges district in Lower-Manhattan? One of the primary reasons was the success of that particular district. It was working and, had it been left alone, might have provided a persuasive case for the most advanced community-control bills. The elections for the local governing board had drawn more than twice as many voters as had voted in a local State Assembly election. The board had hired as its district superintendent a respected supervisor, Rhody McCoy, an educator who knew something about the use of media in instruction and was willing to try a variety of innovative approaches to schooling: team teaching, bilingual learning, a Montessori class, courses in Afro-American history and others. Attendance within the schools of the district had risen substantially and the local district acted as a kind of informal referral service for residents with health and housing problems in order to generate a true feeling of "community," a community with its schools as the centerpiece.

Not only did the district appear to be successful but it had made progress without the U.F.T.'s "More Effective Schools" program, a considerably more expensive approach to urban education. The local board had specifically rejected M.E.S., a move that angered the U.F.T. There is a whole series of offices at the U.F.T.'s Park Avenue South headquarters devoted to proving that M.E.S. works; the union didn't need the local experimental district to prove that M.E.S. wasn't necessary.

Most significantly, however, the Ocean Hill-Brownsville governing board was willing to fight, to do something not even the central school board or John Lindsay was willing to try—challenge the U.F.T. hegemony over public education in New York City. Rhody McCoy could have, as most administrators in the system had done, informally "worked out" the transfer of unwanted teachers with U.F.T. representatives. But at the time, the U.F.T. had no contractual authority over transfers; it would have been a violation of administrative prerogatives of the local and the central board as well as silent and forced tribute to the union, a power without real standing. McCoy and the governing board would not budge; the administrative power over transfer was not for sale. When the

* *Teachers and Power*, pp. 221–23.

suspended teachers and administrators defied McCoy's order of reassignment, he formally charged them with insubordination— something Bernard Donovan was unwilling to do after the teachers in Ocean Hill-Brownsville began taking orders solely from Shanker. When 350 teachers struck the experimental district in support of the original nineteen, McCoy charged them with excessive absences and asked for the invocation of the state's Taylor Law against strikes by public employees—again something Donovan refused to do, although even he could not swallow the U.F.T. statement that the 350 had been "locked out." [The 350 even managed to be paid for their holiday. RJB.] Throughout the crisis, it was McCoy and the local governing board who "played it straight," not Shanker and the U.F.T. The union through "informal negotiation" with the central board had won the right of unlimited transfer *out* of the experimental districts, a violation of its own contract with the central board and an initially devastating blow to the nascent and vulnerable experiment. This certainly was not playing it straight. Inevitably, McCoy and the local board lost; they had, perhaps foolishly, perhaps bravely, perhaps both, challenged the U.F.T. and the union had to destroy them, both to preserve the union's own credibility as the strongest organization in town—a bit like the United States "keeping its commitments" by nearly annihilating a client country—as well as to paint true community control the most awful shade of failure.

The U.F.T., of course, would have been readily content not to engage in such clumsy and obvious slaughter, had either the school board or the political structure done an adequate job in behalf of the union. For the first few acts of the tragedy, Shanker said and did little, viewing the drama warily but passively from the union's Park Avenue perch. That appeared to be the correct approach; after all, any good bureaucrat—and Shanker is that—would know that the central board would do its utmost to prevent amateurs from proving its expendability. Only when it became apparent that the central administration lacked the muscle to kill decentralization did the union become an active belligerent—and only when the demonstration districts expressed their pointed intention of ridding themselves of all past vestiges of failure, union and board alike.*

* *Ibid.*, pp. 233–35.

The U.F.T. after its success in shutting down Ocean Hill-Brownsville went on to amass more power with the City and wreak more havoc upon the schools and the community. It struck four times, once in May 1968 against the Ocean Hill-Brownsville School District, and again in September, October and November against the city as a whole. It defeated the whole trend of the city away from bureaucracy and toward participating community school boards, away from the union solution and toward a development of educational plans which might have worked, given as much community interest as Ocean Hill-Brownsville displayed.

Most important in terms of future implications for other cities across the nation, the U.F.T. exhibited the power of bestowing upon whatever political or governmental agency *it* chose the ultimate responsibility for operating the schools. It never dealt directly with the governing board; it simply refused to recognize it as an interested party and thereby stripped it of its power. The U.F.T. finally dealt with the city administration and the state Education Department to end the strike—forcing the two agencies to create those conditions which were best for the union and to take responsibility for them. In a sense, labor chose its management, a through-the-looking-glass reversal of the despised company union. The union thus becomes the ultimate in unresponsive bureaucracies—it is not itself responsible for the damage it may inflict, but has the power to choose which political subdivision will be responsible. An incredible power. And one that could conceivably not only take the public out of the public schools but also replace it with a private organization so untouchable—and therefore free to take whatever action it chooses according to the divine right of its enlightened leadership—that it will be able to assume quasi-dictatorial powers over the system which it is supposed to be serving.*

What are the implications of such experiences for the groups involved? We do not, of course, imply that every parent-teacher conference ends in disaster, nor that every negotiation among

* *Ibid.*, p. 243.

state, community, parents, union and school leads to an Ocean Hill-Brownsville. The example was cited only to indicate that since there is a boundary between groups because their basic tasks differ, and therefore their views of their own interests differ, there is always a potential for either negotiation and agreement, or impasse and quarrel, which can mount and involve other groups within the system. In such cases, the original concern, the child, may be either forgotten or exploited. The reminder of Ocean Hill-Brownsville illustrates that the danger is no academic matter. Any teacher in a neighborhood where activists and community organizations are alert to sensitive issues is aware that nearly everything that used to be of purely professional interest— curriculum, methods, school placement, transportation—can now be used as kindling to start uncontrollable fires.

Take the simple issue of corporal punishment, a shocking recourse to violence in the face of helplessness by an adult group whom we expect to model and to teach control and the use of the mind to deal with irrationality. Children, unfortunately, and against all sound education practice, have been manhandled and assaulted by teachers or principals for years. In certain communities where corporal punishment has been made illegal, the parent of a child who has been struck can take the abusing teacher to court. Everyone knows, however, the shocking fact that many times in these very communities, legally or illegally, kids are beaten and smacked around in the locker rooms and in the basements. I have myself heard three different principals say "Just don't leave a mark, and don't have a witness—then it's your word against theirs, and guess who'll win?" And guess-who *does* win most often, unless the parents have pull (but children of people with pull don't usually get hit) or there is a community group who will take action.

Currently, two divergent but related things are happening in connection with corporal punishment. The first thing is that the school groups, the teachers and administrators, are so convinced that parents, especially ghetto parents, are for corporal punishment that even the concealment and the lies that used to pretend to virtue where none existed have been dropped by school staff members who now use, and indeed flaunt their use of, the stick, the slap, the fist, and the push. In many schools, especially ghetto schools or those with large bussed-in groups, the hitting and slamming about goes on in the halls and classrooms and in assistant principals' offices, in full view, while awed, frightened and hating children watch and learn how adults really behave when they feel helpless. It goes on while some teachers and counselors, who are as horrified as they ought to be, look on, feeling powerless to do anything for fear of risking their own positions with their colleagues and superiors. Some become apathetic in the face of the mood that exists in and out of schools, fed by politicians, movies, and TV, where violence is the popular mode of action. Not to hit children, by some kind of sleight-of-hand logic, becomes tantamount to "permissiveness," and everyone knows permissiveness is the soft underbelly of the philosophy of liberals, and everybody hates liberals. So corporal punishment may be forbidden by law, but in practice it is given the green light in a large proportion of urban schools and probably in many rural schools as well. The situation has become so flagrant that in the spring of 1972 a joint national meeting of lawyers and mental health people took place under the auspices of the American Civil Liberties Union and the American Ortho-psychiatry Association, which has been trying as a starter to get at least state and local laws against corporal punishment enacted throughout the nation. And we consider ourselves civilized!

What we need, along with new laws, and even more basic to education, is the ability of parents to act on behalf of the children. In a community where there is an active, alert parent group organized in such a way that it is prepared and willing to take action, no teacher or principal would dare take the risk of hitting a child, because he would be sure that either a court suit or personal retribution would follow. Such a community usually represents one economic extreme or the other. It may be a well-grounded middle class group with influential parents involved in the school and an organizational structure geared to put pressure where it counts, or it may be a ghetto community where activists such as the Panthers supply leadership and organization which can exert power. In either of these two kinds of school district, the pendulum can swing in the opposite direction: it has been known to happen that a teacher or principal has been taken to court or even dismissed because of a single loss of temper, or because he has resorted to measures of self-defense after extreme provocation. If —for good or bad reasons—a teacher or principal is unpopular by virtue of need for a sacrificial victim, he may be removed on the basis of a child's story, truthful or projected, if it is vouched for by other children, even if only by the child's clique, and exploited by a parent group that wants to make a point. The teachers' union or the school board may support the staff member and may perhaps give him a job in another district, but he will not be permitted to stay in the community where he has offended; thus his future is in jeopardy. This may sometimes be a good thing. It is also sometimes an evil one.

Just or unjust, the power of community action is a fact. And when wisely used, community action is a powerful group tool for parents, since it is parents whose interests cross the boundaries from community to school through the children. Like all people, property, and land situated on boundary lines, children are the most likely victims at any time of skirmish or battle. To protect children from exploitation by either group, as each pursues its own self-interest, a great deal needs to be done to increase skill in negotiations between parent and community groups on the one hand, and school staff and school administration on the other. In intergroup relationships there is of course no guarantee that practice will make perfect, but practice does produce skill and increased understanding of what is taking place on both overt and covert levels; it can thus minimize disasters.

Perhaps too it can bring about needed change, however gradually and frustratingly. The military hold war games; business and industry often use management consultants to design practice situations where stakes are minimal or even imaginary, but where the feelings aroused can be the very same as those aroused when the stakes are high. Parents and schools too must find practice areas, for there are no greater stakes than the welfare of children. In times of comparative peace or quiescence, school administration and staff, from top to bottom, and parents and their community representatives (including health and welfare agencies, as well as court and local political figures) might get together in comparatively small units of fifty or sixty people to take part in an exercise where the only stake was learning how groups operate with one another and to learn how, and under what conditions, trust among them may be developed. In such an exercise the problems of the delegation of authority might be studied, as well as the consequences of action and inaction. The children might then be in a far better position, and parents and school staff would benefit enormously.

PARENT–TEACHER RELATIONS

But the relationships of most parents and most teachers as individuals are not, in the beginning, anyway, primarily concerned with the underlying or overlying processes of the school system and the culture in which it operates, even though it is this total superstructure that affects their personal interactions. A parent is concerned with John or Beth, with Sue or Don, in the second, fifth, ninth, eleventh grade. The teacher, in dealing with parents, is concerned only with her classroom group.

Although the teacher keeps the entire group as a central focus when talking to a given parent, both teacher and parent are concerned about how the individual child operates in the particular setting. Therefore, a teacher-parent interview has a great potential for each to gain a view of a different world of groups—of home life for the teacher; of school life for the parent. Thus, each learns new things about the child with whom both live. But, in spite of the golden opportunity for personal enhancement and growth, it is sad to find that a majority of teachers and parents dread the parent-teacher interview. And as with all things which humans dread, one or both tend to put off the conferences as long as possible, and sometimes even longer, so that they never occur.

Frequently, the parent-teacher conference is seen by each as a threat to the other. Typically, both are armed, each sure inside himself that there will be criticism and attack from the other, so that all the defenses man has developed for himself are set in action. These defenses so befog or barb the occasion that the end result is too often precisely the opposite of what it had been intended to be—a *con*-ference. The task was set up as the exchange of information; it often ends consciously or unconsciously as a test of ways to conceal facts from each other in order to avoid pain, or at least discomfort for the conferees, the child, or both. In many cases the parent—and this is true as well for the teacher—cannot avoid bringing into the interview the non-present group behind his shoulder. In the case of the teacher, he brings in the principal, the supervisors, the curriculum that is supposed to be taught, the adjurations of the superintendent, the mores and precepts he is expected to convey. The parent brings in his or her invisible group—the family background and life style, relation with (or without) the spouse and the other children, Grandma's and Grandpa's family background, economic class, racial attitudes, and political and philosophical and ethical orientation. Both often feel (and too often rightly) that they are dealing with a hostile, judgmental, alien group. Often, even before meeting for the first time, and with only the child's reactions and stories back home, or his presence and style of behavior and performance at school, as the information channel, parent and teacher greet each other with such set stereotypes of attitude that it is patently impossible for each to hear the other's words without coloring them by the stereotype each has created.

Heard in the Teachers' Lounge about Parents

"What can you expect of these kids? Their parents don't teach them any manners at home."—"How can I teach them to speak right; they hear nothing but street language at home."—"What's the use of calling the parent in for a conference? I've tried three times; she doesn't care how her kids do. They're all a bunch of spoiled brats."—"I don't want to see that Mrs. Jackson. Did you see how she was got up when she came for Judy the other day?" —"I wish I could talk to the James family. Sally's such a sad kid, but when I've seen either the father or mother pick her up at school, they don't say a word, just look off into space or turn away."—"Oh, God, I have my first parents' meeting with the Grays today. I'd like to play sick. Judging by the kid, they must be the uppity kind."

Heard at the Parents' Pre-conference Talk

"I guess Harold's in trouble. They called me for a conference." —"If that teacher would do her job right, she wouldn't have to see me."—"The way those teachers look at me when I pick Stew and Lil up, you'd think I was dirt."—"I'm not going over to talk to that white (black) teacher. What does she know about black (white) kids and what do any of them care?"—"I tried, I really tried to talk to Mrs. Paine about how scared Larry is to go to and from school. The kids beat him up on the way. He's small, you know. But when I call on the phone, she just tells me we've got to toughen him up. Now what's the sense trying to talk to her?"

And so on. Interaction is set up in advance for an impasse. There are teachers and parents who get along; there are even some who enjoy seeing each other and get something from the encounter. But given the oppositional role of the two groups as it is set up, the likelihood of friendly and openly communicative relations between parent and teacher is small.

In large part, the set for opposition can be understood as a group phenomenon. In relations between groups, the family group and the school group are brought together because of a common concern of both—the child. The task at hand, namely the child's growth, is and should be different for each one. A useful way to approach the problem is not, as we are accustomed to do, to blur the boundaries between the two, to try to homogenize them, but instead to clarify the way the tasks of each differ and so see how the roles differ. When these boundaries are made clear, it becomes easier for each participant to keep his own identity, and therefore his own role, to avoid encroaching upon areas which are special, private, or professional, and as such appropriate to one or the other. If clear boundaries are marked, the distrust that exists between groups, in this case between teachers and parents, will diminish to manageable proportions. That is not to say that distrust will vanish—it never does, especially since the boundary concern in this case is the child. For a child has emotional impact for both parties—especially of course for the parent—and tremendous significance for both in terms of personal sense of success or failure, since in both instances doing one's job is so linked to a sense of self, a sense of identity. How one raises one's children is obviously intertwined with one's sense of adequacy as a parent, and doing well on the school job is equally tied to identity and self-image for the teacher. As a result, for each one, parent and teacher, encroachment on his territory as well as judgment of his performance, active or fancied, can affect him anywhere on a range from being mildly upsetting to being devastating. But once it is understood that the common ground, the child and his welfare and development, requires different approaches from each and involves quite different tasks, the intergroup boundary line, the overlapping concern about the growth and development of the total child, can be handled with less threat. Discussion can then be more open and less defensive, and therefore more fruitful.

Each, parent and teacher, feels justified in holding to his own boundary and in not permitting entry into his special domain. Either parent or teacher may, from the communication that takes place, spoken and unspoken, gather clues and insights as to how within his own domain, he may wish to operate differently in order to be most useful to the child, or in fact, as a fringe benefit, to become more competent in general. But each has the right, indeed the duty, to say, "That fraction of what we are dealing with belongs to me, and at this time I do not wish to share responsibility for it; this other section is your domain, but I know something which may be helpful to you. You may use it or not; that is your decision since it falls within your domain."

However, there are certain elements of the child's life in which parent and teacher must plan and work together. Let's take, for example, Katy's behavior in school on Mondays and Fridays, which is directly connected to the turbulent weekend at home, where, since her father died, Grandma has moved in, and life is now new and rough. There is grief to handle and a new hierarchy to deal with. This section of Katy's personal life needs to be dealt with by both parent and teacher so that her life in school can be made more secure, more comprehensible to her, while home is settling into its new circumstances; both can help see to it that her behavior and reactions at school are more clearly understood. Expectation of performance needs to be decided upon together so that it is appropriate to life both at school and at home. A teacher who is not informed about Grandma's having moved in is at a severe disadvantage, and so therefore is Katy. Likewise, a parent who doesn't know that Katy has been stealing things lately is at a disadvantage. The information that each has but does not share may be the very thing that would help Katy over a bad time. Knowing may free mother to act one way and teacher quite another to fulfill their task for Katy's benefit. Nonetheless, boundaries between parent and teacher have to be kept carefully in mind.

Many excellent teachers, like many mental health professionals, have chosen their profession because they want to help others. The need to help, asset though it may be, often gets people into trouble, because it becomes so tempting to blur the boundaries and enter into this or that family's personal life in order to help the child. Sometimes this crossing over the boundary seems for a while to work. Miraculous change or promise of change seems to occur or to be about to occur. It is unlikely this situation will last, and when the promise fails, as it must, the fall from near heaven is harder on both teacher and child than a fall on mere earth. Important as a person may be as teacher, counselor, or therapist, he is not mother or father. He cannot, without adopting whole families and neighborhoods, control the forces at home; in attempting to do so, teachers more often than not fail in their purpose at school.

What happens often is that the child comes to recognize at a sub-aware level this slipping away of boundaries before the teacher does. He knows the promise of rescue cannot be fulfilled, and he often strikes out against the very hand that was offering to feed him. The pull that was to bring about closeness often ends in heightening distance and reaction on both parts. A child becomes aware that the covert message is that in exchange for help given he must grow to the tune of the teacher's expectations, and *that* out of gratitude, not out of his own readiness. He cannot give himself away in this fashion. So disaster and disillusionment ensue.

Of course, we are not here talking of the teacher who sees an underfed, abused or cruelly neglected child, or indeed a child with physical, mental, or emotional disabilities, and reports these findings *to the parent* and the school, using all possible channels at hand to find resources that will ameliorate the difficulty, while working to the extent possible with the family. Such action falls within the boundary of the teacher's responsibility. But the final decision about what to do and how to do it, though it may and should include the teacher as a major contributor, cannot be his. Boundaries relating to such complicated situations are delicate, they need constant redefinition on the teacher's part, and support of the principal and other school personnel involved, such as the school psychologist, the social worker and the nurse. The question here is not whether one should be useful to others; on the contrary, it is one of how to be most useful by doing one's own task. To keep one's role as a professional does not exclude concern or helpfulness. It means rather that one can show most effective concern by remaining the teacher or the counselor so the child has an opportunity to use someone in the outside world for learning, for gaining skills and for gaining identity and a means of negotiating with the world.

Sometimes it is neither the child nor the teacher or other school professional who tries to stretch the boundary, but the parent; and the teacher, out of pity or desire to be nice, allows the parent to encroach upon his territory. A particularly dependent, helpless, or frantic parent may try to use the teacher for his or her own needs. Telephone calls at all hours of the night sometimes beginning by asking the most simple questions: "Is that really the homework you gave Johnnie?" "Is it all right if Mary stays twenty minutes after school?" Sometimes they are pleas to ask the teacher to do what the parent herself cannot do—to tell Susie or Sam not to be fresh, or not to fight with little sister. Sometimes there are desperate outpourings of troubles with the father, tales of desertion, beatings or infidelity; sometimes there are confessions that the parent can't control the child, or that he is sorely worried about him. Sometimes, complaint comes in the form of fury that Judy or Jack is being discriminated against, treated unfairly, overlooked or misjudged. Sometimes, because of something the child has quoted or misquoted or even made up, the parent is mortally insulted and ready to take the issue right up to the mayor if need be. Always, when these calls or invasions before or after school come repetitively, and when they bear a similarity one to another, the teacher can be aware that the parent is trying to put her or him in the role of a surrogate parent, to use the teacher as parent. That such a boundary-bulldozing parent needs help is unquestionable. Perhaps, if properly and tactfully referred to the proper channels, the parent can get the help he or she truly needs. Perhaps, if the teacher fails to get the parent to the right helping person, another school professional—the school psychologist or social worker—can succeed. But the teacher, tactful though he may need to be, also needs to be firm and hold to his boundary. His personal life and school-teaching life cannot be invaded too often, no matter how piteous the case; if it is, the teacher will begin to build up resentment, or become so involved that he finds extricating himself becoming more and more difficult. In addition a teacher's already overloaded multi-task assignment is such that his own adequacy diminishes and is finally exhausted. This is the penalty one pays for allowing oneself to be seduced beyond the boundary lines of job and group. More resignations of potentially good teachers are caused precisely by this overkill of good will than is generally realized.

What can be done to make parent-teacher encounters less fraught with distrust and anxiety so that they can achieve their purpose of enabling parents and teachers to communicate in such a way that both can learn about the needs of the child?

First, as has been said above, one must understand that the teacher and the parent represent two different groups and that even though both are concerned with the child, the job of each differs, and the boundaries differ.

Second, the teacher can learn interview techniques so that her approach neither freezes nor overwhelms the parent. Teachers can enroll in seminars given by people skilled in interview techniques. There the teachers can discuss their interviews, exchange information, act out interviewing, become aware of the way they come across to others, and how that may help or hinder interactions with this or that parent. Covert processes in both parent and teacher can be brought to light. Teachers can learn how to avoid stepping on sore toes, and how to achieve direct non-hostile confrontation; they can learn how to open up some areas and shut down those that are irrelevant or too painful for the parent to bear. Teachers can learn ways of presenting painful information without cruelty and at the same time without deviousness or so much reassurance or camouflage that the parent either doesn't hear the facts that he must hear or gets so over-worried about the hidden stiletto that lies within the words that he makes more of the problem than need be. Interview techniques are rarely gone into in teacher training schools, but they are essential for teachers, counselors, and other specialists who deal with children and parents. They make an ideal way for teachers to get together in a group, since interviewing is a skill that all can use, and one all need help in. Interview techniques make a first-class group task for staff study and for morale-building and communication among staff members as well as between parents and teachers.

A third approach found useful in many schools, especially those whose principals have foresight, is to make parent interviews a routine event at the beginning of the year and again near the end of the year; such a procedure helps get rid of the notion that a call for a parent-teacher conference means that the child is bad, failing or in trouble. Parents and teachers can thus get acquainted before a crisis occurs, at a time when information can be exchanged in a less charged atmosphere. It has been proved time and again (see Marcella Bernstein's doctoral thesis at George

Washington University, 1965) that, though time-consuming, this procedure is well worth the time spent, for it achieves parent goodwill, lessens anxiety and promotes heightened understanding of the child.

Certainly, more than two meetings would achieve even more understanding; though we glibly say that familiarity breeds contempt, in this particular case it may often lessen it. And this is important, since the child, who through no choice of his own sits straddling the fence between the two major factors in his life, home and school, cannot help but catch the tone of the relationship that exists between the two. He is aware of it if there is fear and suspicion, if the teacher holds his family in contempt or if his family is hostile to and suspicious of the teacher. Even when the feelings of one of the adults or the other are unjustified, they cannot help but be transmitted to the child, who may see himself as the cause of friction; this can result in his feeling either overpowerful, or overhelpless, a victim. Both reactions are frightening and destructive. If intense, these relayed feelings may easily color the child's view of society or of his parents' ability to handle relationships, and he may incorporate their suspicion and distrust for life, and eventually become in his turn another difficult, distrusting, embattled or ineffective parent in his turn. For these reasons the meetings are important to all three, parent, child, and teacher. In all three, fear is likely to diminish with more contacts, but since most schools find even the routine meetings—early in the year and late, and pre- and post-crisis meetings—too time-consuming when designed individually, it is highly unlikely that parent-teacher conferences will be scheduled any more frequently for each individual parent or couple. With that in mind, we may consider a fourth approach, one which has the obvious advantage of being less time-consuming in the long run, but at the same time has more potential for achieving the task of better communication and deeper understanding between home and school, the two major forces in the child's life.

This fourth approach is to have meetings with small groups of six to ten parents at a time—groups small enough so there can be easy exchange after the first awkward stiltedness has been overcome. The chance of success increases if the groups have some homogeneity of purpose other than the overall one of having the teachers meet with parents. One way of organizing such groups, for example, is to group parents whose children have something in common—special talents, such as music, art, sports, science, shop, verbal expression, let's say, or special learning disabilities —reading, arithmetic, spelling, writing, study habits, attention-span. Or there might be a group of parents whose children seem to have major difficulties in social relationships or behavior control, or a group whose children are achieving far below potential, or who show emotional strain—withdrawal, drivenness, lying, stealing, cheating, etc. Grouping so that the parents may have something in common at the outset and so learn from one another makes for a greater probability of success.

There are advantages to be gained from small-group parent-teacher conferences for both the parent and the teacher. Of course the quality of the learning for each is likely to increase with the number of sessions. And while one early session is better than none, and one early and one late is better than one, a regular once-a-month meeting is often the best of all. There have even been instances of groups of parents and teachers who have arranged to meet weekly for a school year because the experience, for one or multiple reasons, seemed so worthwhile. In view of the reality of the lack of teacher time, it is difficult to get even a monthly calendar of group meetings going. Yet, time is a remarkably elastic commodity, responsive to motivations and priorities. When things go well, it is amazing how schedules which before had not the slightest area of give can miraculously be made to accommodate parent-teacher conferences—when these are no longer feared. The only way to get at the reality of the time problem is to have at least one such small group of parents meet twice or three times and see how it works. If the group is competently led, it is more than likely the idea will catch on. Some schools have arranged such meetings in place of or along with large PTA monthly meetings. They have a large meeting for the purpose of making announcements at the end, or they use it to have refreshments and social intercourse, but they have at least one small group meeting first. Night meetings have the advantage of attracting more fathers and couples. Some schools use one of the faculty meetings each month for small-group parent conferences in order not to encroach on teacher time. Some principals have found this such a useful plan that with the consent of the parents, they have arranged small-group parent-teacher meetings in the first or last hour of the school day, and have themselves covered activities for the class or assigned specialists or aides to do so while the teacher is busy with the parents.

These efforts have proved worthwhile for the gains that have occurred for both parent and teacher, and through them for the child.

Parent gains are many. The parents, after the initial awkwardness has worn off, find it less frightening to confront the school or a particular teacher in the school when they are with others who feel as they do. They find ways to say things and even think things, or at least to formulate their thoughts in a fashion they could not manage without the input of others. They feel less judged or, when they do feel criticized, they can talk about how that makes them feel, and how it results in anger toward themselves, their spouses, their children, or toward the teacher and the school. They often feel less isolated in dealing with their children and may get suggestions on new ways to work with their children, new insights into what occurs between parent and child or between the child and his school, by hearing other parents who have similar difficulties or ways of relating. Sometimes they make new friends. Often they get different cultural slants and broaden their horizons and thus better comprehend their children's choice of friends and interests. They are more likely to get into a habit of greater openness and are forced to be more direct and more searching about their feelings, thoughts and concerns, and this directness can be transmitted to their children.

The teacher gains too. It is often frightening to a teacher to undertake to lead a parents' group. Because of this, many teachers initially shy away from the task. Experiences of their own in teachers' groups, such as those discussed in Chapters X and XII, help them become aware of what occurs in group process that gets in the way of the task or furthers it. Most teachers find they are less anxious and less unwilling if they have a co-leader, a counselor, a school psychologist or social worker *with whom they get along*, one who hopefully has had some experience in group leadership if the teacher himself is a novice. Co-leadership is helpful in this kind of group. Not only does it give the teacher support, but also it serves a means of checking out what really is happening. Things move so fast in a group that it is impossible to grasp everything, especially those things that take place on the more subtle levels; a good co-leader can help in the task. It is true that co-leadership itself is a difficult maneuver, but when it works, when the two leaders work out their own relationship sufficiently well to make it work, it is doubly rewarding.

The gains for the teacher and his co-leader are many. One is that both learn much about themselves and how they participate in a group, how they come across to others, and what situations arouse their defensiveness, their anger, their hurt. They can learn new ways of looking at children, new different ways of handling the children in class, and gain new understanding of what the child is coping with at home. Moreover, both leaders can learn about their leadership style and ability. They can learn how to get things across to a group whose self-interest and warring feelings of self-protection might otherwise interfere with the task. They can learn how and where their manner of communication is muddy or tactless or easily misunderstood. These are all points of primary importance in teaching children as well as adults; through leading or co-leading groups of parents, leaders can see more clearly how their own virtues and faults interfere with or enhance ability to get heard by the children they teach. True, some teachers—especially teachers of very young children, and also some teachers of adolescents—relate far better to children than to adults. That trait usually has to do with the teacher's own Peter-Pan-never-grow-up wishes, or with a shyness about relating to peers that may derive from teacher's own school experiences; or it may have to do with the teacher's never having come to terms with his own relationship to authority. In any event, through leading small parent-groups teachers have the opportunity to learn about themselves not only as teachers but as adults. They may find they can become more adequate leaders than they think. Seeking to master new skills has the further asset of teaching humility. Teachers, like the children they teach, learn how it feels to work with a new tool and to feel uneasy in using it until time and practice help.

What is most likely to hold teachers back is fear of taking on group leadership. This fear is a reasonable one—and anyone who had no trepidation or second thoughts about the assignment would not be likely to make a very sensitive group leader. Yet, just by virtue of teaching, teachers have acquired some skills in group management which, when they analyze and examine their own procedures, cannot but bring them some understanding of what group leadership entails. Thus, though adults may be more intimidating to teachers than children, the skills of leadership of a group are not alien to them. Different techniques are involved, but many teachers make excellent adult group leaders or co-leaders once they have mastered the special skills required.

The pitfall teachers fall into most frequently in leading groups derives from their training in teaching children. Teachers are taught to preplan and structure—to fill silences, to ask questions, and seek or give answers, to lecture or moralize, to avoid flare-ups and show of anger or tears or even open affection. Although to begin with they will need to present the purpose of the meetings and to convey what they hope to achieve in each meeting, they need a good bit of support to achieve the self-discipline of truly letting the group do something but not everything itself, of allowing some silence, but not allowing a silence to last forever. They need help in learning to allow a degree of anxiety, confusion, and frustration to exist without barging in quickly to make everything seem smooth, pretty, and organized. The other side of this coin is that teachers also need to learn to keep on task, to deal with the forces that are holding up the work without lecturing, scolding, judging, or moralizing. The best training is group experience for oneself. The best safeguard against mishandling, overdirecting or underdirecting, against opening up too much or shutting off too fast, is to have a consultant with group experience who can talk over the sessions with the teacher and his co-leader weekly. Sometimes a school psychologist or social worker can play this role. Sometimes the personnel of mental health facilities in the community are eager to act as consultants. Sometimes, in fact, they themselves like to co-lead a parent group with the teacher. This combination is a useful one, since two different skills, each of which can augment the other, can be used—if, that is, the teacher and the visiting consultant have gotten to know each other and respect each other's contribution.

Bringing into the school someone from an agency who is concerned with the welfare of children and their families builds another bridge between the school and the outside world. If and when it works, such a relationship is of great mutual service; it serves, in fact, not only the school and the agency, but also the community. To make it work, as has been pointed out before in a different context, takes repetitive defining, changing, communicating, and redoing. It requires the clear demarcation of boundaries between the tasks of the agency and those of the school. Often the school starts by rejecting offers of mental health agencies, suspiciously guarding its own troubles as if they were top-secret portfolios, which, if revealed, might threaten the whole institution of school. Afterward, when the representatives of the related agencies (or of private institutions which for their own reasons wish to give service to schools) have proven to be useful, the school often demands more time and service than the consultant, wherever he comes from, can give. Often a school that has originally claimed to have no problem, finds when it is receiving help, that it has in fact heaps of problems, some of which the agency or person can handle, and some of which are entirely inappropriate to its mission. When definitions of purpose, both can-do and can't-do, are set forth clearly and repetitively in Beethoven-like thematic development, that is, stated and restated again and again, it is possible to avoid battles between the school and the agency and to avoid smoldering resentments that finally explode and end by taking away services that might have been of use.

When an agency participates in the leadership of parent groups whether by providing a co-leader or by training the teacher for parent-group leadership, or by offering consultative supervision, the school on its side must be very clear as to what it wants and needs, what will be helpful and what may overload an already top-heavy complex system. For instance, an agency often wants to send school consultants who are themselves in training as resident psychiatrists, intern psychologists, or student social workers. Such personnel may be a great deal more naive than the teachers, certainly about the school milieu. If this is so, more time may be spent in the training of the agency's trainees than is worthwhile for the teacher, the school, or the purpose at hand, including, for instance, the leading of parent groups. The school, which is often used as a guinea pig in research, training, and the pet personnel needs of agencies or private practitioners, has a right it often in its hunger fails to use: the right to insist that it get just what it needs and that it not be burdened with intruders who are there for their own purposes. If the teacher or counselor is an experienced adult-group leader, a trainee may indeed be acceptable and useful as co-therapist, or participating observer, especially when both teacher and trainee get joint supervision from an experienced person from the agency. If the teacher is inexperienced, however, the school should not accept a trainee as consultant, but consider him merely as observer. If a teacher does not feel up to this type of observation, he should feel free to say so and should be given support by the principal. This rule should go for trainees' visits to the classroom as well. Valuable as that experience is to trainees, it can be designed so that only teachers who want to be observed are observed, and the visit is not, as often happens, an encroachment without the teacher's permission. The point here is that to make consultation service worthwhile, the consultees have first to find out, in consultation with the consultant, what it is they want, and then they must see to it they get just that, insofar as their demands are realistic.

Such a modus vivendi may be potential TNT in the relations between school and related community agencies. It should be remembered that it is not usually the clearly stated rules based on reason that make relationships explosive. It is rather the lack of clear statements about where each party stands, about what each party can and cannot do, together with constant re-evaluation, inputs, and checkouts, that makes for difficulties. Constant re-evaluation is particularly necessary for good working relationships; it benefits both agencies and school and, so the community.

The fact that a teacher can find help in carrying out the task of leading small-group parent-teacher conferences has brought us directly back to the matter of intersystem group relations, and back once more to the need for clear boundaries and clear definition of the tasks that either system is prepared to offer or competent to put into practice. Make no mistake, that first task of definition is no easy matter.

Even with skilled leadership at the helm—and that is not always available—there may be political reasons of consequence that make it a touchy matter to air the facts about an agency or a system. For instance, at budget-planning time, directors do not wish their business aired in the press, where the alloters of funds may become aware that all does not smell sweet in the particular garden of the agency or system. If unfavorable information is exposed, money may not be forthcoming to do the things that need to be done if the system is to be overhauled for better functioning. As a result, bosses tend to collude with their staffs, and their staffs with them, in whitewashing their failures or postponing attention to their lacks. In so doing they find it difficult, or even impossible, to come out with statements that can stand the light of day about what they really can do, for to make such statements might reveal what they are not doing that they ought to be doing, or that others believe them to be doing. If this is the case, and all too often it is, concealment and obfuscation not only continue but increase, until even the people within an agency or system don't know what they can and can't do. Then they certainly cannot make any clear statement to other institutions with whom it would be useful, or with whom it is essential, to deal.

Sadly, this is what occurs much of the time; it causes exactly as much trouble as any sensible person could predict without having any special seerlike or scientific predictive capacities. The result is the creation of an impasse between institutions—defensiveness about each one's own functioning, and blame or scapegoating of other institutions. There is obfuscation of all facts, and either magnification of details which are in themselves of minor significance, or production of meaningless generalities in incomprehensible technical terms. Another thing that happens often is a violent explosion from within, such as paralyzed the New York school system a few years back, or an explosion from without, like organized student rebellions and riots that occurred in many places a few years ago.

This is not such a broad jump from where we began as it may seem. For it is precisely the kind of "cop-out" in evaluating one's own system or institution that we are talking about that makes it so difficult to state the facts as they are. This in turn makes intergroup relations crumble and causes the explosions—inner and outer—that we experience. The moral is that all groups—from small groups (parents and individual teachers) to large groups (school system and health department and welfare agency and court and legislature)—must look facts in the face. They must recognize their limitations and assets, try to reorganize, if need be, to do the task that they are in business to do, and at the same time, relate to other agencies who must do the same, each keeping to his own skills and tasks, and working with the others. If boundaries are kept distinct, it becomes possible to achieve the common goal—in the case before us, the total education of our children.

IX

Schoolhouse Groups

IN SCHOOLS, or closely associated with them, one finds an increasing number of varied groups, as different from one another as the basketball team from the Current Problems discussion group. Since the purpose of each differs from the others, the structure too differs, and since the styles, background, attitudes and personality of the leaders of the groups also differ, the groups seem at first glance to have little in common.

Up to now in our discussion of the group life of the school as a social system, we have looked chiefly at the classroom group and its subgroups, both as they function internally and as they deal with other groups. Now we shall concern ourselves with the brocaded fabric that makes up much of the life of the student and the youth. Some of the groups to be discussed meet not in the school building but in clinics, neighborhood centers or private offices; we include them in our discussion because their leaders are associated with the schools, or because they affect the child's learning and behavior in school. In this chapter we shall consider only school-centered groups; the next chapter will deal with treatment groups and training groups whether they meet in the school itself or outside it. In many cases the border between the two kinds of group is tenuous.

THE LECTURE TYPE GROUP

The most familiar kind of group—the one that immediately comes to the mind of anyone who has been through school, and certainly to the minds of those who have gone through college and graduate school—is the lecturer-listener type of group. This is a highly structured group that involves a small number of people addressing a very large number. Seats are usually arranged in straight rows, and the lecturer is set apart from the listeners at a distance. The method is so impersonal that we may have, instead of a live person lecture, a film or video-tape or closed circuit TV program. (Occasionally, depending on the skill of the lecturer —the substitute may be more involving!) After the lecture or film, a teacher will usually, though not always, lead the ensuing discussion. This general format is a tried-and-true method of boring a good number of people, unless the speaker has unusual charismatic or oratorical appeal. It is questionable how much is ever actually learned from lectures.

Many, too many, teachers, even of elementary school groups, approach children in this way in their own classrooms. They sit or stand at their desks and talk *at* the class, interrupting themselves momentarily to call for order, scold a note-writer, or leg pincher or gum-passer, or to ask a sudden question to test attentiveness of individual students; or maybe, just because he is in that position, the lecturer is lonely and wants to hear a voice other than his own. Regardless of the age level of the group, lecturing is certainly not an effective teaching tool if one wants group participation, if one wants to encourage active rather than passive learning and interaction. Even for older children and adults, its usefulness is limited, and it is far more effective when used sparingly and in combination with less didactic, "talking-at" methods. Lecturing can be useful in large groups to give an introduction to a subject or a summation of it.

THE SEMINAR

The seminar is usually thought of as a small group of people who get together with a leader, presumably an expert either in the subject or in group leadership, to study a given field or topic. The seminar can be a one-shot or two-shot arrangement, but usually it goes on meeting at intervals over a longer period. Although the leader or seminar contributor may indeed lecture, ample time is usually allotted for questions and discussion. Often a seminar member presents one aspect of the subject and the leader directs the discussion which follows the presentation and enriches it. A seminar may be converted to a group discussion of feelings or group process, but that is not what most seminars are intended to do.

Some seminars are physically laid out as formally as class lectures, but most, these days, are arranged more informally with seats set up in a circle. Seminars are sometimes held outdoors on a lawn, in the homes of members or even chosen restaurants. One university president came to be known as an innovator in the 1950's when he served sherry at each meeting of his seminar in literature in an effort to recreate the atmosphere of the 18th-century English coffee-house or the French salon. The reference was apt, for ideally that kind of atmosphere is the essence of the seminar: the creation of a love of the good life in an ambiance which, with or without refreshments, includes learning and comfort, an ambiance where someone with special information and ideas holds forth, and others participate informally.

Seminars are usually thought of in relation to college and graduate school, and sometimes nowadays in high schools, as well. However, they are quite appropriate for younger children, and do indeed take place. The progressive secondary school I went to as a pupil was designed around seminars which we called "Labs" or "Laboratories." One did one's own work or research, and then, along with a small group of others who had worked in the same area, reported research and learning as well as questions and puzzlements to the teacher and other small groups. The teacher would lead the discussion and direct us to further study according to our needs. Various participants—sometimes including the teacher—would report on the various phases of the subject. The work that takes place around the desk of one or another teacher in the presently popular learning-center method of teaching is likewise essentially a seminar held with small groups as they are needed or wanted.

The method is a useful one, for the group can be small enough for everyone to participate according to his ability, and small enough, too, for the teacher to see who needs what kind of help. Subgroup dynamics operate in seminar groups, especially if the seminar contains the same people over a period of months; thus both teacher and children can learn how to conduct themselves within a group of manageable size, and so, if the group is successful, develop a group morale and atmosphere. There is often competition—both useful and unuseful—among subgroups and seminars that becomes a major factor in shaping class attitude and informal grouping.

Other special interest groups or clubs are formed by students, usually with faculty advisers, to fit into the structure of the seminar group. In these subgroups each member takes responsibility for becoming more knowledgeable than the others about one or another aspect of the overall subject. Each shares what he has gained with the others, and if all goes well, he and the group learn still more from the discussion that follows.

PROJECT GROUPS

Though seminars do occur at high school and even elementary school levels, project groups are far more common there. A project group, when well conceived, often has the same atmosphere as a seminar. It combines activity and research. Mostly we think of "projects" as operating in the elementary school years, though they do extend upwards. Usually the project is teacher-initiated. Sometimes, in classes where the students genuinely participate in the making of their curriculum, the students themselves suggest projects for their class or initiate a project where a particular personal interest can be deepened or expanded; sometimes a sub-group or even a whole class can be persuaded to join with the initiators. A project group usually revolves around the idea most completely expressed by John Dewey in the phrase "learning by doing." Dewey believed that people learn by experiencing, and our current experience with deprived children, as well as with the more privileged, confirms his hypothesis. Dewey saw the child as a whole with the child's psychology as much a part of his equip-ment for learning as his mind. He observed that a child thinks and hypothesizes, questions and comes through with informed guesses based on seeing, hearing, feeling, smelling and manipulat-ing materials. He saw that the individual's world expands and deepens, that abstraction is grounded on more basic understand-ing when the learner has struggled through the experience on which the abstraction draws. As a result, he developed what we call "the pragmatic approach" to learning. Project learning is an example of Dewey's pragmatic approach. Projects in which stu-dents participate, develop, create, make mistakes and retrace their steps under the guidance of someone with experience and concern for the subject and for learners at the age level he is teaching, Dewey believed to be the optimal way to learn. The more that method is tried, the more it proves to be an effective tool. Three examples will suffice to give the flavor of project-group learning: I choose one from a graduate level course, one from elementary school, and one from high school.

Example 1 In a school of architecture, a project related to the total ecology surrounding housing was planned so that each student (or subgroup of students) chose one animal and built housing and landscaping especially for that animal, so that it could survive and get its food, its proper climate, its pleasure and its shelter with minimal human interference or assistance. Each student or group created an entire mini-world where the animal chosen could function. Thus architecture and ecology were brought together for the whole group; the individual members got together in subgroups to pool their skills and understandings in order to work out individual sections of the project. Lectures and subgroup reports, general and specific readings, were included as the total plan emerged. Some students provided an environment for alligators, iguanas; others for birds, or mice or monkeys or squirrels, or for raccoons or snakes. Such a study might have been modified to suit a group of students in elementary or high school, but it was in fact a graduate level project.

Example 2   A second grade class was studying the services necessary in a city; a special project decided upon was the fire department. Talks by and about firemen were arranged, pictures of equipment were drawn and a series of trips designed, one to a nearby fire station, and one to the harbor where the fire-boat could be toured. A museum in the city had a remarkable collection of fire engines from the past, and the class went to see that. The uncle of one of the boys was a fireman; when the group decided to erect their own model fire station and to keep on hand facsimiles of necessary fire-fighting materials, the uncle was called in as consultant to the group. Art work, shop work, science and social studies, all were involved in the project; it provided good opportunities for leadership within the class. The project required thinking up ideas, reading and research, and a study of history, myths and stories of fact. It included, too, purchasing materials in preparation for presenting the whole to parents and schoolmates.

Example 3   In the innovative high school which I attended, we developed an elective project which was designed to include child-care and the study of human development from conception through the first year of life. A suite of rooms in the school was made into a nursery and two nurses were hired. The city's Day Care Department allotted us four infants to be taken care of by the nurses during the day. The mothers left their babies at the nursery at 8 A.M., went to work, and picked the babies up at 5 P.M. daily. They took care of their own babies over the weekends. A pediatrician, a child psychologist, and an obstetrician donated their seminar services to our class. The pediatrician was paid to supervise the medical care of the children. Those of us who participated formed a subgroup. Our teachers were the nurses, the physicians and the psychologist; they showed us films and talked with us in small groups about the care of the babies, about the mothering process, and about ourselves as surrogate-parents and as people who might seek future careers with children. We learned what to do, how to do it, what it all meant, and where it all came from. With supervision from our teachers, we made up the babies' formulas, diapered, dressed and bathed the infants, and played with them for two hours of our school day. We read and reported on our reading; we talked about the babies and also about ourselves, about our future as mothers and about our own not too remote childhood past. There was no subject in or out of the standard curriculum that we did not find we used during this year's commitment, from history, anthropology and biology to physical education and English. As an only child, without experience of babies, I learned not to be afraid of diapering and bathing a baby. The subgroup of those who elected the course became a close one. It was as if we all had a secret life in common. We knew a bit more about ourselves and life, and found it easier to talk over sexual problems and questions we had only worried about or fantasied about in the past. This was in 1933!

The structure of project groups is informal. During planning and progress-report and review periods, members are likely to be sitting about in a circular or other informal arrangement. At other times the group members are usually not sitting—they're moving about, grouped wherever appropriate materials, reference books, telephones, and anything else that's needed may be situated. There are frequent small subgroup huddles. The teacher or project managers are, or should be, centrally and visibly located, so that they can be conferred with at any given moment of the allotted project time, which may be anywhere from one period a day to the whole day. For this reason, it is advisable for the teacher to have in mind an approximate time-bounded notion of how long the project is to last. Flexibility is essential, of course, but depending on the nature of the project and how it goes—on how passionately involved the group, or most of it, is, or how bored—a guess about the time is helpful. The age of the children often determines the time scale—younger children are able to sustain enthusiasm for only a very short time; older ones are able, as a rule, to work on a project for a month or even a semester. Many projects have had diminished effect because they were either too quick and spotty to develop a real commitment, or too long and too endlessly incomplete to sustain involvement. It is sometimes wise to allow a passionate subgroup to go on with a sort of postgraduate work on a project in "elective" time, if what they are getting out of it seems worth the effort, while the rest of the group turns its attention to something else.

It happens also, from time to time, that certain rigid or withdrawn children translate a particular project into their own inner-life symbols and can't let go. The teacher must watch out for the children in his class who get too caught up in a project and persevere in it too long. Consultation with a psychologist on this kind of occurrence is sometimes useful. But for most children, the project method is valuable: it motivates and teaches in ways less forgettable than those of many another method.

We have talked of the project groups as they occur in classroom settings. The same format, with similar flexibility and breakdowns into subgroups based on interest or expertise, operates in a theater club or theater production. In fact, many of the special-interest clubs of the secondary schools—clubs for the study of art, camera, film, science, cosmetics, carpentry, dance and so on —operate, or should do so, in a framework of project-group flexibility.

THE TEAM

Important as it is to develop sufficient flexibility to lead or to follow in many kinds of groups, it is invariably true that some people learn or teach better in the more rigidly structured situations, while others do better with more leeway for individuality as in the project group. The schools use many kinds of structure; the job they seem to find most difficult, although it would be both beneficial and possible, is to develop a process of selection of teachers and learners that would fit a given kind of basic-group structure to the kind of task that is best done in that structure.

Team structure is different in task, and therefore quite different in organization, from the structure needed in a lecture, seminar or project group. By examining the way team structure, in the most rigid sense of the term, is used in the school system and in the world, we may come to understand both the uses and misuses of this kind of group structure.

Project groups which permit freedom of motion use the body as an adjunct to the mind in experiencing learning; for athletic and physical education groups, use of the body—coordination of body and mind—is central to learning, and the use of academic learning peripheral.

To some people athletic team groups are extremely threatening because a structure which is by its very nature so clearly interdependent, which is, so to speak, under the orders of the captain and the coach, is generally inimical to personalities who must do all, control all, and be all on their own terms. The ski-centered character in the popular semi-true movie *Downhill Racer* is a remarkably subtle analysis of the basically unrelated quality of the Super-star, of the evolution of that quality and its effects. Champion though the hero is, it turns out that other lives are risked, and some lost, because of him; he is awkwardly unable to love, be loved, or share with anyone, and he is always excluded, even from his own inner circle, the ski team and its managers. But the team, apart from the hero, is an illustration of the close ties and warm feelings that can be generated when team structure really works.

In its extreme form the structure of this kind of group is clear. There is a boss at the head—the coach or manager; a team beneath, which has a captain to take the lead on the field of battle; an arena, the rink, the court, the field, etc. The responsibility is only partly the captain's; that goes mainly to the coach or team manager or whatever he is called. He sets the rules for his group, and these rules—as we see in Jason Miller's brilliant team-study, *That Championship Season*, where winning is the name of the game not only on the basketball court, but also in every aspect of adult life—often overstep the boundaries of the given activity and involve the entire life of the team member—his diet, his sleep schedule, his leisure and his sex life. Team "Thou shalt not" and "Thou shalt" are as strictly adhered to as the laws of many religious orders, if not more so. It is very clear that the fate of all depends on each in accomplishing the task—the task of being proficient in the sport chosen and to win above all others. Since the entire lives of all of the group are involved with all the others for the duration of the season, it is not hard to see why a fall from grace—a failure of discipline, an egotistical play that sacrifices the goal—is a devastating occurrence, far greater than any game in itself. The atmosphere and culture of this kind of group is, in fact, very similar to the outer discipline, self-suppression, interdependency of every detail, that is expected in the military, where war games become real and the survival of all is at stake.

It is this kind of discipline, the discipline of many working as one, that is often astounding and beautiful to watch—although it is not without terror that one sees how machinelike a performance a dress parade or a chorus line or an unbeatable baseball nine can become. One wonders both how much autonomy has been given up for good, and whether, if it became necessary, the individual members could make up their own minds or have actually given over their thinking, deciding and initiative to the coach. It is because of this group structure too that when a team has a bad season the coach is fired and maybe the captain, too, but not so usually the team members, as if to demonstrate where responsibility lies. It also demonstrates, however, the fact that when people work together in a disciplined way, under skillful, motivating leadership, a creative project can be brilliantly achieved.

This structure of ultimate discipline is exactly that of a bombing crew, an infantry battalion, a ship's crew. Its goal is to win—even at the cost of individual fates or lives. The task itself is more important than the group it is inextricably bound up with. In getting the task done, the individual's importance is subservient to the group's. It is for this reason that the leadership—the officer in the military, the coach in the playing fields—must command loyalty, even, many times, loyalty without question. All reservations have to be suppressed, and delegation to authority of decision and task deployment of the group members must be as complete as possible.

Time and again the study of such groups, especially the military counterparts, has yielded significant information. We find that it only *seems* that the group, whose whole task depends on teamsmanship and the authority of one person, works best with a bunch of sheeplike ninnies or automaton-like robots. In point of fact, the survival potential or the victory potential when the ninny or the robot standard is adhered to is very low. Each instant in a battle or a contest, whether on the war front, on the playing field or in the staff conference room, is packed with the necessity to make decisions. A team or battalion which depends on one another's judgment fares very badly indeed if its members, or even one of its members, having loyally given over all decision-making to the coach or captain, finds he cannot without superior orders or prior approval move from the spot he is on. The robot-ninny the group has created is roundly cursed and told, "You don't have the sense you were born with." And this is literally true: The robot has indeed abdicated that sense, misunderstanding the concept that, though overall decisions are to be leader-made, he is responsible for himself and for others who depend on him while in the fray. The question becomes: what happens if his judgment is atrophied by disuse and infantilization?

Since many classrooms and many administrative offices are run using the Team-Coach, Captain-of-the-Ship, Commander-of-the-Battalion approach, the school system creates its own dependency structure and then marvels at the confusion and mayhem that occur when these objects of "snap to it and do it without question" edicts prove helpless when left on their own, or rebellious and incompetent even when reasonable orders are given. Such team members cannot maintain any degree of autonomy and self-determination in the face of a mass-onslaught. I once saw the extremely bright chief of a school special-services department give his personnel the word about a radical change in policy with clear, intelligent explanations. When someone questioned him, either because of puzzlement or critical attitude, or simple lack of certainty, about whether the change was for real or just another nod to the higher-ups, he was put down with belittling and exasperated sarcasm and taken sharply to task. And yet the chief wondered why no one spoke up, why no one could carry out his new orders—orders which gave each of the personnel decision-making authority! The truth is that, with some reason, no one trusted the gift of responsibility, and few knew how to use it even if trust had been warranted.

A further danger of this kind of group structure is that it lends itself overwhelmingly to manipulation by the charismatic leader. A man or woman who can invoke, whether sternly or quietly, the "Come into my arms, little children, I will take care of you; there is a price, but come, I will take care" has it made with those who long for just such leadership. As the war movies—of all wars— and the sports movies have shown us, that appeal works best among men if the leader sounds gruff, rough, tough, and uncaring, but hides a heart of golden butter underneath. The ideal is the "Ah, I knew you could do it, pals" (team crew) as the leader lies wounded and dying, or just fired by the trustees, but with his team victorious. What happens in tomorrow's skirmish if the leader does die and the team has no ready substitute is a problem that has the potential for sparking a more tragic tale.

The extreme danger in this approach is that it may lead to a Hitlerian type of automatic followership with a Fuehrer on top. The shocking number of Watergate witnesses who claimed they did what they did because the top leader needed them to is a case in point. But when led wisely, the team approach can be an exhilarating and useful method of learning to manage interdependent human relations. The model offered can make for creative experiences and close friendships, if each member of the group is aware of his own responsibility and mission. The advantage of the team is that it is a group-form set for action. Moreover, there is special appeal in the closeness which is so coveted in these impersonal times—closeness at least among teammates, and sometimes also between leader and team. There is in the relationship, too, an encouragement of dependency and interdependency, which appeals deeply to the inner need of all of us to look for guidance, help, and answers, and is catered to along with the lovely escape hatch of "It's his fault, not mine," in the team approach from dodge-ball to Army. This dependency is strong enough to make it worthwhile for many people, especially dependent personalities, to give up the painful processes of ultimate decision-making.

SPECIAL LEARNING AND REMEDIAL GROUPS

There are always some children in any class who have a great deal of trouble in learning academic skills. Among them we find many types:

The bright who cannot symbolize or verbalize because of poor training or lacks in their backgrounds, because of emotional blocks, or because of specific disabilities such as handedness, eye-forms, hearing loss or brain damage, whether of the minimal sort which does not show up on tests, or the more severe and obvious types which leave a child epileptic, spastic, or aphasic.

The dull, who may or may not be brain-damaged, but whose capacity for attention, generalization, abstraction, and retention is less than that of the children described above or that of children without such troubles. It is sometimes exceedingly difficult—though still quite possible—to tell the difference between the mentally, the physically, and the emotionally handicapped. In many cases the categories overlap, and the child who could not learn originally because he could not hear, and therefore could not attend, and therefore got in great trouble in school before adequate diagnosis was arrived at, is likely to have acquired on his way through life a good many emotional blocks to learning as well.

Some children, who may to a classroom teacher seem just as disabled as any of the above, may simply not be suited to the curriculum and methods used in the school. Such a child may need more individual attention, different kinds of materials to work with, special instruction and help in relating to others because of some lack or difficulty at home. He may have been physically or mentally abused or traumatized; he may need foster-care placement and a tailor-made education program while his parents get help—if they are there to help and are able to be helped.

A fourth category includes the delinquents, or those who have got into trouble with the law. Delinquents may belong to any one of the other categories listed here, or they may have no observable learning problems. They do always have some relationship problems, and these often interfere with school learning.

These four categories include within them millions of children. Of these more are boys than girls. It happens frequently that a class of children with a learning disability has but one girl. To be one of anything in a group—black, white, yellow, red, male, female—is tremendously difficult. Everything related to oneness or difference tends to be played out in a group. Being "special" may attract a lot of flack, or it may attract spoiling; neither extreme reflects a realistic picture of the world. Whether the different one responds by becoming a scapegoat, a prima donna, an isolate or, in despair, relinquishes the personal attributes that make the difference—sex, race, culture—the experience is destructive. In order to avoid that, it is far better to mix ages, and even some disabilities than to isolate the child; for differences that can be shared and spread about may actually assist learning. Difference that is borne alone increases isolation or defensiveness or denial, none of which help either the educative process or the emotional growth.

In discussing the structure of learning-disability groups, we draw a somewhat arbitrary line between the groups discussed here and the treatment groups, mental health groups, and training groups discussed in the next chapter. When the disabilities are very severe or incapacitating, settings away from regular schools are, or should be, created. Anywhere along the continuum from day schools to residential treatment centers and hospitals and incarcerative or rehabilitative institutions, we find children with one or another kind of grave disability. The methods of grouping and handling such children, as well as the deployment of staff and types of help required, are all closely related to, and often overlap, the special class within the regular school setting which we are concentrating on in this chapter. Often children who are in the one setting ought to be in the other, if only diagnostic and treatment services were better and more plentiful. It is a general rule that if a child can stay within his home and neighborhood and community without damage to himself or others, it is usually, though not always, better to have him do so. The extent to which staying at home is possible is determined by the awareness of the educators and specialists of the community of what the child's needs are, and by their ability to convince parents and budget committees that bringing the best possible special-education services into the schools is far less expensive, both to parents and to the city, county or state, than setting up bigger and bigger institutions to provide for more and more deviants and disabled—products, in many cases, of the very society which now forces them into banishment. In this chapter we consider only the basic group structure of special classes within schools for the children suffering from disabilities.

In cases of all learning disabilities, regardless of diagnosis or cause, it is necessary to have small groups. Damaged children need individual instruction and tailor-made programs. But they also need *not* to be isolated from other children and adults. Small groups are the answer—some as small as four children per teacher, some as large as ten per teacher. Rarely is it profitable to have more than twelve. When there are more than four, more than one adult is needed so that the child who is having a particularly difficult time, either with controls or with depression or withdrawal, can be taken aside and helped, or at least temporarily removed from the mainstream of the group activity and treated with a Life Space Interview,* without disturbing the rest of the group and without punitive import.

* Cf. pp. 250–253 below for definition and discussion of this technique.

The tasks of these groups are different from those of "regular" classes, and this is the primary thing the "special education" teacher must truly and thoroughly understand. But this is precisely what many educators fail to understand. For instance, many principals choose a skilled teacher who has been very successful with the children in a regular class and assign him to a special class. This is often tragic, for many an expert teacher is wasted or de-skilled in working with the disabled. The teacher may come in sure he can teach anyone, and find that "these kids" defeat him. ("These kids" are especially talented at defeating people with expectations of output and Achievement with a capital A.) He may feel resentful, guilty, pitying and helpless all at once, and all of these quite natural feelings are exactly the ingredients "these kids" in all their different diagnostic categories, have aroused in their parents and teachers before. And so the children are again defeated and even more confirmed in their conviction that they are unable to learn.

The task of the special teacher is to find ways to approach the particular group assigned, whatever the diagnosis—ways to help the children learn the process of learning, each making use of his own style of interpretation of stimuli from the outside world. In comprehending the complex body of knowledge needed to work well with a special education class, the teacher must be aware that every child, from mongoloid to severely epileptic, from autistic to impulsively homicidal, is much of the time just a child, with the same needs for group play, for mental and physical development, for social intercourse, for legitimate praise and limit-setting, as the so-called normal child. An entire school year may be very profitably taken up with mostly teaching the group of children:

  to live in a small group together;
  to relate to the adults in charge;
  to deal with other classes of children when they meet them in
    halls and assemblies, in playgrounds and in other joint activi-
    ties (opportunities for which ought to exist);
  to relate to society at large on trips and in visits from parents
    and school visitors, and
  to follow directions.

Those five items would make an excellent first-year core curriculum for the group; it might well in some cases take two years. As success is achieved in this five-fold task, academic skills usually come along apace. The major need at the beginning is the core of learning how to learn and how to relate, how to accept one's differences and one's similarities with the rest of the human race.

To lead such a group takes empathy and understanding. What it does not call for is pity or indulgence. It does take a high degree of inner-core self-certainty within the teacher, so that he is not discouraged at lack of progress or achievement. It takes awareness of adult-group covert forces, so that the teacher can tolerate being shunted away by the rest of the staff—many of whom, in primitive unconscious fashion, will be afraid of the children in the special class, and through guilt by association, be suspicious also of the teacher, as if epilepsy or mental disorder or autism could be contagious! One very human difficulty which occurs in a special-education group is that success, though gratifying, can be experienced by the children as terrifying, as well. What more will be expected of us if we learn such-and-such? How much more will be asked of us? Is achievement the only way we can gain acceptance and love? These children are too well-versed in the experience of rejection and hostility and love with a sales-tag attached—covert or overt—not to be wary even of success. The teacher of such a group has to expect to be tested to limits, and to be disappointed without ultimate discouragement. There actually are people who can manage this. It takes both native temperament and training to put their skills to use.

It is clear that the groups must be extremely flexible and informal. Since, in all these disabilities, the attention-span tends to be very short, or, contrariwise, perseverative—that is, such that an activity once started cannot be stopped without adult intervention—change of group format at many times in the day is of the essence. For instance, early in the morning, sitting still and focusing on one person, one task, however small, may be the lesson of the moment; for this a group, even of four, may be lined up in a row or circle behind desks all facing the teacher with minimal stimulation from outside, all focusing on the teacher in the center. Each child may need help in carrying out the task of, let's say, coloring-in a stenciled map of the schoolroom in order to give the children a contained sense of their own immediate geography. One child may need help in physically holding the crayons, another, more advanced, in keeping within the lines, a third in not going to pieces when his crayon breaks, and still another one who has learned to write, in spelling out labels for his map. A brain-damaged child may—it often happens—vomit because of the tenseness generated by the task. An autistic child may be off in his own world of live steam-shovels and be acting out the part of a crane on the floor, and another may insist on holding the crayons in his mouth because he is at that moment being a bear. If a child is deaf, the lesson may be one in watching the teacher's face-muscle movements to make sure the task is comprehended and so on. But whatever the group is concentrated on, the task should be short and complete in itself.

Later, when that first task is done, the group may re-form in a totally different structure, and do something physical and free to relieve tension—perhaps a favorite game outdoors or in. (Ideally, classrooms for such classes should open on to an outdoor play space.) After that, the group may be engaged in the project of making a puppet stage and so be grouped around a table where different materials are already placed so that each child can do what he is able to do—sawing, hammering, drawing, measuring or perhaps sewing. Later still, a discussion may occur about what makes people laugh and what makes them cry, and the teacher may sit on the floor with the group circled informally about him.

A major tool for the special class, one which serves to preserve the group and take care of individual needs, is the Life Space Interview. This technique is useful particularly for the emotionally disturbed, but actually it helps in any class where upset or disturbance arises at any time for any reason. The Life Space Interview is a technique originally developed by Fritz Redl and David Wineman; it is in essence on-the-spot therapy. It must be carried out by someone trained, who is, or instantly can be, on the spot. This may be the teacher himself, a "crisis teacher" within calling distance, an available and trained aide, a counselor or principal or assistant. The child who is in trouble (or, sometimes, the whole group, where there is a group disturbance) is taken away from the immediate scene—either out into the hall, or into an alcove of the room or a special small room; after some calm settles in, the child is led to talk or draw or mime what has happened—what was going on inside himself, or what he perceived, or misperceived to be going on. Without sabotaging the teacher in charge, the interviewer behaves in such a fashion as to help the child pull himself together again and express his difficulty. As in any form of therapy, the more the interviewer and the child have been together —the more the child's behavior and reactions will make a pattern and conform to his inner life—the more the interviewer can be helpful to the child, and work out how to get him back into the group with no one losing face.

Every special class should have a Life Space interviewer, either the teacher himself, with somebody to come in and take his place in class while he interviews, or a trained staff member or assistant. In this way the group can proceed as a group. The group itself can also, when appropriate, be in on some of the results of an interview with one of its members. For example, the interviewer may say, "Johnnie's mother is going to the hospital tonight, so he's feeling scared, and when Dick mentioned his mother, it all came in on Johnnie, and he began to hit Dick. When Johnnie's scared, you know, he hits out." A group talk about mothers and their being sick may ensue, or there may be silent acceptance, and the class may go back to reading the story about freight trains in preparation for the group trip to the trainyards, but now with more understanding of Johnnie, themselves, and the mutuality of group life.

Another aspect of the special classes within a regular school structure which affects the group life is the advisability of having the children, as far as they are able to do without undue stress, join the regular classes. A child, for instance, however disabled, may be particularly talented in music; he may love to sing or play the drums or the recorder, and may do that well. For this child, joining a regular music class, glee club or band may be a privilege which helps him bridge the gap between disability and normality. It may be the key to motivate him so that his disability is overcome or at least diminished. Whether or not this happens, the experience of participating with regular groups in the area of his gifts—music or carpentry, dance or mathematics or baseball—is so important that his whole schedule should be reorganized, if need be, to allow for the possibility. For broadening of group experience while still in a protected environment is an essential aspect of consolidating gains. Hopefully, each child in a group, given a school environment which can accept this—a too rare situation—will have some way of going into the regular class, with the support of an assistant teacher or even, if possible, alone.

The more a special-class teacher has made a cohesive group structure of his or her small group so that almost all decisions and actions are brought up for group awareness, the more the individual child will have the social support necessary to risk himself in the regular-class world. Because these are small groups, a teacher can make many opportunities for group participation in decision-making, while not burdening the class with authority decisions and the limit-setting which should be his own responsibility.

What usually happens with a skillful teacher who is emotionally well suited to the task of teaching a particular category of disabled children (despite the discouragement and the slow—indeed sometimes for long periods imperceptible—progress) is that he would not change places with ordinary classroom teachers. He likes the close relationship with his small group, the sense of commitment, his interrelationship with the other personnel involved—psychologist, social worker, parents, physiotherapists, reading specialists, speech specialists, physicians and nurses. The whole child–team approach so necessary in dealing with the disabilities of these children is a challenge and a satisfaction. After going through the long hard road of a year or more with such a group, to see growth and change where for so long growth had appeared nonexistent or so "one step forward and two back" as to persuade one that change would never occur, is to experience a miracle that for the special-education devotee is worth all the pain and the self-examination and struggle that has had to take place while working with a disabled group.

In the next chapters we take up the subject of treatment and training groups. Much of what is said there, especially about treatment settings, applies as well to the special-education teacher within the regular school setting.

X

Treatment Groups

LIVING SOMETIMES brings to children, as it also sometimes does to adults, problems of such a nature that they may become immobilized. Anxiety or panic besets them to such an extent that they cannot concentrate, and even when they appear to be doing their work, they can neither comprehend or retain it. Like as not, they are unable to sit still long enough to hear the task assigned, let alone to pursue it. When these problems come only from the outside and are temporary—let's say, when a child's parents have separated, or his father has lost his job; or when his mother is ill or the gang has ostracized him or when a beloved pet has died—tension abounds in the family, and the child may become morose or cross. He may feel ignored, belittled, picked on, rejected or unworthy. Or he may be recovering from a bad flu or suffering from undernourishment, both of which conditions make for low tolerance of anxiety, easy loss of temper and clouds of depression. These things he will get over; but if they go on too long beyond their causes, in order to keep the situation from becoming worse, to keep what began as superficial from turning into a deepset response, the child often needs help, usually of a temporary nature.

Help for problems of this kind may be given as therapy within the school building, or it may be given in a clinic or private office outside the school. In most cases recognition that a child needs help comes first from the school. In these instances, therapy is usually preceded by parent conferences and a diagnostic work-up by a school psychologist, a referral clinic or a private facility. In the latter cases, the school needs to have some way of determining whether the child is actually getting help outside and if so of what kind; it needs to know whether the therapist wants to keep in touch with the school or not. The therapy decided on may be individual and may or may not include the family or it may be in a group of peers. There are sometimes special and good reasons for treatment to be individual, but if these are not apparent, this kind of child will probably be very well able to use a group, for in a group he can discover that, as well as his peers, the adults involved can help him gain insight.

If the problems are in fact largely born of circumstance, this type of child tends to be that boon to group therapists, the child who himself takes to therapy as a thirsty man to water, and who is able also to be helpful to others in the group. When he leaves the group, he has learned something more about himself, about his interpersonal style. He has become more aware of the habitual ways in which he has defended himself in situations that make him anxious, and of how he comes across to others; he gains, as well, many more insights that can be of use to him throughout his life. If he is too young for such self-recognition and ability to do something about it, hopefully his parents, through parallel or collaborative group work, will have gained the ability to hear his cues and act upon them, and to seek counseling themselves. At the time of crisis, the problems of this group of children *feel* to them no less bad or intense than those of far more distressed children, and sometimes their actions in class are as disturbing or even more so, but the distress lasts less long, and the situation, if caught and recognized, does far less damage to the child or the class, and can be handled more readily. This type of child is well served both by short-term group psychotherapy where some unconscious material can be dealt with, some basic needs served, and coping mechanisms explored, and by inter-active groups such as sensitivity training offers. These groups can meet either in or out of school. There are many kinds of therapy groups. I will describe the basic ones briefly.

NON-TREATMENT GROUPS

What do we mean by the term "non-treatment group"? Most commonly, the kind of circumstances that beset a youth above the age of twelve may be alleviated by responsibly led encounter or sensitivity groups in which the group concentrates on its collective behavior and feelings in the here and now, groups in which the individual members get and give feedback on what is happening to them, from and with each other, as well as from and to the adult leader(s).

The leaders of such groups usually behave and dress in a very open and familiar manner. They not only use their own feelings, as every good therapist does, but relay these feelings and the behavior they generate to the individuals in the group in order to indicate how what a person is doing may make others feel. The leaders and the group attempt to explore alternative modes of behavior which might be more successful, or at least more satisfying and so presumably more easing to one's own soul and relationships. Groups serve as a laboratory: they offer a safe place to try on different roles to see which ones fit one's own temperament and needs most usefully. Different leaders use different styles and techniques, but in general the sensitivity or "encounter" type of group attempts to deal with problems in the here and now, largely using past material only where it seems relevant to present behavior or feelings. It emphasizes relationships, closeness, caring, as therapeutic tools to help the individual. Though it often arouses unconscious or reminiscent material and sets up anxiety-provoking happenings, it is not a sine qua non of the sensitivity group dogma that the unconscious be looked at as it is in most psychodynamic therapy or in the Tavistock Model groups. The aim is to enable an individual to see himself and others in a group, and to get help from the group and the leader toward personal growth and development. This is often all that is needed to alleviate the pain and paralysis that derive from these circumstances and to allow them to come close enough to the surface, in time and place, to be looked at and appraised.

Adolescents as well as adults who are shy of "psychotherapy" are often very willing to try this kind of experience. It is particularly apt for adolescents, with their loneliness, their struggle to find themselves, their dependence on group approval and their need to test out adult authority. The search for the self fits in well with the identity struggle adolescents face. When led by skillful leaders, such a group does well in helping the person without deepset problems who needs to grapple with developmental changes, which by themselves at crisis periods of growth (such as adolescence or aging) can cause great anguish.

Sensitivity or encounter groups are often held in the school, though sometimes they are held outside. It is essential that if the school is the sponsoring agency the leaders have some contact with the counselor and teacher—not to breach confidentiality, but so that school people can be made aware that the child is working on his problems, and that while he is doing so, his behavior in class may, for a while, seem more tense or dreamy, and even, at times, bizarre. It is equally important, or more so, that the parents be fully aware of the groups their children are in. It needs to be made absolutely sure that the parents have given their permission. Again, with younger children especially, the group's value is enhanced appreciably if the parents too are involved in a group, or in individual counseling experience.

Sensitivity and encounter groups are also used widely for staff training, and will be discussed in that context in Chapter XII. Although "sensitivity" and "encounter" groups may differ in technique, the goal of *individual* growth through interaction is paramount in both kinds of group. The difference between the two depends on the particular school of thought or techniques used by the leaders.*

Leaders of the two types of group differ not only because of differing professional interests but also because of different theoretical biases. Right now, the largest number form a cluster around what is called "Gestalt" and "transactional therapy." "Gestalt" is represented in the practices of the late Fritz Perls and Laura Perls. "Transactional therapy" is exemplified by Eric Berne in his *Games People Play*. A similar kind of eliciting interaction and insight is that of Virginia Satir who emphasizes a role-playing dramatic approach. Her interests have been largely in family therapy, where the family is seen as a group, but her methods have since been extended to other groups as well.

"Marathon" groups—groups based on the principle that when people are tired their usual sets or behavior patterns can be broken down more easily, and that insight and change can thus occur—are used by most sensitivity and encounter leaders. Sessions may run anywhere from eight to forty-eight hours at a stretch. Some more conventional groups who meet regularly once a week for one and a half hours include a few modified marathons in which the participants can go home to sleep for brief periods. For many reasons such exercises are clearly inappropriate for young children.

There can be dangers for adolescents (in fact for everyone) in the extremist types of group. Some adolescents can't take the kind of closeness forced on them, because they are not yet sufficiently clear about their own identity and unity as persons to have whatever patterns they have developed for themselves battered down without time to assimilate the why and the how and

---

* The National Training Labs launched the sensitivity groups. National Training Labs is an organization associated with the National Education Association. Its program is based on the work of Kurt Lewin; its founders are Leland Bradford, Ronald Lippitt and Kenneth Benne. Sensitivity training has gone through many phases since its inception, and now has centers throughout the country. Its staff and trainees are active in many groups, some in business, many in education and training, some in therapy, and some as an expression of social concern.

the what it all means. Many, who in their daily lives are overexposed to badgering, cannot take the force of group-badgering which insists that a person feel what the group thinks he should-ought to-must feel. He may not feel what the group wants him to feel and may either fake it—which is not useful—or get group-pressured into feelings, phoney or real, he can't deal with. Another danger, when these groups are adapted to children, lies in precisely that quality which appeals to adolescents and to many adults. Since one of the goals is to develop closeness, intimacy, sharing, the procedures involve the breaking down of existing boundaries. But such boundaries are needed, especially by young children, to give some steering power, some individual sense of how the skin separates one person from another, of where the limits of do and don't, can and can't really fall.

Where boundaries are not a problem, such groups are appealing and useful, and when they are led by people who know adolescents, they are particularly useful with that age group. They can be invaluable to facilitate open communication, to help one realize feelings, to make one aware that the supposedly unacceptable parts of oneself are often liberating and energy-producing. A responsible leader of a sensitivity type of group for adolescents in the school or outside would give careful attention to the problem of who should join and who should be eliminated. He would be careful not to mix adults who are emotionally adolescent with chronological adolescents.

A leader may use many Gestalt and transactional techniques, but he must not allow the activity to reach a point where the adolescents are forced into a closeness they cannot tolerate, or led into sexual fantasies or acting-out which would make them too frightened or too guilty. Fooling around with people's defenses while setting loose group forces is at best a precarious business. The safeguards lie in the leadership. Still, keeping this in mind, groups which concern themselves with the three areas of particular moment to adolescents—peer relations, self, and authority—can be invaluable aids.

Before we leave the subject of sensitivity groups for school-age children, it should be said that in modified form a sensitivity group may be useful in the earlier years as far down as the second or third grade. It may include all or only some members of a class; and it can be a useful device when included as a means to teach sex education or social values and to stimulate intellectual growth as well.

PSYCHOTHERAPY GROUPS

There are certain children whose problems have deeper roots than those we have so far discussed. In their lives too, circumstances may arise which cause traumas, and these may bring to light or exacerbate pre-existent difficulties. It requires careful diagnostic procedures to distinguish the problems with deep roots from the more superficial ones. Children with deep-rooted problems fit well into psychotherapy groups.

To pass over the perennial debate about whether the problems that beset humans are rooted in physical constitution, chemical imbalance, genetic fault, environmental happenstance or cultural pressures, let us agree that all these factors do exist and do create stresses. It is rare to be able to say with any validity that a particular individual's misery or mis-adaptation is caused by one aspect and not by the others. Whatever the causes, the difficulties in living exist, and all we can do is take the best information we have available and try to find the best way we now know to work with a particular child, given his assets as well as his liabilities. We do know *some things* beyond trial-and-error methods. If the chosen mode of approach does not work, we try another and another, or we combine two or more, or we eliminate the ones that don't work. Since people are the instruments of these methods, we have to consider not only the receiver of treatment, but the giver as well—and most of all, in nearly all therapies, no matter how mechanical or "controlled," we have to look at the relationship that exists between the giver and the receiver of treatment. Moreover, at the same time that we become more sophisticated in what we know, we have learned that with all humans, but particularly with children, we have to look at the homes they live in, the culture and values they absorb, and the school and the people who teach and treat them. With this assortment of factors in mind, we can proceed to review—we can only skim over them—the various types of therapy where groups become a central aspect of treatment.

Many times it has become clear that certain children do far better in working out their problems—no matter how deep-seated —in a group with children roughly about their own age level than in individual therapy. Their fear of adults is mitigated and their fear of exposure is lessened by the knowledge that others have problems too. Groups confront difficulties in relationships with peers, a prime cause of problems. From these confrontations, understanding, whether vocalized or acted upon, can be gained. For children, a group is a more everyday setting than what Fritz Redl calls the "pressurized cabin" atmosphere of the therapist alone with one child, in a situation outside the context of daily life. Sometimes groups are made up of children with the same kinds of problems. Most often it has been found that a mixture of many kinds of children, exhibiting many different kinds of behavior and exemplifying within themselves a variety of inner dynamics, do better together, than children all of one kind or type. Depending on the need, family and group treatment are offered either simultaneously or in sequence. If the therapists of each— the family and the group—collaborate closely, this can be very successful.

Sometimes a child is so emotionally deprived, or so beset by his inner dynamics, that he requires individual one-to-one treatment. He may need only this form of treatment, or he may need it as a prelude to group therapy. The group therapy then becomes a safe testing ground for what he has learned, a kind of graduation exercise from individual treatment, where the child makes transition from the complete attention of one adult to the more difficult and more usual situation where one must share adult attention, and find a way to have one's own needs met while leaving room for the needs of others. Sometimes a child is so fearful of adults, so tight and clammed-up, that he can better manage to get help from a group of peers than from one adult. If this is all he needs, well and good. If he needs more, the group may serve as a prelude or a support to his using individual therapy either after the group, or along with it.

Family Therapy

Since the family constitutes the central group in anyone's life, but especially in the life of the young, and since the younger one is, the more closely one tends to replicate relationships known, heard, hated or yearned for, in the original family, we find family-group sessions useful in diagnosing the major cause of a child's trouble and in getting at the characteristic modes of family interaction. Since family therapy is a relatively new form of treatment, there are many theories about it, some conflicting and some overlapping.

The least group-centered of the lot is the Systems Approach represented by Dr. Murray Bowen. In this approach, the family is understood to be a group, but is not treated as one. Instead, the therapist sees the mother and father and treats them as a couple, first talking and listening to one, then to the other—allowing some dialogue between them, but not using group process. Like all the theories of family therapy, the Systems Approach sees the child who is in trouble, the child because of whom the family comes for help, as "The Index Member" of the family, the one in whom the family trouble is stored. The child is seen as acting out the unconscious—or at least unspoken—difficulties of the family. To Bowen and his group the clue to the difficulty is to be found in a detailed and thorough study of the genealogy and present network of the family—their physical story, their economic status, their job choices and educational histories, their divorces and deaths and illnesses. The further back one can go and the more widely one can study the offshoots of the family, the better for the purposes of this kind of approach. Therefore, even though the Bowenites say with passion that they eschew the treatment of the central family as a group, they are, curiously enough, ready to engage in the study of unusually large groups, not to offer them therapy, but rather to use them as information sources. The literature of this type of therapy abounds in fascinating studies of family happenings: reunions, births, funerals, weddings, anniversaries and birthday parties. The patients are asked to study these rites and occasions to determine patterns; some therapists try, when possible, to get themselves invited so that they may explore and see at first-hand what goes on. In this way the large live family is used as a group tool.

Network Theory

There is only one other branch of psychological treatment I know of that uses the large group, and it uses the group for therapy. That branch is Network Theory, a new outgrowth of family therapy that is used in families where the crises derive from sticky chronic conditions that have not yielded to other forms of treatment, no matter how lengthy or how drastic. Such treatments may have ranged from long years of individual treatment to hospitalizations; they may have moved from group to family therapy and back, with all stages in between. The formulator of Network Theory is Dr. Ross Speck.

In this form of treatment, the organizing therapist and a team of therapists act as consultants to the family in trouble for a definite and short-term series of "network" meetings, anywhere from two to about six in number. For example, a mother and daughter in a family have such severe trouble that neither can leave the other alone. Neither can let the other live separately; yet neither can live with the other without terrible battles. Thus serious destruction ominously hovers over them as well as over the rest of the family and their friends. Suicide and murder attempts are not unusual in such severe situations, whether between husband and wife, or between parent and child. The two central figures, together with the whole family, are asked to invite to a group meeting everyone they know—relatives, ex-wives, lovers, teachers, friends, doctors, counselors, service people who have become involved, bosses—any and everyone. The bigger the group, the theory goes, the better: it dilutes the problem. The idea is to get all these people involved and so to generate a mild form of the anxiety that has been so severely aroused in the focal pair of miserable people. After group anxiety has been aroused—and that's not hard to get going in a large group—and the feelings expressed, the group breaks up—in the same room—into committees (small groups) each to tackle one aspect of how they can help with the problem. The notion is that in this way the spiraling trials and failures of the focal couple can be broken into, diluted, and monitored by a concerned multitude; the family-trap is thus hopefully broken by sheer weight of concerted pressure from all sides. A further concept here is that the extreme differences between the pair in trouble, by being taken on by a network of people, can be worked out by compromise, and through compromise alternate ways of acting and reacting be found, if the support of a large enough group is insured. After setting up these "networks," the team of therapists vanishes—as any good business consultant does after he has finished doing all he has contracted to do for the firm. If therapy is needed, either the committees of the network give it, or they see to it that it is arranged for. If housing, a job, school placement, or money is needed, ways of taking care of the problem are worked out. In this context, one of the most fascinating and unusual things Network Theory offers is the use of the chaos engendered by a large group as a therapeutic tool. Gossip too is used, as one offshoot of ways to get opinions whether sound and based on fact, or not. Network Theory suggests an intriguing but as yet unworked-out possibility of using this kind of treatment for school children in deep trouble with their peers or the staff, or for crisis (with a capital C!) in the staff itself.

Some other forms of family therapy, although they differ from one another, can be talked of together, since the therapists who offer them conceive the family as a group and use the interaction between members as a treatment tool. Some are more group-process oriented than others, but all use the way a family interacts and the roles each is supposed to play for the other and for themselves as a key to the problems of the child in trouble—the Index Member—and the family as a whole. Some family therapists insist on home visits to see the family in its habitat. Some do most of their work in offices. Some invite in-laws and grandparents and close family friends, if this seems important; others stick to the core family. Some use speech alone; others use art and psycho-drama and role-playing and a technique called family-sculpturing. In family-sculpturing one derives a whole family situation or character from the interaction of therapist and one family member, creating the script with body movement and words.

Family therapy as a systematized way of dealing with people in trouble grew out of work with families in which there was a very damaged schizophrenic son or daughter, often one who was hospitalized. Time and again it became clear that on those occasions when the family was seen in combination with the sick child, the family guilt about that child seemed not to give way even when the child got better. It came to light that the group guilt had a genuine reason for existing beyond the constant use-less jumping back and forth between periods of mea-culpa and woe-saying, and periods of anger and withdrawal of all interest. The proof-of-the-pudding was seen time and time again as lying in the fact that when the sick one (the Index Member) got well, the family as a whole would fall apart, or would appear to be in danger of doing so, until either the sick one got sick again, or the family dealt with its problem otherwise. Without outside help it would seem each member felt he could not afford to take on his own problems and allow the elected one a measure of health without responsibility for keeping the whole rickety struc-ture from collapsing. A second proof was seen in the great num-ber of families (any school, like any mental health agency, knows the number is legion) in which as soon as one child who has come as "The Patient" has been treated, and has become well, another family member, usually a sibling, at once gets into trouble just as bad as the first child's, or even worse. The thera-pists developing this form of therapy began with hospitalized schizophrenic patients whose families illustrated this group phe-nomenon to the extreme; it was taken up soon thereafter by agencies where the repetitive pattern of breakdown in the family, a re-catching of the disease after "the cure" of one member, was part of a vast intake picture. Names often associated with exploration in this field are: Ackerman, Wynn, Shapiro, Bloch, Jackson, Whittaker, Minuchen, Rycoff and Paul; many of these (along with Bowen) are still working in the field, as are many others.

The reason why I have given this detailed summary here is that the record indicates how a common and damaging group phenomenon can affect the core group structure, the family, as well as people outside the family group. One member of a group is made the scapegoat—that is, he is sacrificed to keep the group together, to take away the pain and unacceptable feelings from others in the group, thus dumping the pain on the chosen group member. We have seen this phenomenon in the classroom of the teacher who is shaky about her own leadership, or the teacher whose personality does not allow expression of hostility, affection, rage, or fear. The cure for such scapegoating in any group, just as in family therapy, is to try to get each member, along with the leadership, to own his "unacceptable" feelings by exploring them, and to help each member not to allow himself to play the lethal game of being the scapegoat or sacrificial lamb.

THREE SPECIAL FORMS OF GROUP PSYCHOTHERAPY

There have been two broad lines of thinking out of which group therapy as it is practiced today has developed. The first has come from the medical model or the psychoanalytic school; in this each patient comes with his individual problems as he would for individual treatment, but is seen within a group. The group happily profits from listening to one of its members work on his problems with the trained leader. The group members may have more or less opportunity to react to the material presented, depending on the convictions of the group leader. With some group leaders—those whose interest is more in group interaction —the group that is listening may be led to relate to the problems with their own experience and insights, and thus play more of a role in being therapeutic agents; with others, the procedure is largely a dialogue, with the leader engaged with one member after another.

This "classical" approach, as it is called, is typically represented by Slavson, the man who is the father of activity groups for youngsters. Its leaders are all professionals, usually trained in individual one-to-one treatment, who have come to group therapy later in their experience.

The second broad line of thinking may be represented by such groups as Alcoholics Anonymous and Synanon. Here people with a common problem get together to keep guard over each other, with the conviction that the force of a group whose common experience binds them together can help each member in times of stress or temptation. The group mitigates loneliness, satisfies dependency and serves as a cathartic agency. It tries to mobilize itself, often by faith either in an overseeing agent, such as God, or, if not God, the group itself and its leadership. The leaders here are often people from the ranks of the group, though sometimes professional leaders will be brought in to work alone or in unison with the indigenous leaders. The power of the group has been seen to be extraordinarily helpful for motivated individuals, especially for those given to an addiction of some sort: alcohol, drugs, obesity, gambling, smoking and the like. (About the only type of group that has not so far been constructed on these principles is a group to deal with people who have become addicted to groups as a substitute for direct life experience.) Here the group is paramount, and group process is the therapeutic tool. Dependency is the prime mover and the attempt is to transfer the dependency from a drug or a consuming obsessive pattern to the group. At this stage this therapy may be likened to methadone treatment as a means to get someone off the habit. Later, at least in some cases, the goal may be to free the person from gripping dependency needs, but for some it is clear that, once formed, the group must always be behind one to rescue one and to use one as rescuer in turn. Thus, along with caring for dependency needs, this type of group makes for a lifestyle, a social life, a release from isolation and loneliness; it is a route for helping and being helped that makes an individual feel needed and necessary.

The Bion-type group is quite different from the first two (see Chapter III) yet in some ways combines elements of both: for here the psychoanalytic unconscious material is basic and so is the treatment of the *group* as an entity. Treatment is of the group as a group; it is not focused on individuals. Thus, group process here too is paramount. The leader is trained in group behavior, covert and overt, and the recognition of covert processes is a sine qua non of insight. Dependency may be one phase of the process, but others are considered equally important as life-factors: Fight, Flight and Pairing must be continually dealt with as well for the group to do its work and become a work-group. In Bion group therapy, in contrast to group education, the task is allowing individuals within a group structure to deal with conscious and unconscious ways of coping with life, and thereby to free them from crippling aspects of their lives by offering alternatives.

These three broad categories of group psychotherapy cover most of the types of groups that are now used in therapy, including behavior modification groups, hypnosis groups, and drug-induced groups, as well as activity groups, art and music and body therapy groups, psychodrama and scream therapy groups. Some theories and some techniques are applicable to classroom teaching; however, since the task is a quite different one, the application needs to be effected with discrimination and care to avoid confusion of goals. Having said so much, I believe it is clear that the sensitivity and encounter groups talked of above fit better into the second and third categories than the first. The Gestalt (despite the fact that the word itself means "the whole") fits better into the first category, since in Gestalt groups people are treated in a coupling between leader and subject with the rest of the members of the group looking on, relatively inactive until their turns arrive. The network group, whether its developers are conscious of that fact or not, is in some ways more Bionesque; in others, more like communes and self-help groups.

In view of the existence of all this potpourri of group structures, it is difficult to know which child in trouble will fit into what group and why. That decision is best left to the diagnostic process once the child is referred. The trouble is that conventional diagnosis seems to be getting rustier all the time. Since the school is nowadays laden with looking after a child's behavior as well as his intellectual development, and since that behavior is linked to the use of his intelligence, and both to his inner dynamics and the stress of developmental changes, it would seem mandatory that the school, or one of its delegates—teacher or counselor—be automatically included in the diagnostic process. Though this is indeed sometimes done, especially if the treatment planned is to come from within the school, it is not done often enough. True, teachers and counselors could use more skill in sharpening their observations and translating them, but if their summaries were included automatically along with records of testing and interviewing, we could cut down considerably on mistaken placement in both classroom and treatment modality, and the damaging consequences of doing the wrong thing or nothing would be much mitigated.

As a rule adolescents who need treatment do better in a group than in individual treatment, but there are many exceptions. Many younger children do better in a group or in family sessions than in individual therapy, since individual therapy often divides their loyalties and their ability to work out ways of relating to peers and parents. Here too there are many exceptions. In both cases the exceptions depend on the amount of pressure internal forces are placing on the child. If those forces tend to be so all-consuming that the child cannot deal with a group, or so idiosyncratic that no group seems appropriate, or if they are such as to lead him to destroy any group he is part of, then individual treatment is mandatory. Most workers still think first of individual therapy and then of group in diagnostic placement. It is useful to have diagnosis include a group experience of two or more sessions; that would make it possible to judge whether a child would do better with individual or group treatment, and if group treatment is indicated, might tell what kind of group the child would do best in.

In making a decision about the kind of treatment group to send a child to, if indeed he is to be sent to any group, the school could add essential information concerning the extent to which the child fears classmates, how he handles himself in those toughest of all periods in the school day—the transition periods—and how he acts in the lunchroom, playground, study hall or rest rooms. What is his concentration span? Can he get started? and once started, can he stop? Does he talk excessively? How does he show how he feels—or does he? How does he play? How does he win and how does he lose? What is his attendance record like? his health record? Does the nurse have data? The gym teacher? Is he one who waits in the principal's office, and if so for what kinds of offense? What role does he play in the classroom—bully, scapegoat, clown, or sad sack? Do his parents come to meetings? What are their superficial attitudes toward him? How does he make the teacher feel—pitying, furious, indulgent, amused, bewildered? Is he over-intellectual? Is everything always the other guy's fault? If so, would an art therapy group or a psychodrama group help? Is he a loner or a mixer or a leader? If any of these, a low-keyed talk group might be a good choice. What developmental phase has he reached? Does he need work in behavior control, or does he need the chance to explore his body and mind in an activity group or encounter group? Are parental pressures such that he needs a place to help him relax and meet only minimal demands, or does he require higher expectations of himself? Is he ashamed of being tall, small, fat, dumb, bright, different? Is his or her sexual development a terror to him, and the thought of sex a nightmare? Does he try to act older or younger than his years? Does he attach himself to one person? Does he bribe or steal or brag to get friends? All of these are questions to which an alert teacher can contribute answers for the use of the diagnostician, along with the picture his parents give of how he behaves at home. Both accounts, compared with what the psychologist or psychiatrist finds, tell us how the child sees himself, how others see him, what his emotional and mental capacities are. The composite picture may indicate what group he will fit into and be able to use, and whether individual treatment should be considered simultaneously or uniquely.

All of the above assumes that a teacher or counselor, the school social worker and the psychologist all agree that a child would benefit by help. A conference of school people that decides that Tessa has really been crying too many days in class, or that Louis has been running into the locker room to hide under people's coats too many times, will strengthen the recommendations given at a parent conference, and will give the person responsible for diagnosis and placement a clearer prescription as to how to proceed and what kind of treatment to seek.

BEHAVIOR MODIFICATION

We have not gone into the various kinds of therapy—those which may be offered in or out of school—which are based on principles of Behavior Modification. This particular form of therapy has become more and more popular among psychologists and in schools in these last years. There are a complex set of reasons why Behavior Modification therapeutic techniques are particularly popular in the schools. Schools have good pragmatic reasons for being concerned with behavior. "Deportment," as it used to be called, has always been the teacher's concern, and the teacher is often rated on how well her children behave. Misbehavior is usually defined as anything that "doesn't go" in Mr. N's or Miss M's classroom or in Mrs. P's or Mr. Q's school. Behavior is rarely seen as the psychologists see it—as any action or reaction, verbal or otherwise, that responds to stimuli from the environment. Behavior is even more rarely seen from the psychodynamic point of view—as not only reactive to outside stimuli, but as symptomatic of what is going on in the inside world of the child to make him perceive outside stimuli as he does and make him react to them as he does. Behavior Modification gives school people a tool they can apply to many situations in the realms of both cognitive learning and "deportment." Since Behavior Modification therapy derives from learning theory, the psychologist's domain, it is a natural alliance between education and psychology. It can deal with the behavior that bothers the teacher at the moment; it need not concern itself with bringing in past happenings in the family or personal history.

Behavior Modification is an outgrowth of Pavlovian conditioning psychology in which animals were taught to produce a number of responses by means of punishment or reward. By the same means they were taught to avoid other behavior, to "unlearn" it. The process of "unlearning" was called "extinction" (of a habit or response). Pavlovian theory was later applied to people—both reward and punishment have been used to teach new modes of behavior or new cognitive material. In the Soviet Union, Pavlovian theory is the basis for most psychological therapy. It is often used both here and abroad to make extinct various patterns considered undesirable, such as stuttering and smoking and drug-taking.

In its more sophisticated form, now in use in some parts of this country, Behavior Modification involves a thorough inquiry into a child's total pattern of behavior, and an even more detailed exploration of the problem that is of particular concern—for example, school-phobia (which lends itself well to this form of treatment) or poor study habits, or not being able to control actions, anger, or body movement. The detailed inquiry tells the therapist all he can learn from everyone involved—child, parent, teacher, friends—about the patterns of behavior and what kind of thing sets the problem in motion. It also tells him what is seen as a *reward* in the case of a particular child. The famous M & M candy may work for some small children, but it may not work at all for others—it certainly does not work for older children. Money may work for some, records for others; chits to be used toward the purchase of a guitar or a motorcycle, or a TV or a sleeping bag or a trip to the seashore, may work for a good many. Once a program is worked out, detailed as any program designed for a computer, and once a reward system is evolved, the plan can be put into effect. From then on, any avoidable stimulus that would work to upset the new learning is avoided; any stimulus that would work toward the goal is encouraged. This means, for instance, that if a given piece of behavior is considered undesirable and therefore to be made extinct, it must be ignored; in behavioral terms, not the slightest word is said about it, for ignoring is "punishment." If such an act is performed, a scolding, or even a mention, may act as a reward in the form of attention-getting, and the aim is literally to get the child to forget it. After each success, rewards appropriate to the particular child, or tokens that will mount up to realize the reward, are given because desired behavior requires attention to impress it on the child. After the behavior is "conditioned," harder and harder assignments are made until the desired goal is reached. Though rewards continue to be given, it takes more and more work to get them. The goal is finally to have the wanted behavior so ingrained, and the satisfaction from it so clear, that rewards are no longer needed to "reinforce" the learning. The success of the process is measured by what happens when rewards and programming stop. Is the new learning really learned or do old patterns re-emerge in an orgy of backsliding? How much reinforcement is needed, and at what intervals? Results vary.

Many behavior modification people began as purists, insisting that all that was needed was the program and the reward. Though punishment in the form of shock, electric or verbal, has been used in some instances—electric shock with, for example, autistic children; psychological shock, visual or oral, in a remedial reading institute for children with learning disabilities—punishment is not really commonly used. This is partly because there are some data that tend to prove people respond more lastingly to reward than to shock; there is too the fact that public opinion reacts more favorably to the use of rewards than to the use of punishment.

Behavior Modification has been found to be most successful when carried out in groups, since the presence of the group and competition among members seem to act as reinforcements in themselves.

More recently Behavior Modification people have found it most helpful when working with children and youth, rather than with rats, cats and dogs, to "reinforce" the learning by means of adding talks with the group leader—a kind of combined psychodynamic and Behavior Modification practice. Clearly, since the leader or the people who are directing the program dictate what must be done with the children, this kind of group falls within the dependency AA-type model. But of course, the leaders must be professionals, well-trained in Behavior Modification techniques.

There has been considerable success with this method, especially when the relationship between the group leader and the children is seen as being as basic to the treatment as are the program and the reward-systems themselves. But the method does not work for all children. For some it does not work at all; for others, results may be temporary. It does seem to work particularly well for many children with severe learning disabilities, especially those whose psychological problems appear to be more the result than the cause of school failure—children whose inability to conquer a basic skill has led to severe feelings of incompetence and apathy.

For the successful use of Behavior Modification in groups, no matter where they are, within the classroom or as an addition to the class offices outside the school, it is essential that parents be involved. The younger the child, the more important is this axiom. The reason is obvious. The purpose is to get rid of certain behaviors or learnings and to instill new or different ones, and this is to be achieved by completely ignoring the old pattern and continuously reinforcing the new. If then the child goes home and is scolded or punished for the very behavior that is to be assiduously ignored and is ignored in the behavior that is to get immediate notice and reward, the outcome will at best be highly questionable. Parents are usually seen either singly or, more economically and more usually, in groups. They are given explanations of what is going on in the treatment of their children, and told why and how they must help, and what will hinder progress. These parent groups are basically educational in function, but they may and often do turn into discussions of dynamic issues, such as feelings, causes, traps parents fall into, and traps they themselves set, with or without awareness.

The danger lies in the fact that since Behavior Modification *seems* easy to do, it is often looked at as a panacea for all troubles, instead of as simply a tool—one tool among many—to approach some problems, but not all. It also causes many people to be concerned about the obvious possibilities for misuse, for Behavior Modification carries about with it an Orwellian, brainwashing character, generating fear that someone up there or out there will decide what people ought to think, how they ought to act, what they ought to like; the fear that someone's thinking—the psychologist's, the teacher's, the dictator's—will "condition" all of us to be robot-automatons, all uniform assembly-line products. Particularly frightening is the political misuse the technique can be put to—e.g., in the service of the status quo or of a dictatorship or a religious fanaticism.

Nevertheless, with proper monitoring and caution, and in the hands of people who are aware that they are using potential dynamite, Behavior Modification can be a helpful group tool in the classroom and in the clinic. As a group, delinquents or children caught in the immobilizing trap of unusual learning disabilities are often particularly appropriate choices for a program of Behavior Modification when it is combined with an understanding of what is going on and why, so that they may have some awareness about what is happening to them. But this is true of any theory.

Before we leave the subject of Behavior Modification, it should be said that in diluted form, and not in its pure culture, this technique is frequently used in all of the groups we are to be concerned with in the rest of this chapter, especially at the early stages of group formation and definition of the task and the methods. This is true particularly with those groups of children who have a hard time with impulse control and sitting still. For instance, at the outset of a program, even though the methods chosen for the group are psychodynamic, an activity group leader may distribute Cokes to the children to reward a few minutes of sitting silent so that he can suggest to the children what activity is available today and where the materials for it are. The handing out of Cokes is a diluted form of reward, but it serves its purpose. The collaboration of a group psychotherapist with someone who knows Behavior Modification techniques has proved successful with persons who are hyperactive, or those who suffer from apathy and withdrawal.

Once it is decided that a child (or a youth) needs a group, the problem becomes what kind of group to choose and what kind of group leadership will best meet the needs of this child at this particular stage of his physical, mental and emotional development.

Many children have a hard time talking, especially about their feelings. So of course do many adults, especially men who have been trained not to talk about their feelings. To make it possible for such children (or adults) to benefit by psychotherapy, an education or re-education job must be undertaken to open them to treatment—much as a surgeon will not operate until the patient is in good enough health to tolerate an anesthetic and the strain of the surgery. In psychotherapy, ability to receive therapy is even more important, for the treatment depends entirely upon the give-and-take process between patient and therapist. Unlike other treatments, it cannot be done *to* a patient; it must be done with him. The unhappy myth that the psychiatrist knows all, that the psychologist comes equipped with a crystal ball, is often encouraged by the practitioners themselves with their mystique-laden jargon and props. Given a therapist who is able and willing to give up this voice-from-on-high role, group process can break the myths down. Even in adult or pure talking-groups, it becomes impossible to keep up the myth of unseen voices making wise, oracular comments. Children's therapy has always been a nail in the cross of this mystique, since from its inception child-therapy forms of play have substituted for or have supplemented talk. Messages about feelings and circumstances of life are given through toys, puppets, games, pictures, charades and other materials as clearly as through words, or even more clearly. The therapist, depending on whether he came from the Anna Freud, Melanie Klein, or Virginia Axline schools of training, may talk a little or a lot, may interpret or only reflect what the messages given out by the child's use of material mean, but it is still the child who expresses the messages by his play or by his use of materials.

Play and materials, as much as or more than talk, are the language of children. This is especially true of slum or ghetto children whose parents are beset with work and weariness, and who themselves have not been trained to use words as either tool or weapon, and therefore find the demand that they say how they feel overwhelming.*

Even if language were available as a tool, even if in itself learning abstraction and symbolization were more familiar, the question of using these techniques with people whom you have no reason to trust becomes a gigantic hurdle. Why should any child trust a strange adult with his feelings when clearly his family, whom he is expected to trust, have not understood them or been able to use them—when his teachers, with whom he is at least acquainted, seem not to be able to understand them, and when these very feelings appear to be the reason he is in enough trouble to need special help? Besides, he probably isn't sufficiently at home with his own feelings to know what they are, let alone to name them. Even God took a few days before he named things in the world, so the troubled child, especially the nonverbally educated child, has legitimate precedent! It becomes the therapist's job to ease the pathways of communication and hack out new paths where none existed before.

A group therapist may, for a time, have a hectic and bewildering experience, but his task is made easier by the fact that he is dealing with a group, who by their manner and interests and separate means, suggest materials, games, images, which he can follow up and use as channels for getting feelings expressed and dealt with. Interestingly enough, a by-product of successful therapy is usually the ability of a child to use speech more ably than

* See John Dewey and Alfred North Whitehead, as well as Joseph Barrett's "Cognitive Thought and Affect in Organizational Experience" in *Science and Psychoanalysis*, Vol. 12, N. Y., Gruner Stratton, 1965; and James McWhinner, "Forms of Language Usage in Adolescence and Their Relationships to Disturbed Behavior and Its Treatment" in G. Caplan and S. Lebovic (Eds.), *Adolescence: Psychosocial Perspective*. N. Y.: Basic Books, Inc. 1969.

ever before, not only in the realm of feelings, but as a tool for thinking—that is, for solving cognitive problems as well as emotional ones. The therapy, itself, if successful, is educative, and the therapist (along with the group) has been the teacher. This is amusing, because many therapists vigorously deny their teaching role just as they too often object to the teacher's playing a therapeutic role. Yet many of the children without any intervention other than psychotherapy in their lives, do far better in the conceptual school subjects after therapy. One may say that this is true because their emotional problems have been sufficiently solved to allow them to use their energy in school study; it is hard to disentangle emotional from intellectual effort, but there is much evidence to indicate that the mere ability to translate feelings and thought into words is indeed a successful by-product of the group venture.

Keeping all this in mind, we turn now to those forms of group therapy that use materials as the focal point of group organization, and where words only supplement or come out of the materials being used. The group leader, depending on his point of view and personal style, may interpret much or little. His interpretations will, to be sure, affect the course of the ideas and the problems produced, but the primary point here is that the group itself use the materials to state and to work on the problems of its members.

ACTIVITY GROUPS

Slavson, as I mentioned earlier, was the grandfather of activity group theory. F. Redl, W. Morse and many others could also be mentioned as utilizing a natural child-group structure in the service of treatment. Such a group, often called a club, may meet together at regular intervals, anywhere from once a week for a few hours, to several afternoons or evenings a week after school, or in school or at a designated camp. The group is together because all the members exhibit some kind of behavior which troubles either them or, more often, their schools, homes, or community. They may meet indoors or out; there is usually a room or "clubhouse" set apart for their use. They may, with the leader's help, or at first on the leader's initiative, find projects that they are interested in—building a playing field, fixing over the clubhouse, etc. They may play checkers, monopoly, pool, card games, baseball, basketball, etc. They may box, trampoline-jump, learn acrobatics or dance. They may work in crafts and make things in wood, plastic, clay, basketry. They may cook or sew or sing. The activities, though directed and sometimes suggested by the group leader(s), derive from the age-level interests and needs of the members. At first, it is unlikely that they will, no matter what their ages, all be able to do the same thing at the same time. That may come in time, if it comes. How they win, how they lose at games, the effect on them of competition, how they cheat and how they get found out, how they steal or lie within the group— all these things are significant and make great group material to work on. How do they handle a fight? Do they look for a fight, start one, run from one—always get licked, always bully, or get bullied? How do they handle the use of tools, a tool that won't work, an object that will not work? How does a member act if the object was broken by himself, by another group member, by the group leader? Observations based on these questions offer a direct route to basic problems. How do the members handle the problems of attendance—their own or other people's? How do they handle lateness or no-shows, trips that are postponed, defections of particular pals, switches in loyalties, their own inclusion or exclusion and that of others, new members, the loss of old members, change of adult leadership? How are crises handled— crises that arise out of the group itself or in their lives? How do they relate to the leader, to the others in times of stress or need, to their own needs or to the needs of others? These are all basic problems to everyone; with skillful handling and appropriate interpretation or restraint of interpretation, depending on the state and readiness of that particular child at that particular time, working them out is the therapy.

Activity groups can be geared for children as young as three and four, and as old as eighteen and nineteen. The materials used, the games played, the projects engaged in, will differ of course according to age, sexual development and sex interest, but, if well led, groups of this kind are excellent for children and young people of all ages. The age range needs to be fairly homogeneous, though in day-camp settings or residential-camp settings where there is a sufficient number of group workers or leaders so that subgroups can be formed and so that the older members can, as part of their advanced treatment, help younger or newer ones, the age range can profitably be quite wide.

Leading activity groups is a demanding job. It requires certain skill and a certain kind of temperament. In many cases, the kind of ability to handle children exhibited by talented recreation teachers, nursery-school teachers and camp counselors is more valuable than the more intellectualized talent of the garden-variety psychotherapist. In other words, the prime essential here is a feel for children at a given age level, ease with them and enjoyment of them, and the kind of sense of humor that children understand and can share and respond to. In addition to such a temperament in its various phases, what is most important is empathy with what it feels like to be a child and in trouble—in trouble beyond the power of a child to mend or alter. Actual skill at games, crafts, arts, can be learned. But imagination, the ability to use ideas, the flexibility to let something you have planned drop and to take on something that seems more youth- or child-motivated—these are rarer traits, harder to use and equally necessary to success in this field. Many sophisticated psychiatrists who are good at other forms of therapy are not comfortable in this kind of group and need training to relax into para-verbal modes. Many times it has been found helpful to use group leaders who are themselves relatively untrained in psychiatric know-how or in psychologic know-what-for as the major leaders, under the supervision of a psychiatrist or psychologist or with the professional taking the role of assistant. In such groups co-workers or teams of leaders are especially useful. Collaboration and supervision time is of the essence, since with the best will in the world, and even with the help of tape recorders and videotape, one person cannot help but miss much significant material. Lest I be misunderstood, let me add that I am not saying that trained therapists should never lead activity groups, but simply that they need more training and some re-educating to do so, for their professional training itself has in many cases trained them out of or beyond the flexibility and ease with the nonverbal messages and language of childhood that are required. This kind of retraining is essential to any good group leadership, especially with children and young people.

ART THERAPY GROUPS

Over the past years, art therapy has grown up to be an entity in itself. It has left the area of occupational therapy and now has its own theory and practices, and of course its own group differences in point of view. It could be said that art therapy began through acceptance of Hermann Rorschach's projective tests, tests in which diagnosis is based in significant part on how the client perceived the world. Perceptions, anxieties, distortions, conflicts, and quality of mind were revealed by what one read into the white cards on which there were only ink blots in black and mixed colors. As the projective tests grew and multiplied, material from them yielded much useful data about the functioning and non-functioning of adults and children alike. The study was further advanced by the use of many additional kinds of materials: story pictures, self-created pictures of persons, houses, trees, etc. Models were provided with which people, especially children, would create mini worlds according to their own perceptions; mosaic blocks were introduced too, and games and mazes and comments on films, scenes and anything imaginable.

What a person creates is clearly a projection of himself. Any artist knows this. Conceal himself as he may school himself to do through techniques and skill, somewhere the personality shines through—if one can read the message, even the message the person does not intend to give. That message may come through to anyone, but the skilled psychologist is especially trained to read it. The less skilled a person is in using a medium to express himself, the more clearly he reveals himself. For that reason, especially in pure diagnosis, it is better, when using drawing, painting, or clay productions, to have one of those many people who say "I can't draw anything" or "I never touch a paint brush" than an aspiring Picasso. What one is after is not a product, but a communication from the inside of a person.

This seeming paradox is relevant to the selection of an art-therapy group, especially for children and youth. The group leader may want children who like to use art materials. Those that do like to tend to be better at it than those who turn away from these media. Yet one doesn't necessarily want skilled artists; indeed, it is more difficult to read the messages of those who are so naturally skillful that they can glibly cover over and conceal their inner selves. The dilemma is a far more conscious one among art therapists than among therapists who deal with verbal wares. It is true one hears of too great ease or glibness with words, of intellectualizing as a form of resistance, of talking too much in order not to say anything important, but people are not excluded from talk groups because of their verbal skills. Still, it might be wise to get verbally gifted people into art, dance, or pantomime activity therapy. The point I am making here is twofold: (1) simply being willing to use art materials is enough to admit one into an art group; and, (2) the quality of the products, though sometimes surprisingly good, is not the important thing. The important thing in an art-therapy group is the same as in other groups: the decision about what to do; the time it takes to get started; the throwaways, the erasures and crossings out, the slips and errors, the mess; the disgust and frustration; the rage with the leader, with others, with oneself; the envy expressed; the comments before, during, and after a picture or other art form is made; as well as the fun, joy, recognition and even ectasy over finding new ways to express one's feelings and thoughts. The heaviness of the lines, the overlap of colors, the personal symbolism of the colors selected, and the personal forms, abstract and/or concrete, that emerge to express oneself and one's own image; the mood of the pictures and the changes in that mood; the joint interpretations and comments of the group; the kind of contribution each member makes to a joint production such as a group mural or group clay structure: all of these are the essentials out of which the therapy grows. The group therapists—at least one of whom should be cognizant of and comfortable with the use of art materials, and one, or preferably both, of whom should be aware of the processes of personality development and its pathology—may, depending on their point of view, interpret much or little. They may use group processes and group awareness; they may be direct or indirect in their approach. They may wish to limber people up with body or at least arm exercises; they may or may not use music; they may meet many times a week or once a week. They may themselves see individuals in the group aside from the art-therapy sessions for talk sessions, or they may prefer not to do so, but rather to send individuals elsewhere if, through the art groups, material comes up that the child needs extra work on, as indeed often happens. When this occurs, the leaders, if they are group-wise, will let the group know what is happening, so that the issues arising out of being special, or the worries over having problems, can emerge. Having more come up than can be handled in one session a week, let's say, can be a common group concern.

Many art therapists leave the choice of subject completely free. Others, especially those working with school age and adolescent children, find it useful to assign topics to serve as a basis for drawing, painting, modeling, or sculpting. The following suggestions have been found to be useful to groups, both because they get children unstuck from the "I don't know what to draw" defeat before it defeats them, and because the topics are such excellent starters for group discussions:

Make pictures of all the people you live with, or of your family; label the people. Draw something happy, something sad, something frightening, exciting, or funny. Make an angry picture; make a happy one. Make a picture of the group. Make a picture of someone in the group you think could help you. Let's make a joint picture about fun, about dating, about girls and boys, about parents or teachers. These pictures can be either realistic or abstract. When I was first involved in this sort of work, I thought it would be hard to get children to use art media abstractly. I was dead wrong. Children catch on right away, and the comments that are made about their own and other people's abstract pictures or products are tremendously revealing and helpful in the group. So impressive are the results of well-led art-therapy groups for ghetto children, for torn-apart adolescents, for tied-up, constricted children, for children who find talking—especially to adults—next to impossible, that I would like to see all adults who want to become therapists go through an art-therapy experience. They would not only find out much about themselves and about the children they think uncommunicative, but would find themselves more in touch with a children's world.

MUSIC AND DANCE THERAPY GROUPS

The same principles that operate in art therapy operate also in the use of dance or music as therapy. Just as in the case of art, music and dance were first used with hospitalized patients. It was found that many patients who could not and would not communicate in words would do so when they were allowed to use one of these other expressive forms. We have found that catatonic schizophrenics—patients whose body postures are so rigidly held that they seem (but often only seem) not to take in stimuli, and who do in fact emit no reactions or next to none—react especially well to the use of music, rhythm and body movement. In doing so, they often assume postures and positions or go into patterns of movement that relay to the insightful therapist what they are experiencing in their inner world; they may even give some clues as to how they got that way.

When dance and music therapy was taken out of the hospital and into psychiatric offices and some schools, we established the truth of something that had been guessed before, and even applied by a few experimentally minded, gifted teachers: that brain-damaged children and hyperactive children, especially those with minimal brain damage, respond extraordinarily well to music and dance treatment. Aside from the gains that can be achieved, first toward communication and through that toward relationship with the therapists and other group members, it is a useful cue to teachers that music and body movement can be used well in the classroom for this kind of child. There is something so basic in telling what is going on in oneself by physical stance, kinesthetic sensation and rhythmic movement, that children like the very ill respond to it (once their embarrassment or awkwardness is overcome) with ease. Likewise, there is a part of all of us that helps us reach out of ourselves and respond to the sounds and rhythms, tunes and harmonies, related to nature. A good leader, with the help of music and dance, can set this element in ourselves in motion more easily in a group. Helping patients to do the choreography is as therapeutic as it is revealing.

It is important in using these forms, whether interpretive as in dance or listening, or active as in choreography and instrument playing, that boundaries be set to fit the personality of the group members. That is to say, hyperactive children and brain-damaged children with few controls need more formalized, less free, dance and music forms, while rigid, inhibited, tense youngsters require greater freedom. For this reason, the group leaders (or at least one of them) must be aware, beyond their use of music and dance, of the significance of the disturbance the children are burdened with, so as not to exacerbate the difficulty while they are trying to alleviate it.

WRITING AND READING THERAPY

It seems paradoxical that many of the people who most love words and what they can do, and who depend on writing words or reading them as their major solace, often have so much trouble communicating orally, face to face with other people. Yet that is true for many. Among this group are many adolescents. Experience has shown that often those who fear any face-to-face encounter, especially in a group, respond well, *even in a group*, when they are allowed to write at home or alone in privacy, and then share what they have written with the group. They may be asked, too, to write comments on what they have read, and to share these as well. Sometimes, at the beginning of such a group, anonymity is used to ensure privacy for the shy person. The progress of the group can in part be measured by the willingness of the members to own their productions and ideas. At the end of such a group, we may hope to find that the members are able to say what they feel to one another and in front of one another, without needing a piece of paper with words on it to protect them or to hide behind. Sometimes in such groups, journals are kept and shared—the teens are diary-keeping years. Sometimes the device is used of having letters written either from one member to another, or by a group member to the group leaders or to the group as a whole. This brings to mind a story told about Abe Burrows: In talking to a class of aspiring writers at the University of Pennsylvania, he answered their questions about how to write by advising practice. "Write," he said. "Write all the time. Write letters. Try writing home!" People in writing-therapy groups write. Some write poetry, some stories or essays or scenes from plays. They experiment with forms old and new. They write to one another and collaborate with one another. They try group writing and group reading. It is often an exciting experience which develops skills in thinking as well as writing. It gives a community of interest and a pathway out of isolation, loneliness, shyness and self-consciousness. Stutterers, whose trouble often lies in self-consciousness and hostility, do particularly well in such groups. Writing becomes an avenue for the expression of difficult feelings such as anger, hurt, competitiveness and affection. The difference between such a group and a good writing seminar is that the task of the group is therapeutic, and therefore the quality of the product, which is sometimes first class and sometimes pretty awful, is secondary to the fact of communication itself. The important thing is getting to be at home with one's own feelings and being able to own them in public, changing one's attitudes so as to be able to live a more satisfying life within oneself and among others.

PSYCHODRAMA

Of all the therapies which use nonverbal (as well as verbal) ways of expressing feelings, conflicts and dilemmas, probably the best-known and most widely used is psychodrama. Since this form requires group participation, whether playing a role in a play or being part of the actively engaged audience, it is essentially a group form. Many people have developed psychodrama in many ways and have adapted the technique, or parts of it, to their own uses. Curiously, the term is not generally associated with the name of its founder, Moreno, though he has written extensively on the theory, practice, and application of psychodrama. Moreno heads an institute where he trains people to use the technique, and he has trained many psychodrama leaders in hospitals and institutions and agencies all over the country, and in fact, in foreign countries as well. There are too many skilled followers of Moreno's ideas to mention here, and too many innovators whose work is based on his. Suffice it to say the field is still being explored, and uses for the method broadened and deepened. Gestalt theory and transactional theory use snatches of psychodrama in their exercises and in their dream work. Transactional therapy also uses the technique to demonstrate the games that take place among people and to indicate less dangerous alternatives than those employed in these games. Virginia Satir and her school use psychodrama in family therapy in the technique known as family sculpturing. Other groups use it too in moments or full sessions of role-playing. (See Viola Spolin's *Theatre Games.*)

Essentially psychodrama is an opportunity for people to "act out" in a useful way their fantasies, dreams, fears and preoccupations, on the one hand, and the situations which do already, or which later on may, give them trouble, on the other. For example, a member of a group might report a dream and have various members of the group act out parts of his dream. Perhaps they switch roles in the middle, perhaps not. The dreamer may act as director and actor or as either one, or he may serve as audience.

Fritz Perl and others exploited the technique of using objects: the chairs and cars and attic windows in the dream are mimed by the dreamer and personified by him. Another example: a child may report an obsessive fear of dogs. He is asked to choose others to help him, and all with him act out his fear, which may be general or may have arisen out of a frightening experience. Or a youth may be going to an interview that means a great deal to him—a job, college-admission, a first date with a girl he likes. He tells the group his concerns and with him they act out the interview or date.

The uses of psychodrama for children or youth of all ages are many. Children like to play-act and like making their own plays as they go along, so it is a popular activity. Children like to create their own experiences and feel them out in a safe place away from outside criticism and belittling. One adaptation has been used by a theatrical group in which the players are actors and respond to requests from an audience of children: Act out this or that. The actors do so, and the children respond. One can deal with material once it has emerged, and the audience helps get the problem posed and sees solutions being added before their eyes. There is no age above three that cannot use psychodrama as therapy.

It is amazing to note the different feelings one gets by becoming for a moment another person or object in one's own life-drama. Attitudes and patterns of thought alter and are often helpful.

XI

Live-in Groups

SOME OF the children who are in our schools shouldn't be there. It is true that if our schools were better staffed and equipped, if the staff were more appropriately trained and were given more genuinely supportive services, if the curriculum, methods and group placement were made to fit the varying needs of children who learn differently from others, we would undoubtedly have far fewer children who can't accept school and whom the schools can't accept. But even with all these ifs, there are some children who are too disturbed or too damaged to be able to tolerate any school program at all—children whose attendance brings destruction on themselves and the class. These severe cases are a minority, but they do exist.

Roughly 60 per cent of schoolchildren can succeed in schools without special help. Another 30 per cent need special help within the school system and/or from outside supportive services. But 10 per cent of our children cannot make it in any regular school no matter what help is given. Of this 10 per cent, perhaps 3 per cent more could manage in very special classes within a regular setting, but we are then still left with 7 per cent who cannot manage, no matter what special arrangements are made.

Minority groups, especially black groups, assert—and some of our most sophisticated educators agree with them, as I do, fully—that our schools have, in the great majority of cases, dealt unfairly with them, have discriminated in favor of the white middle class and against the poor, who are, many of them, from minority groups. The schools have suspended from school or even expelled children who were having trouble; as a result, the child who was having *some* trouble comes to have much more. A child who needs special help in adapting to school and in learning essential skills is many times pushed out of school so often that neither adaptation nor skill-learning is possible. It is also true that what has in the past (and often, unhappily, in the present too) been labeled as a child's disturbance, or that of his family, has in fact been the effect of the use of a different language and modes of expression different from those familiar to us. There is no question that much of the curriculum and some of our teaching methods as well do not take into account individual differences and needs. Not enough money is spent on remedial programs and on supportive school mental and physical health programs; where money is given, it is often not used to the best advantage. It is this kind of situation that makes the collaborative group action discussed earlier so essential. Nonetheless, notwithstanding the fact that these truths are only all too evident, it still remains true that some children cannot make it *even if they could be given ideal conditions*; they certainly cannot manage as things are today. To keep such children in the classroom because of a particular political stance, or because of ignorance, fear, or denial of emotional disturbance, makes for mayhem and misery all around.

We in America, as a conglomerate of large groups, can learn much from some of the smaller countries—Sweden, Norway, Denmark, Holland and Israel, for example—about recognizing the needs of the very disturbed or damaged child and implementing services to meet them. That would enable us to save much of the money and effort that now goes into the building of big, impersonal "training schools"—a euphemism for reform schools and junior prison systems. Rarely does any child sent to these schools learn what we would like him to learn; he is far more likely to learn instead the very things we sent him away *not* to learn. Since with more and better treatment centers we would be caring elsewhere for the very ill, we could plan more effectively for the care within the school setting of the disturbed who are not quite so ill, and thus we would not need so many training schools.

In the countries mentioned above, and indeed in some places in our own country too, residential treatment centers do not necessarily call for elaborate, expensive structures. Such centers are often small, manageable, homelike units, as large perhaps as a large family home. The people who direct them may be trained psychiatrists or psychologists or they may be special-education teachers; they may employ trained child-care workers, or people with a natural talent for handling upset children who are being trained as they proceed—much as in our best para-professional programs. In the latter case, the directors may want to hire a specialist as a regular consultant or to do specific tasks. These centers attempt to create a therapeutic milieu within a modest setting, where there is adequate indoor and outdoor space for living, learning, playing and brooding. In such settings, both here and abroad, treatment is not seen only as individual psychotherapy or group therapy, nor only as the administration of appropriate medically supervised drugs, nor only the instituting of special teaching methods and curriculum: it is instead the whole life of the center; the whole day and night of the child is considered his treatment. He may have within that whole any or all of the forms of treatment listed, but the milieu itself is the paramount agent of cure.

The first stage, which at a treatment center may take weeks rather than days, is a long thorough diagnosis. It exposes a child to all the customary diagnostic tools—the ordinary battery of educational and psychological tests and an interview for him and his parents with a psychiatrist and/or social worker. But more, it includes talks with those who have known him over the years: teachers, grandparents, pediatricians, close relatives. Then the child is observed day in and day out for a few trial weeks at the institution. This study notices his co-ordinating patterns—how he wakes up, how he eats, dresses, plays, concentrates, loses his temper, cries, works, or fails to work, with other children or adults; it notes how he goes to sleep, and whether and when he has nightmares or night terrors. In these diagnostic weeks the child also has a physical and neurological examination, and a thorough check on vision and hearing. These will tell his teachers how he needs to be approached, how taught, what group he will fit in with, what his red flags of anxiety are and what forms his comforts take.

The results are called a "prescriptive program"; it is, in fact, a *group diagnosis*, involving both the group he leaves behind and the group he enters: a group of adult inquirers and interested people, and a group of children with whom he will live, either twenty-four hours a day, or, if it is a day school, all day. A first task is to decide whether he will be better off living at home and attending day school, or better off in a residential setting. This unfortunately is often a matter of economics, but it should at least in theory be determined in part by the child's life circumstances, by whether his parent or parents are available to work with—available that is, in both psychological and geographical terms. Sometimes parents and children are so caught up with one another that they need to be separated, at least for a while. Both may be worked with, but geographical space and distance may be needed to break the vicious cycle of mutual destruction that has arisen between them. Sometimes, however, the opposite is true—the two may need to become better acquainted, and this may require the unifying help of trained workers.

One kind of child who needs the extreme day or residential kind of treatment is the autistic child. The autistic child's relationships with other humans are tenuous or distorted at best; at worst, such children do not relate to people but rather to objects, like a toy or a door or a horse. Their speech, though it may have developed well in early life, may have retreated to a bizarre use of words, or may have become non-existent, for part of their disease is failure to use words to communicate. Sometimes autistic children use grunts or animal sounds or weird cries or moans.

Their gestures tend to be jerky, though often, despite clumsiness in ordinary motions such as walking, throwing or catching, they engage in some intricate pattern of motion with more skill and ease than a normally coordinated person could muster. They seem to start and stop moving automatically, as if, in order to move, an engine outside themselves must turn them on and off. Bruno Bettelheim has described in detail their typical gestures of "doodling-in" and "doodling-out"—the phrases are descriptive of the complicated and skillfully executed series of motions by which a string, a piece of gum, a toy, may be used to convey something. By the form these gestures take it is possible, though difficult, to know what is being communicated and why these gestures mean to the child what they do mean.

Autistic children cannot possibly learn to deal with their illness in regular schools. Both they and schizophrenic children need special care and special programs. The terms we are using here are not very precise, but many feel that what we call childhood schizophrenia is a disease that develops later than autism. The prognosis for the schizophrenic child, in contrast to that for the autistic child, is more hopeful, since the later a disease appears, the more reference points of contact with the world have been established. Many people feel that in at least some cases both the phenomenon of autism and that of childhood schizophrenia have a constitutional or organic or chemical base.

In addition to the autistic child and the childhood schizophrenic, there are certain brain-damaged children who cannot function at home, either because they themselves are too disabled or because their presence sacrifices the rest of the family. There are, too, severely retarded children who need, as do the brain-damaged children, special care and special training within the limits of their disabilities and assets. There are also, especially in the age bracket between three and fifteen, some hyperaggressive children whose damage to themselves and others, if they remain at home and in regular schools, can be too costly for society to let them stay at home.

Another portmanteau category is that of "delinquent" children;

these may fall as well into any of the categories already listed. Some of them may simply have had disabling experiences in their family or other relationships; sometimes they are abused children who have survived tortures. In other cases, the abuse they have undergone may have been of a more subtle character than physical suffering. The behavior of such children is erratic, impulse-ridden and without control. (See F. Redl, *The Aggressive Child.*) All have one thing in common: they have got into trouble with the law, the school or the community.

Special care may be needed too by certain of the feeble-minded, especially those whose deficiencies result in strikingly different behavior patterns. While mongoloid children tend to be placid, pleasant, cheerful and cooperative, the cerebral-palsied child may have suffered damage that makes him irritable; lack of muscular control may cause such a child to clutch and claw when angered without being able to stop. It may cause him to vomit when anxious. Some may be partially cared for at home; some not.

These days we come upon more and more adolescents and young adults who need residential or at least day treatment away from home. Often the real need of such young people arises out of their use of heavy drugs such as heroin, cocaine, LSD, amphetamines or "speed." The more set the addiction, the longer the stay in residence usually recommended. But at this time our facilities are bursting with adolescents. Old adult hospitals that have heretofore refused to take such "children" are now forced by circumstance to do so, and there is a frantic attempt to transform existing programs, which may or may not suit the young people we are considering, into programs which plan for adolescent needs by emphasizing group work, either for skill-learning or for communication needs. Because of the prevalence of drug cases, more and more adolescent units are being developed, and more and more programs, centering especially around group-ward decisions and group-ward discussions, are being formulated. Though they vary considerably, most such programs have learned much from places like Synanon about the importance of group action to help members of the addictive group through the rough times. We have found that in many cases, the use of drugs was only a precipitating event that led to the uncovering of a pre-existent disturbance underneath; in other cases, the drugs seem to have done the major damage.

It is true that it takes quite sophisticated diagnostic tools (sometimes, unfortunately, colored by the biases of the experts involved) to say whether a patient has one kind of disturbance or another. Is he severely retarded? Does he have either visible or invisible organic damage? Is the problem a matter of genetics, and if so, to what extent? Is the patient severely retarded because of mental deficiency or because of mental distortion? The group of adults who make up the diagnostic team or staff group are sometimes hard put to it to be sure of their judgments. All too frequently confusion makes for misplacement, which is distressing because psycho-educational prescriptive programs for one type of child are, or should be, quite different from those for other types. Where does each child fit in? But, in the end, assuming that a correct diagnosis has been made by a neurologist, psychiatrist, psychologist, teacher, pediatrician and social worker, with the help of the parents, and, if it appears appropriate, also the grandparents, the child finally is placed at some special treatment facility, and phase one is over.

Now let us examine available treatment centers and grade them on a scale from bad to best. No matter what the diagnostic category, the child who is placed in a large mental hospital is usually unlucky, for his illness is such that he needs every reinforcement and special treatment known to us, and it is unlikely that he will, in the typical hospital, be given a full-time milieu program. Not only that—he may be put into a ward where there are also adults and senile patients. His schooling, if any, will be peripheral, not integrated with his treatment; it may involve only the hiring of a teacher from the nearby school system, a few dabs of occupational therapy, and the use of the yard or exercise facilities, if there are any such things. Sometimes, though too rarely, there is a children's ward separate from the rest of the hospital. In such cases, a milieu approach is possible. The hospital can, if it is not too caught up in interdisciplinary status warfare and politics, integrate and supplement a children's program—if the staff can be given special training on the subjects of the development of child play, learning and group interaction—about all of which most adult mental hospital staff usually know very little. With a good director for the children's branch, the staff can learn much from the teachers, and the teachers can learn much about the children's life patterns. If the hospital then adds special consultants, use of the occupational therapy department, and the help of some of the recovering patients from other wards who are skilled with children, it could evolve a pretty fair program.

Next in the rising scale, are the large institutions for children. As in the case of the hospital, whether the design is for brain-damaged, feeble-minded, severely disturbed, autistic, schizophrenic or hyperaggressive children, the mere fact that it is a large institution runs counter to the need of every child for personally directed warmth, a homelike setting and nurture. Some institutions try to get around this by having systems of separate cottages in which the programs and staff of each cottage are reasonably independent of the others. In this arrangement, the relations of staff to children are more contained, and a child can learn, with more security than in a constantly changing ward system, whom he can, and whom he cannot, relate to, and where to go to find help of various sorts. In such self-contained cottage systems, a staff under effective guidance and training can learn how to create a group milieu approach. They can learn what is involved in the group meeting that takes place daily with both staff and children attending. After diagnosis and prescriptions have been decided, the staff can learn how to plan programs with the children and how far to go in offering alternatives to the various children. They can discuss Lucy's night-time terrors, and the death of the favorite guinea pig; the treatment of the cats, and how the new climbing equipment was broken; why John is not attending the group meeting, or why everyone dislikes Mr. May, the new child-care worker.

Some of the staff will show talent for Life Space interviewing— a technique that will be explained later on—and will be given special training in the use of that essential therapeutic technique, for it can calm down and preserve a child who has become distraught, as well as preserve a group that is endangered by one member's disruption, or a group that has used one member as a reason to go into group chaos. In this country, some of the best known of these cottage institutions for children are Menninger's in Kansas, Southward in Connecticut, Vineland in New Jersey, Langley Porter in San Francisco, Hawthorne-Cedar Knolls and Berkshire in New York, Hawthorne in Michigan, the Eastern Psychiatric Institute of Pennsylvania, the Brown School in Texas, the Ann Pendleton Home in Rhode Island, and many others.

In a cottage setting it is possible to see the importance of the various patterns of each child in the routines of daily life—particularly his eating and waking patterns, and his going-to-sleep rituals. It is possible to register dreams and nightmares, to learn what toys or games have special significance; what activities generate peace and coziness, and which combinations of kids are poison and which fruitful; what certain teachers, counselors or child-care workers (or whatever the day- and night-time staff is called) mean to each child and to the group.

Much like the principal in a school, the director or head counselor of the cottage or unit will determine the kind of milieu the children will live in and what attitude the staff will have toward each other and toward the children. Since in all group structure, no matter what is said, the leadership determines underlying attitudes about what is important, what is not, what goes and what does not, the more in tune the staff leadership is and the more aware, the more consistent the life-mode of the cottage will be, and the more secure everyone in it.

An institution which depends on other units for its budget and its staffing cannot be as independent or as autonomous in carrying out its treatment philosophy as a small residential or day-treatment center. In these days especially, budget troubles which affect staff or program are inevitable for *all* mental health facilities for children. It would seem that mental health expenditure is to the nation's budget priorities what caviar is to the budget of a young couple. Whatever the case, the smaller residential treatment-centers tend to be able, when adequately financed, to create a more personal and homelike atmosphere. There are some excellent small private units dotted over the country—alas, too few and far between to take care of all the needs.

Similarly, though there are some especially fine treatment-center day-schools, there is a great range in quality among schools. Some few are excellent, some good, some are barely adequate, some horrendously bad. All tend to be expensive and all suffer from budgetary lacks. Since a very large staff is needed to make a proper facility, the cost of running such places is always very high. Even when treatment centers are under the aegis of hospitals or universities which help staff them, the costs are still beyond the reach of most people. In places that are state-supported or city-subscribed-to, availability of money, always tight, tends to be a political football, and when politics gains control of professional, clinical decisions, the results are often disastrous for children. This is true even for our sickest children: their fates and lives depend to a large extent on the politics and economics of the nation. It is significant that in the more socialistic countries of Scandinavia and Great Britain, facilities tend to be smaller and often also better than the general run of our own, despite our great wealth.

MILIEU TREATMENT

We have several times referred to the term Milieu Treatment, and have briefly defined it. We now examine the concept in detail.

Milieu treatment takes in every living moment of a child's life. Each child's behavior and moods, on a ward or in a cottage, are looked at and reviewed daily. If the setting is group-oriented, that behavior is seen in the light of what is going on about the child in relation to both the staff group on duty at the time, and the peer group. If a child goes off to special tutoring and comes back depressed and somber, group discussions with the tutor try to determine whether it was failure, frustration or success (as it often is) that has depressed the child; was it the mood of the tutor he caught, or was there a demand by the tutor that he couldn't, or wouldn't, answer? If the child goes off to an individual therapy hour, how willingly or reluctantly he does so is noted. He may be pressed to mention his nightmares of the night before; if he does not do so, he knows the counselor may mention them, for in a good milieu setting, though there is a genuine attempt to provide privacy, where secrets sabotage his cure, if he can't tell them, an adult may, with his knowledge. A fight with a counselor, a crush on a nurse, a plot with a peer, all are subjects for the group discussion period. The charge of "unfair" treatment may be brought up. The therapeutic holding of a child may be seen by the other children as hurting and overpowering the child; in such a case, the counselor may discuss with the children why he held the child as he did. The group may confer about the mutual responsibility of child and counselor for the effect of a given event.

An atmosphere of trust is mandatory in a milieu setting. Openness is required of the child-care workers about their own reactions within the group, so that what they do with the children and each other may be consistent; at the same time room must be left for human error. In this way, even after a messy mishandling, all can pick themselves up and behave without recrimination or repressed shame for past errors. Thus the workers indicate to the children by their *actions*, not words, that failure as well as success is not permanent, that failure is indeed something that one can learn from, if it is examined openly. Acceptance of error, of failure, as part of the human condition, can be effected only when the staff group is well directed and supervised. If such direction is achieved, the children benefit.

How does milieu treatment work? Here are some examples: Intake of food is such a basic need among us and so connected with our earliest relationship that mealtimes have great significance. At meals, Mary's gluttony and Bill's use of food as a weapon can be handled directly, with boundaries of acceptable behavior set and acted upon. Again, in class-time Pete, who is today falling apart at the impossible challenge of reading a page that was easy to read yesterday, can at once be rescued; he can be taken out of class by a child-care worker and the event eventually discussed.

It is in the context of such routines that the Life Space Interview is of particular significance. The Life Space Interview is an on-the-spot intervention because of an event in the child's daily life that is causing him or others distress. The technique is one developed by Fritz Redl and David Wineman. The child is taken out, taken aside from the group. He is calmed down by silence or by physical affection, if he can accept it, or by a game, or by just being together with an undemanding but present adult. Then, when he is ready to talk, the incident—the reason why he was temporarily removed from the group—is discussed with him. What can the incident mean? What is he feeling? Talk can be a way to cope, a better way than hitting oneself or others, or flying into a tantrum or a sulk. When the counselor thinks the child ready, he is returned to the group, and the incident, written up in the nursing notes. How he is received back into the group is part of the therapeutic management so vital to treatment—there should be acceptance without scolding or judgment being meted out.

For example, take this paragraph from some nursery notes of a severely depressed child who, while hospitalized, had set fire to three houses, one a home for the blind and aged. He was a child whose rage at the world burned within an iceberg exterior, but once in a while exploded.

On the way back to the ward after the gym David called out, "I'm first." The counsellor asked him what he was first for. David said he didn't know, but he was first in everything. Cliff, another boy, intervened and challenged him, saying he was better at spying and identifying foreign cars than David. David broke from the line and began to pummel Cliff unmercifully. When stopped, David began to cry, he cried for forty minutes straight, sobbing and writhing on the floor as the counsellor sat by him, quietly soothing him. The group had gone on to the group meeting before dinner. David only was able to join the group at the end of dinner when he had recuperated and had had a Life Space Interview. David then had dinner.

Only much later in treatment did the tears and their importance become clear to the therapist and the child-care workers, and then to David himself, but this event and the Life Space Interview attending it gave one of many, many clues to his needs and his reactions that finally, after three years, led to his cure.*

In a milieu setting there are frequent informal meetings to plan schedules, etc. Here are some notes that show how such meetings work:

Today Rick said he didn't want to go on the supper camping trip to the river. The counsellor said "Fine," but if Rick wasn't going, it meant that Phil would have to stay home with him, and Phil was the driver on the trip because Rita and Sam and Tillie didn't have insurance coverage to drive, and so they planned the games on the trip. Chuck said, "Rick spoiled everything, why didn't he come?" Rick said he was scared of the rapids and he had nightmares about them and there were evil spirits that would jump out at him. Rita asked Rick what would make him feel safe if he went. Rick said only if Sam stayed with him up on the bluff away from the rapids, and if no one made him look at the rapids—it was looking that made the bad spirits come out. Sam asked the group if they would let him stay with Rick and not be in their games. All the boys but Jerry said yes. Jerry said he needed Sam with him. The other boys argued with him, and Jerry agreed. So the trip was on. The boys decided they could finish their school jobs by snack time and they all would be ready to go by four o'clock. Alan was asked by Rita if he thought he needed help to get ready on time, he had a hard time being on time. Alan said he'd try better. Chuck made fun of him and imitated him. The group laughed. Alan began to scream. Sam took Alan out for a short Life Space Interview while the group asked Chuck why he had baited Alan. They came back. [Notes from Hillcrest Children Center, Residence Director Edward Gibson.]

Later, after the trip, and before bedtime, another group discussion about the trip and the day would take place. It would discuss

* *The School Centered Life Space Interview*—edt. by Newman, Redl, Washington School of Psychiatry, D.C. 1966 (pamphlet).

Frank's fury when he lost his sneaker and Sam's having had to hold him so he wouldn't hurt himself. It would say how well the cooking had gone. Mary would bring up the loss of all the matches, and the group would discuss who might have taken them. No evening television would be played until the matches were found.

The unit we have just discussed was made up of severely disturbed, hyperaggressive and phobic children. In different contexts, and with different material brought up for discussion, the same format of planning and interchange would hold for other groups, such as brain-damaged and retarded children. In certain areas, teen-agers would be given far more autonomy in deciding their own programs and their own group-leadership. Milieu treatment is tailored to the group being treated. In other words, the unit becomes a group, with each member dependent on all the others, and all having to live with one another's needs and peculiarities. Treatment at the center, though it may be offered as an addition to school and individual therapy, includes all that goes on every day, and every hour, in every way.

The treatment of addicted persons is particularly dependent on groups as the major intervention. The hypothesis in these cases is that dependency and loneliness and isolation are essential traits of the addict, and that if the dependence is made a mutual one in which everyone is concerned for everyone else, loneliness and with it dependency on drugs will be diminished. The lethargy, the lack of concern for making one's own choices, and for setting the direction in one's own development, so typical of drug abusers, is attacked by the group, and thus the downs and discouragement of a single member on any given day are neutralized by group forces. "The changes" that are gone through are experienced with the understanding, but not the indulgence, of others. The central nature of the cure lies in forcing the concept of responsibility for one's decisions on oneself, and in the curative effect of helping others who have similar problems. The leaders of the drug treatment group are often ex-addicts, sometimes with, or sometimes without, a professional as an active co-leader. The Life Space Interviews may be given either by a professional or by the youths themselves in consultation with the paid leader, professional or not.

The group attacks practical issues along with dynamics. For example, they may discuss how to get along in a job realistic enough to be safe as a stepping-stone back to the world. The terror of failing and far more often the terror of succeeding, are explored by the group at great length. The group is concerned for the mood and the health of its members. After returning home, a member may still be in a phase of group life so intense that unless his family is aware of his feelings and state of mind, and aware also of their own feelings about him and themselves, it is unlikely he will be able to withstand home pressures without returning to the drug. For that reason, the best programs work with family groups and adult groups, as well as with the addicts themselves. Such a carefully planned program of follow-up activities in helping others keeps the stability of the group going even after it has terminated its residence or day program.

HALFWAY HOUSES

Halfway houses are designed especially for those people— adults or the young—who have been in hospitals and now need support and assistance in getting back into the social, academic and work worlds, or for those who are waiting to be hospitalized and cannot live at home. The halfway house gives such people shelter and protection of both a material and a psychological character. Sometimes they make hospitalization unnecessary.

Halfway houses tend to be small. They usually have some sort of system which reduces the cost for a person who is working on a job or going to school. They nearly always insist that the residents see a therapist outside the halfway house. As with all institutions, some are good, some poor. The quality depends on the personality, knowledge, basic insight and management capacities of the director. Some have excellent programs of an occupational therapy type that foster vocational alternatives and the achievement of new skills or the refurbishing of old forgotten interests. Many have daily group meetings, or at least meet several times a week; many encourage the live-in members to take responsibility for the living arrangements and programming. The administration provides on-the-spot counseling, emergency intervention, and some vocational or academic guidance. Their directors have access to medical and psychological consultation.

These days there are many adolescents who need to be outside their homes in an open but protected environment. Because of drug abuse, or because of damaging relationships with their parents, or because of seemingly irreconcilable conflicts between their values, attitudes, and mode of dress and behavior and those of the older generation, they have found living at home with their parents impossible; their parents often feel the same way. In the lower economic groups, such young people are often sent to the courts as "unmanageable" and then placed in foster homes or "Training Schools." In the middle and upper-middle classes, sometimes, halfway houses are used to house such youths. In these cases, "halfway" does not mean halfway between the hospital and the world, but rather halfway between home and an institution, or halfway between home and "the street." Usually the program is similar to that offered the post-hospitalized patient. Rewards are offered for work done, including schoolwork. Therapy is usually insisted upon.

A later development for the handling of certain of these troubled young people is the Group Foster Home. This type of facility serves runaways some of whom have deep underlying disturbances, and some of whom are simply unable to fit into or go along with the mode of life their parents want for them; it may care as well for those who cannot bear the amount of distress involved in their family life. In such homes basic structure and care are given by house parents. Programming and group discussion are set up. The Foster Parents often seek or are given professional consultation to help them to find appropriate interventions. These houses, if well run, can be fine preventive and therapeutic agents.

There are, also, of course, structures run by the youths themselves—communes in which the young live together, however loosely, and formulate their own patterns of behavior and modes of group operation. The range of communes goes from highly group-structured to a kind of juvenile flophouse. Some are excellent. Some are distinctly loose in structure and unprotective of individual needs.

What I have given here is only a sampling of the many kinds of live-in group-centered facilities we see nowadays. By choice or necessity, we make do with them in our present society. As in all the other situations we have discussed, the smaller and more cohesive the group, the easier it is to get the task done well. It would be a great contribution to society if more good small facilities, constantly evaluated, were locally or federally supported. It would save people, property, and lives.

XII

Training in Group Leadership

ALL THOSE who lead any group—from playgroup leader to school principal—have been members of some groups. But not all those who have been members of a group are necessarily able to lead a group. The task determines the quality of leadership required, but only the group members can determine whether the leader, however competent he may be, will be able to do his job.

Everyone has been a member of more than one group—a family or classroom group, the in-or-out-groups of peers, or the work groups one belongs to—so that no one comes to the task of leading a group without some sort of experience and conceptualization of what it means to be a leader. No teacher could survive for a day in a class had he not some knowledge of how to get a group together to do a task. But instinctive knowledge is not enough. The power of group forces and the necessary shifts in the kind of leadership needed require both awareness and skill in applying one's knowledge to educate a group of children or adults; to counsel, guide or cure a group of children or adults, or to direct program, policy and people.

For these reasons, almost everyone, to achieve skill in group leadership, requires training. The training can be fun, personally enriching, arduous, painful or frightening, but, whatever its emotional effect, it is essential to one's job as a group leader. Training in understanding the groups one deals with has been markedly lacking or superficial in most colleges, graduate schools, and even in many specialized training institutes and in-service training programs.

A major hurdle for teachers (and others in leadership positions) is establishing the authority with which one handles people in a classroom, on a playground, on a trip or in a lunch room. This authority, in popular if inaccurate school jargon, is called "discipline"—an ambiguous word, which evokes in many people's minds a picture of whips, raised voices, scoldings, and the meting out of punishment and judgments on behavior. A good disciplinarian is seen as a strict or "tough" teacher. A teacher is often told that he would be a good teacher if only he knew how to discipline a group, or that he does know how to discipline a group, but doesn't scold or punish like others in the school. That last may be said with shock or with admiration. Conversely, one hears that a particular teacher is a good disciplinarian, but that his kids don't learn much—which means he punishes and maintains quiet, but either has few skills to impart or doesn't know how to motivate or explain the task to the children. In either case, a teacher is being evaluated on the basis of his authority in group management. Many teachers who might have a great deal to give to their students leave teaching because of their lack of authority in group management and lack of training in this area. What is often missed is that when one has the ability or skills, native or trained, to lead a group, the group itself often is able to take care of the great number of garden-variety "discipline problems" that the teacher of a regular class meets with.

Like "discipline," "authority" is a word that is often used ambiguously. It is often used to mean something that is given, something put upon one, like a scepter or a crown, or it is seen as an evil, associated with strict fathers and dictatorial rulers. In this book the word is used in its original etymological sense: coming as it does from the latin *auctor*—author—it designates one who has something to communicate, one who claims ownership and responsibility for his words and deeds, one whose imprint is upon what he says and does. In terms of a task to be done and a group to do it, authority is the freedom of anyone in the group to work, and the ability of the leader to take responsibility for the consequences, the ability to get a job done in the best way one knows how with the group of people at hand. By this definition, authority can be vested in every member of the group, as he comprehends the task, learns it, and tries to work at it. The authority vested in the leader, or teacher, is the special responsibility to facilitate getting work done. In terms of these definitions, the authority of the leader lasts only as long as he can make the work of the group go.

Discipline thus becomes for the group a matter of being able to forgo for the moment byways that are irrelevant to the task. But discipline can sometimes become a matter of searching the byways people must delve into as a necessary preparation for getting a job done. It is often difficult to know in advance which byway is likely to be task-productive and which task-defeating. If there are members who are not able, for personal reasons, or because of momentary dynamics, to let the group do its job, the leader may have to exclude those people for the moment in order to keep the group on task. That would be "discipline" intended to help the group, not punishment for the strayers from the task. Or, discipline might be the teacher's or leader's attempt to help the group as a whole work out the dynamics that are interfering with the task, so that they become ready to work. Discipline is a means of allowing a group to carry out its mission. It is everybody's concern, but it is the leader's special responsibility. The way it is handled indicates the quality of authority in the leadership. The way one gains inner authority is, as a rule, by training. Some few people seem to be born with authority, but not many. For most, authority is learned.

The most effective method of learning group process is experience—experience gained in groups whose major task is to study their own behavior with a consultant who, by his manner, his interpretations, and interventions will help them in this task. Such an experience, even though all effort is directed toward group relationship, becomes a matter of self-exploration as well as of exploration of group behavior. It invariably taps the complex feelings everyone brings to his relation to authority. It is important, therefore, to know when a person can, and should, risk exposing himself to such mind-stretching. There are times in an individual's life when because of personal disequilibrium such exploration can be too upsetting. There are also people so frightened of change, so rigidly ensconced in their defenses, that they refuse such exploration by not joining a study-group in the first place, or by remaining in the group corporeally only. Most people, however, find the study of group behavior extraordinarily rewarding, despite the shaking up it gives one's preconceived notions. To be able to "look a fact in the face, like a child" as William James has said, by confronting reality and tearing away the layers of fantasy and supposition based on bias and personal inner needs, is to have parts of one's world change before one's very eyes.

Participation in one or many groups seems to have become an initiation rite of adult middle-class life today. Many such groups are used by an impersonal, automated society to stimulate or at least simulate closeness, caring, "togetherness," and to give an opportunity for expression of the rage and passion which people feel have become atrophied by disuse—a kind of societal permission to regress. Some of this avid interest in groups derives from the awareness that since human life is essentially group life, it is better to become aware of the ingredients that make up group process, group dynamics, leadership, followership, and role-taking within different groups. Consciousness of this need has become the more pressing because there is within a group not only a search for one's own identity but also, for some at least, a safeguard against being manipulated by group forces or charismatic leadership. For others, group experience becomes a guide to power to manipulate and influence. For still others, it is a way to learn competence in getting work done in a group and for providing for change as change becomes necessary and meaningful without acceding to unwanted group manipulation.

Increasingly, in more and more centers of higher learning,

graduate and undergraduate, some kind of group experience is offered. Because of the immense popularity of sensitivity, awareness and encounter groups in this country, most of the experiences offered have been of these types. They have the advantage, if successful, of showing a person how he comes across to others and how he reacts to others. They also show him certain group phenomena—for instance, the changing of a group mood, or the dependence of the group on a leader, and the need, once there is a leader, to cut him down. From Christ to Malcolm X to the Kennedys, it is the same story. In much milder form, this last phenomenon is hard to miss in the study of any group, as are also the rivalries for leadership, or the shifting alignments of pairs of people within the group. Useful as these groups are when they are well led, they are far more geared to concentration on individual reactions to all that is occurring than to awareness of the group as an entity. Gains in knowledge from them can be considerable if the leadership is skilled—if, in fact, the leadership has just the kind of authority and discipline to hold the group to the task of the group, and keep it from being waylaid by dramatics or enticed into byways of personal aberration or revelation.

There are training or learning groups which offer a more group-centered approach. For those who are eager to find out about small group relations, large group relations, and the relationships among groups in relation to problems of leadership, authority and responsibility, the groups developed at the Tavistock Institute in London and brought to this country by the A. K. Rice Institute of Group Relations (Washington School of Psychiatry) are particularly valuable, being notably group-directed. This kind of experience is often given in a residential conference lasting anywhere from a long weekend to a five- or six-day period or even sometimes for a period of ten days or two weeks. They are, in short form, sometimes given in nonresidential settings as well. The experience consists of exercises of different types designed to offer a laboratory for study of the various forms of group behavior, in small or large groups, and between and among groups. Time is then given to apply one's learning to one's own work situation.

The experience itself, though strictly group-directed, offers the individual a chance to explore his own overt and covert responses in an eye-opening fashion. A good description of the experience is given in John Fowles' novel *The Magus*.

Both kinds of group experience are good training. Each yields a different product, since the tasks differ, and either one can be experienced without the other. Ideally, however, both kinds should be offered in training for group leadership.

No matter what the kind of group training experience offered, group powers are such that the credentials of leadership become very important and should be inquired into before participating in any kind of group, no matter of what theory or practice, no matter whether designed for treatment, for education or for training.

Experiencing membership in one or more groups is unquestionably the most effective training for leadership, but there are other ways of learning. Didactic seminars on group problems and group theory, on types and variety of leadership, and on the roles within a group, can be particularly useful when coupled with experiential learning. In a seminar each participant may be asked to bring in a complete report on the group he or she is concerned with. A critical analysis or "supervision" of the group reported on follows, with all group members participating and relating the situation reported to their own groups. This can be helpful, much as an individual case conference is helpful; only, with a group, the recounting is more complex, since the interrelationships of group members, the shifting roles and moods must all be accounted for. Indeed, a good seminar leader will need to spend much time, as part of basic training, in indicating how to report a group without getting lost in the microscopic elements of individual roles or the fascination of biographical detail. Interesting and significant as these may be, if a group is being reported on, the flavor of the group needs to be seen as underlying all events before individual interactions can be discussed.

I have found a convenient guide in recording and reporting a group to include the following questions: What was the beginning of the group like? Who was present? Who absent? Who was late? Where did people sit? What were the nonverbal mannerisms displayed? How long a silence was there at the start? Who and what began the discussion? When was the subject changed? Who changed it and how? What was the central theme of the group sessions being reported? Which members expressed it, and what were the others doing and how were they reacting? Were there rival issues? Did they get dealt with? What were the byways and avoidances that were used to detour the main issues? What were the group roles—were they the same as last time, or did they shift? How did the group end? What feeling did you, the leader, have about it? How were you, the leader, feeling throughout? When were you uncomfortable? How many times did you intervene and what was the nature of your interventions? What were the reasons for these interventions? How did the group react toward you? After you have made this group report, tell about the individuals: What role do you feel each individual played in the group and for the group? What is your supporting evidence? How did you play into what was going on?

Films, videotape, audiotape and demonstration groups with subsequent analysis are most useful as aids in learning to report and analyze a group in this group-focused way. To help the trainees catch nonverbal messages, watching a film or videotape or demonstration group through a one-way screen without the sound on is a fruitful device. A group-case seminar can be a good tool for learning.

NONVERBAL GROUP TRAINING

People whose lives center about human relations tend to be a verbal group. For that very reason, experiences of a primarily non-verbal nature can illuminate for them areas hitherto neglected. For instance, to get a group of teachers, psychiatrists, or other trainees together, supply them with easels, large paper and pastels; after some simple loosening-up arm and body exercises, tell them to do a scribble, and then to develop a picture from the scribble and title it. The group's discussion of its products is frequently a revelatory experience. Having the group do first a realistic picture of the group, and then an abstract picture of it, can throw new light on the conceptualization of individuals and on group inter-action. People being given such training may be told to use colors, lines, or forms, to tell how they see other people in the group, perhaps reds or oranges with jagged and curving lines for an exciting, flamboyant person; blue or lavender in long, smooth or gently wavy lines for a cool, serene person; black or gray blobs for a depressed type. When these representations are seen through-out the room, people not only come to comprehend how they are seen by others, but also discover the pattern of group roles. The less skilled in art, the better for the purpose of the group, since one of the ideas is to show people what their students or patients experience in doing something unfamiliar, something new. The talk among the group in all such exercises is amazingly fruitful and revealing.

Another aspect of group training which gets away from purely verbal expression is the use of body movement. Since exercises from this area are borrowed directly from the mime theater and choreographic ballet, it is particularly useful to call in someone knowledgeable in those disciplines to collaborate with the group-minded person doing the training. First, the group is loosened up and made less self-conscious by simple tasks, such as standing in a circle with one person turning to the person adjacent and mak-ing a sound and a movement to relay any feeling one chooses. It might be a scream with the body clutched up in fear, or a yell of triumph and a leap or whatever one thinks of. Sound and movement here are simultaneous and of equal importance. The next person imitates the first one's sound and movement, repeat-ing it until the first person is satisfied that the second has caught the feeling that was being conveyed. Then the second person chooses a feeling of his own to express by using his voice and body and directs that to the other person adjacent to him, and so on around the circle.

After the group has stopped its nervous giggles and sotto-voce self-deprecatory remarks and got into the work, any number of exercises can follow: e.g., the setting up of individual statues and group statues; the creating of a group machine of the Rube Gold-berg type to do a given job that the leader suggests—for example, a machine to dig a gigantic subway or plow up ten thousand acres.

Mirroring is a particularly useful activity. Someone acts as if he were doing something in front of a full-length mirror, and simultaneously with his doing so, his partner acts as if he were the mirror, doing everything the partner does, imitating each facial expression and motion. There is nothing quite so effective in getting to know another person's pace, feeling, tone, and even mood, than putting oneself into his body posture and motion pat-tern. This kind of behavior, as a matter of fact, is described by the late psychoanalyst Frieda Fromm-Reichmann; in order to relate and feel with uncommunicating schizophrenic patients, she would follow them around a room, doing as they did, jumping from desk to bureau to floor, crouching in corners and leaping onto the bed. Any actor knows that in getting into a role in a play, body movements can make the feeling one wants come alive. It is a substantiation of the James-Lange theory of emotion which postulates that a man is not afraid and runs because he sees a bear, but instead, runs from the bear, and then since he is running away, he feels afraid.

These exercises bring out many aspects of individual feelings and group process: tenderness, neediness, loneliness, boundaries between people, control, frustration, fear, and sadness. They help people know others and themselves by tapping sources in them-selves not commonly used. The ingenuity of the leader will in large part determine their effectiveness.

Closely related to the use of art, body movement and mime in training staff to understand leadership and group functioning, is the use of psychodrama and role playing. These methods com-bine movement, speech and projection. They can be employed as a whole-group exercise or consistently woven into the context of the talk group when the situation calls for it. Psychodrama is particularly good for the "as-if" situation so useful in training.

Students and teachers and administrators have long used psy-chodrama to play out anticipated worries over events: a fight

with one's spouse, an interaction with a teacher over a report
card, or, in the case of a teacher, an interaction with a particularly troublesome child or a noncomprehending principal; with a
guidance counselor, the psychodrama may play out an upcoming
interview with an irate parent, and with a superintendent, an
interview with the budget committee. Likewise, psychodrama may
be used to review situations that have worked out either badly or
extraordinarily well, as a recapitulation to analyze with the group
the ingredients that helped determine the outcome. Sometimes
psychodrama is used to loosen up group members and allow them
to use or develop imagination, humor and insight, and thus a
sense of proportion and awareness. They are used therapeutically
by working through an unresolved situation or relationship from
the past.

Psychodrama techniques can be used to train people to understand what is occurring in the groups they participate in or lead,
and to understand also their own difficulties. For instance, there
might be a teacher's (or principal's or counselor's) anticipation
of having to address a group of protesting parents. Fears and
fantasies can all be acted out with the person involved either
acting in or directing the playlet. He may pick others to represent
his unspoken thoughts—a kind of *Strange Interlude* dialogue made
personal. The purpose is to bring one's chimeras or dilemmas to
life and to confront them. In training groups, psychodrama gives
the trainee insight into the force of the unconscious and its quite
remarkable imaginative storytelling abilities, qualities that exist
within himself, but have often heretofore been untapped. He
may come to see that the unconscious, instead of being a dread
enemy, is a force one can learn to consult with, and so he can come
to deal with a group more effectively. In fact, by keeping in
touch with the unconscious, a teacher can deal successfully with
the difficult or upset children in his class, a principal with troublesome teachers.

A basic aspect of training for leading groups is the understanding of the roles being played out in a group. When one is a participant in a study group concerned with the study of itself, it is

easy to see the repetitiveness of the roles that are taken. Not all the possible roles are taken in all groups, but some always are. The nature and personality of the leader and of the group will determine what roles will predominate. Which individuals (children or adult) in the group will be likely to take the bait for one role rather than another depends on the individuals themselves. Yet, though it is certainly true that certain individuals find it almost impossible to resist taking on a role that the group proffers, it is amazing to see that when one of these does, by resolve or by accident, refuse to take up the offered role, someone else will inevitably take it on, should the group dynamics require that it exist in order that the group may do, or avoid, its task, or try to engage the leader in the situation.

It is as if when people get together in a group, they create an atmosphere which makes it necessary for certain roles to be played out. It is then as if these roles hover in the air like an invisible cloud over the group and wait to be chosen by someone. If person A won't or can't adopt a particular role, person B or C will, and so on, until all the roles necessary for the purposes of fulfilling the conscious and unconscious needs of the group are taken, or until either the task or the leadership changes, and the roles alter with the change. It can be seen as a kind of quantum-theory total reaction in which the group energy is assigned in different ways but without preplanned design. Someone will be the clown, someone the pathetic, helpless, needy one, someone the outsider, someone the fight-starter, someone the pollyanna, and someone the peacemaker, someone the scapegoat, and someone the bastard. If the clown, for some reason, sees he does not need to get attention by being a clown and wants to be the solemn one, and the group allows him to do so, suddenly the nay-sayer becomes the clown and the do-gooder the nay-sayer.

What is particularly damaging to individuals in a group (and therefore of particular significance for teachers to learn to prevent) is not the playing out of roles, but the freezing of roles (as has been mentioned in earlier chapters). Where a freezing of roles occurs, Jimmy must always be the scapegoat—even if he is able, given support, to relinquish that position; group pressure on him ends in his capitulation and he resigns himself to being the scape-goat. Roles taken are sometimes very difficult to throw off, especially when they repeat the roles played by an individual in his family. Freezing of roles results in one's having a picture of himself as always the loser, or always the helping one, or always the schlemiel, or the arrogant, hated one. Moreover, this is as true of staffs as of students. There develops a fatalistic attitude about it so that even before a new group is set, the person slips into his accustomed role, as if that were his only identity, as if his other needs and qualities were never to be allowed to emerge. Overcoming confusion between a member's own identity and group pressure on him calls for a kind of dynamic of effort, care and understanding by the leader, and perhaps also a different placement to allow the individual an expansion of possibilities.

The kind of frightening, cemented-in experience a child may feel if he is always in the same role—as if he could not afford to risk being outside completely—can be experienced by the teacher or leader in a study group, when he sees himself as locked into a role he wishes to grow out of or no longer wants to claim. Psychodrama role-playing or intensive talk groups can, with work, thaw out the frozen situation and offer alternatives. When that happens, a person who has been trained can be on guard against the power in a group that freezes roles and can learn to keep some psychological antifreeze on hand at all times for himself and his students or group members.

It is fascinating to a group leader to discover by training what kind of group he generates: Is there something about the leader that makes for extra weights of dependency that last beyond usefulness? If so, perhaps that leader ought to look into whether he is only functioning comfortably when people need him, so that under his leadership, helpless ways become even more helpless, and fights come up as group members begin to gain strength and independence. Indications are that such a leader had better work on problems of separation, and come to recognize the fact that his identity as a leader does not have to rest on the neediness of other people. Does a leader constantly generate fight-groups with rivalrous roles, bully and scapegoat, patsy and overlord? If so, perhaps that group leader should examine his own need to have his group work out battles raging in himself that he cannot cope with or resolve. Interestingly enough, it is often the seemingly placid, non-aggressive type of leader who generates fight-groups, since often he has hidden the awareness of the fight within himself from view. A group is sure to give him away.

There are certain roles that come up again and again in almost every group. Training by participation and by post-mortem discussions of videotaped groups or films or demonstration groups, analysis of one's own groups, and experience in the observation of groups, along with experience in role-playing, should help the group leader or teacher recognize the dynamics involved in these roles. Then he may be able to accomplish the difficult feat of knowing what is going on, not only after the fact, but also during it; he may even be able sometimes to predict what will probably happen. The roles in groups are many-faceted; the players wear many masks. They appear when the group needs them either to serve or to waylay the work task. By training one can familiarize himself with group roles. Shorn of the niceties, these are *some* common group roles:

The Monopolizer: The adult monopolizer may appear as the person who comes in and, with a perfunctory question to another member, proceeds to talk in great floods of words, sometimes meaningful, sometimes mere sound-without-content. When someone responds to the flow by a question or a contribution of his own, the monopolizer skillfully brings the talk back to his own interest. When the leader intervenes, the monopolizer may ignore the intervention, may effusively agree with the leader, or may be quiet momentarily, only to dive into a new flow the second a silence comes. The monopolizer may monopolize by expressing his own views or by feigning interest in the other person's problems and using them as a launching pad for his own theme, or he may do it by dramatics, by being pitiful and needy, or by argument and "yes-butting" as an answer to every comment made by others.

A child may take the role of monopolizer by non-stop talk, legitimized or not by being called on, or he may do it by noise, by whispers at every sentence spoken by others, by continually starting rows, or by complaining, but most of all, he monopolizes by clowning—by being the funny man or the class fool.

In any case, the leader is hard put to it to stop the monopolizer. He may notice that the rest of the group is glassy-eyed with boredom, or is Pied-Pipered a million miles away from the group task, or is angry that their own needs are again sacrificed to the monopolizer's, or may be ready to quit. Still, it is not easy to find an appropriate stopper. The dynamics of such a role is the need for control or attention, or both. The phenomenon often appears most notably when the monopolizer feels himself to be most vulnerable. His acting is often exactly opposite to what it appears to be—it is, that is, a non-communication, a cover-up for saying something by means of saying or doing other things.

The cure does not come easily. Training is needed to deal with both the understanding and the management of the monopolizer. The group itself has to be enlisted to help, for the monopolizing could not continue to occur, no matter how polite the members, if the group too were not colluding in letting it happen, perhaps because they too want to avoid getting down to the work at hand. When they have their boredom or irritation pointed out to them and see that the group is as paralyzed as the individual members, they see to it that the monopolizer, if not silenced, is cut short, and they are no longer controlled by this controlling device. Thus both group and monopolizer are liberated.

The other side of this coin shows up as *The Oh-So-Sorry One,* who virtually apologizes for being alive and deprecates his every comment. "I hate to take up the group's time; I know what I have to say isn't as important as what others want to say—oh, they should go ahead, I'll wait . . ." This role is often a come-on, a plea for a written guarantee of acceptance, an insurance that the water is at 80 degrees before one will put a toe in it. It often conceals as much hostility and/or need as the monopolizer does; it indicates a severe lack of trust or an attitude where one keeps oneself to oneself because of fear that others will inevitably misuse what one gives.

It is just as difficult to manage the "sorry" one as the monopolizer. If the act is a phoney, the leader needs to elicit group support in calling on the person to stop his "I'm sorry for living" preliminary routine. "You must promise me," a teacher once said to one of this ilk, "not to apologize. You must promise not even to apologize for apologizing." If the apology is not a phoney, then the leader must take care to nurture and water any sign of group acceptance of the sufferer; to cheer on any straight statement that does not qualify or put down the person; to remark, without overpraise, on any act of competence. With a child especially, the need is so great for acceptance, the self-doubt so pervasive, that at the first rough tone the person flees like a rabbit, before criticism can set in. Training can help a teacher or group leader to deal with this phenomenon of groups.

The Competitor is the member who wants to lead and will fight off any members who might appear to be rivals, by showing what he hopes is strength often in exhibitionist ways, and offering his protection to all members he considers too weak to rival him. By setting up alignments with these, he tries to collect supporters. Most of the initial battles are tests of strength; for the real prize he is after is to dethrone the present leader. However, his dilemma is, that though to defeat the leader is what he thinks he wants, he is usually utterly flustered and panicked if he succeeds in his attempts. And quite rightly, for he then has a mutiny on his hands and is in the direct line of fire from all other contenders. He soon learns that he who grabs for leadership may mobilize an entire group against him, and so he is fearful that his own aggressive competitiveness will boomerang tenfold.

In dealing with the competitor, the leader, while leaving room for leadership to develop through competition, demonstrates that it is not really so grimly awful to want to compete. By training, one can familiarize oneself with one's own theory of competition.

A craftier contender is *The Power Behind the Throne*—the group member who prods and pushes others to do his fighting for him and is always innocently doing nothing when he is confronted. This contender needs more careful watching than the Competitor, for his need to go at things deviously, in a Machiavellian way, while it might be useful in some areas—for instance, in a political convention—would indicate that the adults around him as he grew up left him few direct channels for getting his needs fulfilled. He needs to have the group become aware of his game so that they may cause him to lead when that is appropriate, and stop him from devious maneuvers when his leading is not appropriate. It often takes subtlety in training to recognize, let alone handle, this kind of clue.

The Helpless One or *The Patient* is the role taken by people who are for the time being dependent and unable to decide for themselves. Salvation for them is got not by what one has but by what one lacks. A group often chooses a victim or a casualty for this role, and such a person, though in fact often quite competent, may, in order to get group approval actually render himself incompetent. Indications are that such a person is so starved for acceptance, so lonely or awkward with others, that he will offer himself up as a group sacrifice to get love. The penalty is that he does not just pretend to be incompetent, he actually becomes so.

This is dangerous business, and a group leader needs to find ways to help the victim escape being chosen for the role without casting himself in the role of the Great Protector. To allow a person to stand on a very weak pair of feet when he is about to be tackled by a group means that the leader has either to introduce some better way to fall or to provide some tools for coping. A useful technique is to set up a subgroup in which such a person can, with a minimum number of people, learn confidence in a situation where the large group is not on hand to overpower him. With children a teacher can manipulate seating arrangements and partners in work projects. Even with training, however, it is hard to keep a group from electing a group member to be sick in order to preserve the group's health, or weak to preserve its strength.

The Bully and *The Scapegoat* are as dependent on each other as a heel is on the toe. The Bully cannot bully without a Scapegoat and vice-versa. The dynamic needs of each are not so far apart from each other. At the base of the need is usually despair that one can get anything one needs, like love or acceptance, without overpowering or being overpowered. Love to such an individual means attention. It means clobbering and getting clob-

bered; it reasons thus: love comes with strength; strength is to
overpower; to gain love, I will overpower or be overpowered.
Behind both roles are fear of being unlovable and unfamiliarity
with the forms of closeness that are based on equality. Confusion
of sex with power is often at the root of such trouble. There is as
much reason to separate the scapegoat as the bully from the
group. As a matter of fact, a needy scapegoat always manages
to provoke the Bully. There is a part in all of us that asks,
begs, to be clobbered. When hit, the born scapegoat takes on the
other's self-punishing desires. The scapegoat needs help in stopping his plea to be hit—verbally or physically. The bully needs
a group who will not let him get away with his bullying. To
develop such a group means helping each member of the group to
accept the bullying part of himself so that all the bullying doesn't
have to be placed on, let us say, Arthur. Then the group will see
to it that Arthur tangles only with his equals, not with the
weaker among them. Training for the dynamics and the management of these familiar roles is an invaluable classroom aid.

Then there is the fringe member of the group, *The Reluctant
Bystander*—who seems, even in the way he sits and in his choice
of a place to sit, half in, half out. He is either by the window or
the door, usually with his chair leaning back or crouched into
himself over a desk. He may come to life when called upon; but
for the most part, he seems not quite "with it," but poised for
flight. Indeed, a group may frighten him; he may be unused to
others, or changed about so often that he doesn't dare risk relationships. He may have got from his family the notion that he is
better, sicker, blacker, brighter, dumber, than the others, so that
he sees to it that his position leaves him where he can flee if need
be, or he asks to have an engraved invitation to get in. Sometimes there are ways, by noting his personal interests or the times
when he responds to something, to offer him the engraved invitation. Whether he does not feel welcome or is not welcoming is a
moot point that can be determined in time. It may be both. Training helps the leader help him with skills to enter into the group.
Just how to help is an aspect that takes observation of the
bystander's approach to things and people to insure that what

one helps him with fits his own pace and style better than the casual "Why don't you just get on in there, buddy?" which is unlikely to help. For the group, the bystander performs the role of the outsider which is present in part of all of them—the part that wishes to be outside, in bed—anywhere but where it is in the here-and-now. The role has to do with being *special* and relates to fence-straddling as well.

GROUP SYNDROMES

There are in addition to group roles and much connected with them certain configurations I call group syndromes—waves of behavior that take place in one guise or another within groups as a whole. It is useful for trainees to be familiar with these "waves" so the dynamics of what the group is expressing through them can be recognized and dealt with. I have titled these happenings to indicate the way they strike me. Here is a sampling:

The Ancient Mariner Syndrome is the phenomenon of a person so loaded with something on his mind that he (or she) "stoppeth one of three" at various times—that is, he must stop the group, stop the class, stop and tell the tale, before he can get back to work or let the group do so. A wise teacher or leader will recognize the urgency of the need, and will let the tale be told as a catharsis for trauma or for preoccupation. It may be—and this is often the case—that the pressure is such that the person needs an individual interview: Perhaps something dreadful has happened at home, such as a death or an act of violence, or it may be the surging of a development urge, such as a sexual preoccupation and fear of acting upon it, a terror of lightning, or being in love—all may need to be talked about, and depending on the composition of the group, the talking can be done either in the group, or away from it in Life Space Interviews, but requires limit setting with adults as well as children.

The Thomas Mann Syndrome is one in which the person who is trying to explain something—an experience, a feeling, the reasons for a decision—has to go to the very source of things before coming to the point. It is as if it were more important to be thoroughly understood than to get one's point across. The dynamics here come, to simplify, from a yearning to share one's feelings, a loneliness that must be breached, a quite true sense that no communication from one person to another can ever be complete, and a denial of that truth in a desire for closeness and understanding. To criticize such a person sarcastically or impatiently is to widen the gap between the said and the felt; what is important here is to help the person know when he has been understood pretty well by group affirmation, and then to help him be more appropriately concise. This syndrome, though it may monopolize the attention of the group for a time, is not the same as being a monopolizer, since it only happens when one has touched an area of deep meaning for a particular person, or when the sense of isolation has overwhelmed him. The cue here is loneliness and the need for acceptance and help to recognize limits or boundaries between people without giving up communication. There is also a related need to be right and to cover all contingencies.

The Samson Agonistes Syndrome is one which occurs when someone in a group has suffered some bitter frustration, failure or disappointment. At such a time, with rage that has not been sufficiently acknowledged or dealt with, the person may well act out, or say: "OK, if I can't have what I want"—which may in fact be impossible—"I will see to it that the whole structure falls." This phenomenon is usually quite unconscious, and until the group or events of life have made it evident, it is not accepted by the current Samson. The working through of the conflicts includes the need to have one's life's wish complete, to leave nothing for others to carry on with in their own way grief at separation save. Handling this kind of dynamic requires special training; it takes insight to understand and verbalize the emotional content of the situation the bitterness of defeat or fear of being alone.

The *Who Killed Cock Robin Syndrome* is one in which the members of the group chorus one after the other, "Not I"—and yet in the group, as in the rhyme, Cock Robin lies there dead. And

someone killed him. Who? Group denial may be universal, sometimes because each member believes himself to be, if not completely innocent, yet largely guiltless—not having shot the arrow.
Or all may deny guilt because their code insists they protect the
culprit and unite in not tattling on one another. The truth is that
the guilt over the occurrence, whatever it is, should actually be
shared by many if not all, since all set the mood for Cock Robin's
murder, no matter who pulled the bow-string. If the event took
place as part of a group occurrence, then those most involved
acted even for those in the group who didn't happen to be there,
and those who may have wanted to act so but didn't. Handling
this syndrome too requires special training.

Let me simply list some other common syndromes which one
can handle better if one has the training:

In *The Sleeping Beauty Syndrome* the person waits passively
until awakened by the group, and nothing, but nothing, can arouse
him (or her) until a solution has taken place; he simply sleeps
(metaphorically) through it all, giving nothing, seeming to take
nothing—waiting for the group to act.

In the *Revelation and Awakening Syndrome* someone comes
in and announces that his whole life is changed from this day
forth. He has seen the light. He now understands what has been
repeated to him for weeks. From now on, life will be different.
In actuality, insights sometimes do strike like lightning, illuminat-
ing a whole group of facts; and change sometimes can and does
take place in a flash. But more often defenses against change are
such that, though the insights are gained with passion, they are
frequently forgotten in a short while, and what was to have been
the beginning of a new life turns out to be the same old one,
until the insight is recalled and worked through with less revelation and more slow hard labor.

In the *Winner of the Hundred Neediest Cases Syndrome* people in a group actually vie with one another as to who has the
most terrible troubles or burdens to carry. With children, it may
sound like this: "I got a worse cut than you did. I had four
stitches put in; you only had three." In certain groups, especially
treatment groups where the leader concentrates on those in trou-

ble, the competition for attention and sympathy take the form of vying for Win, Place and Show in the race for the most misery.

The Uncle Vanya or Chekhovian Syndrome is one that can drive group leaders or classroom teachers wild. Whether with adults or children, it goes in such a way that every few minutes a group member states his or her ills and distress, and complains again and again without (one soon discovers) the least determination or effort to change the situation and do something about the complaints. I have named this syndrome for the character in Chekhov who repeats ad nauseum throughout, "Oh, how my feet ache," without ever going to a podiatrist.

I could list hundreds more. A proper training program would get the trainees to discover the syndromes their own group exhibit and to discuss the group forces that required those syndromes rather than others.

OBSERVATION

At least one other aspect of training should be mentioned, for though it is too often neglected, it can, if used well, be a great help to those seeking to learn about group forces and group process. Sophisticated observation can be a tremendously helpful tool. By "sophisticated" I mean more than simply going into a classroom or a treatment group or parents' meeting or staff meeting, and sitting there, watching and listening. Instead, those being trained need first to be primed as to what specifically they are to look for.

One observation assignment might be to watch carefully all that happens in the first ten minutes of the meetings of eight different groups to find out about beginnings and their significance. Another assignment might be to tell, after watching and listening to whole groups, what major issues were covered in the particular class, therapy group, or meeting. It may be that in a particular observation all interactions with the leader are to be noted and nothing else; or the seating positions may be marked over a period of seven group sessions; or the nonverbal cues of gestures, tone of voice, shifting of positions noted in relation to subject matter and time sequence. A trainee might be asked to make sociometric charts of positive and negative reactions among group members to follow emerging member leadership, or totally shifting group moods. Used in this way, observation becomes a tool to sharpen perception of groups at a time or place away from the magnetic pull of involvement in the actions of particular individuals. After observation of this sort has been well learned, an overall observation of the total group, with indication of the roles played by various individuals over a time period, can be of great help, especially if applied after training when the new way of looking at one's own groups has been achieved. Best results for people being trained come not from observing their own groups right off the bat, unless perhaps by videotape, but rather from seeing a variety of groups. The styles of group life and group problems then begin to take on a pattern that can be made very useful. Like note-making or record-keeping, observation can serve training needs best if different areas of group life are focused on one at a time. The choice of a variety of groups to observe broadens one's understanding of the concept that while every group differs from all others, there are nevertheless certain common themes in most groups that emerge clearly enough for one to be able to apply them in one's own group.

There are, of course, many aspects of training for group management that have not been discussed here, but basically the message of this chapter is that people who lead groups need to understand the various phenomena that occur within them and the forces that are set in motion to direct or to pressure the group so that its work gets done. If that understanding is there, it is possible to apply it to oneself as a group leader and as a group member. By so doing, one's task both in terms of learning and of relationships becomes more workable and more satisfying. Curriculum and even adequate bibliography have not yet been fully developed for dealing with training problems; that work is barely begun. But the fact is that by experiencing groups, studying them and observing them, one can in time achieve competence.

It is my conviction that every school system should incorporate group training as an essential of in-service training. The group-training program should provide group experiences of both the sensitivity and the Tavistock or A. K. Rice kind. Staff may attend groups outside the system, if the groups and their leadership have been investigated to gauge the responsibility of the leadership, or the groups may be brought into the system itself. Seminars, workshops and observations should be part of the year's program. Competent consultants, within the system or outside it, should be asked to attend meetings and point out when and how the group slides off its task; they can thus help develop more awareness of the particular problems of the group. I would wager that if this were done, awareness of group phenomena would be raised considerably, and that would raise the learning level, production and creativity in any group from classroom to school board very greatly. It is not simply a question of the usual small study group that is necessary. It is equally essential, since most school staff is part of a larger and complicated institutional system, to include exercises that study behavior and forces that emerge in large groups and those that hold sway between and among groups. Otherwise one limits essential understanding to deal with the education systems.

Conclusion

The Meaning of It All

IN THIS book we have sampled many groups that abound in or around schools. Looked at from outside, the groups may appear much like colonies of ants, each busy with its own immediate task and so intent upon it that related groups, layered above and below, are considered only when interests overlap and collide. Unlike ants, however, human group members in the school system, as in all our social systems, become aware that in pursuit of their special section of the task the overall purpose may, and often does, get lost. Being human, group members are able to think, feel, judge and be judged. When they are judged as a group and found wanting, they tend to muster all the defenses that human beings and human groups have managed to concoct. Some of these are productive in achieving overall group goals; many are not. When attacked, groups of humans tend to cling to their own group view, right or wrong, rather than change to something new and different. Group members tend to get together and point the finger at other groups within their own system or outside it. They tend, when threatened, to deny, to become secretive or suspicious, to avoid communication and opportunities to plan jointly with other groups within the system to repair the damage and make new groupings to achieve their goals.

The dilemmas of these groups are common to all human group members in all of society; they are not simply dilemmas of the groups in schools. The problem that makes it imperative to do something about *school groups,* as apart from other groups, lies in the fact that the overall task of schools is the education of children, and the children represent society's survival or demise.

While what school groups do, or fail to do, about their mandate reflects society's accumulated past with its information and values, what is more important is that in their struggles to approach their tasks, and their solutions and pseudo-solutions, they invariably represent the present state of society and its institutions, and especially the particular way society organizes its energies. The peculiar turmoil of today, with its contradictory needs and conflicting values, is mirrored in the school system's agony in working out its own intra- and inter-group problems as it attempts to do its task. The school is in a particularly vulnerable position, for other of society's institutions have delegated to it the responsibility of preserving society's future. If it looks back, like Lot's wife it turns to salt, becoming fixed, lifeless and immovable. If it looks too far ahead, groups within the school system itself (teachers and administrators) and groups outside the system too (parents and legislative bodies) find themselves unable to keep up with it, so that, like many forerunners, it is likely to be unheard and therefore ineffective.

The balance point is hard to find and harder to maintain, especially in the light of the basic conservativeness inherent in all human groups. "Conservative" here is used in its most basic sense —that of seeking to "save" or maintain things as they are—and herein may lie one of the large hurdles that stand in the way of school leaders who seek to make changes, even when those changes are clearly necessary to achieve their goals. For there is a dynamic which operates in human beings to defend their own present, to deny their death. All tend to be envious of the young, especially we in our youth-minded culture; the more that envy is suppressed, the more it may come out where we least want it, destroying our ability to work on behalf of those who will succeed us, those who remind us that our time of full powers will soon come to an end, and that we will die, while they still live. Thus, in society's making scapegoats of its schools, and in the school's inability to pull itself together to do its required job of objective self-evaluation and responsible innovation and implementation, it may well be that unconscious forces of life-and-death are at work to prevent us from accomplishing our true task, a task indeed in essence present-oriented, but actually also future-directed. And that task is precisely the task schools are established to do: educating the children so that they have skills and the flexibility to adapt to change.

One of the major problems which groups always have had is that of overcoming the unconscious forces which block task-performance. It is a rule of group dynamics that simply to override these forces—much as we might like to, for they are indeed time-consuming—is impossible, unworkable, and leads only to defeat in any case except immediate emergency situations. It may be that it is the opportunity to avoid, if only temporarily, the facing of unconscious forces that accounts for the mountainous number of emergencies, real and contrived, that appear when an attempt is made to force immediate group action in situations that might better have been handled by prevention.

Whether or not the suppositions hypothesized in the paragraphs above have as much validity as I attribute to them may be a matter of argument. What is not arguable is this line of thought:

1. The school is the social-system unit whose mandate it is to educate children so that accumulated knowledge of our society may be transmitted and so insure the culture's survival.

2. Our schools are made up of a great many groups of human beings, each of which is supposed to do a particular part of the job.

3. As the complexity of groups mounts, the ease of communication and joint planning decreases, and the whole complex cannot function unless each group is aware of its place in the total design, and machinery is provided for each to deal with the other groups, directly or indirectly.

4. To manage this difficult job of communication, it is essential that the leaders of the various groups in the hierarchy be sophisticated about group action, both intra-action and interaction. Without sophistication about covert as well as overt group forces,

the system as a whole is likely to become immobilized and the task—the education of our children—to be altogether defeated.

It was to contribute to a sophisticated awareness of the constitution, dynamics and effects of various school groups that this book was written.

The question may certainly be asked: What beyond writing a book would I do to implement this sophistication of all school personnel, including not only staff but parents and community people interested and involved in schools? My answer would be to begin by redefining the task:

I have said that the task is to educate the child. This means:

1. Leading the child from a state of dependency, where most decisions are made for him, into a state of independency and autonomy where he makes the decisions—as far, that is to say, as human life, which is group life, permits, and where the needs of others are considered and the need of each individual to maintain meaningful relationships is understood;

2. Leading the child from a "tax-exempt" state of not being responsible for his behavior and its consequences into a state of taking full responsibility for his behavior and the results of his acts;

3. Leading the child from a state of potentiality to a state of actualization of at least some of his capacities;

4. Leading the child from unawareness and lack of knowledge and skills to awareness, knowledge and command of skills, according to his ability to learn to use these skills and his own gifts;

5. Leading the child from a state where he must, by virtue of his age, accept the status in which he finds himself, into a state where he is flexible enough to adapt to changes, and also to initiate change himself where change becomes necessary or desirable;

6. Leading the child into a state where he can use his humanness to further his job satisfaction and his sense of self, his sense of adequacy, while still maintaining his ability to consider others and adapt to them by granting them equal rights; and

7. Teaching the child to be able to use both his mind and his

heart without forsaking one for the other, in order that he may enrich his universe.

If these seven processes were achieved, or even approached, I would believe that the task of educating children had been successfully carried out, and that the future of our society was well served. So far, these goals have not been achieved. This is largely because the educators—and the word includes all members of the system, from teachers to superintendents—need to teach themselves before they can teach others.

But assuming the school staff was taught, and the task defined as I have specified, I would then bring together the responsible group directing the school system with representatives of other groups within the system—teachers, counselors, principals and school psychologists, along with social workers, nurses, *and* representatives of people from the community—to determine how this or that specific community, given its particular culture and its special needs, could best achieve its task within the conditions operative in the community. The ways chosen would not necessarily be the same even for neighboring communities—they might well have different needs, and so the curriculum, methods and staffing pattern might be quite different. Variety of facilities allows room for differences in how people learn and how they express themselves. The basic goals might be the same, but the pathways to them might be quite divergent, and each might be successful with the school population it sought to serve. Freedom from uniformity would insure far greater room for task achievement both for staff and children; it would give greater responsibility and autonomy to each individual system to provide for its own needs. That would be a kind of Jeffersonian democracy applied to education.

Once having established goals by group meetings, I would want to see all staff members directly involved with the children, or with other staff members, form training groups in which their own group behavior would be studied. Out of this study, leadership up and down the line, as well as responsible followership, would, it may be assumed, develop, and the particular province of each of the trained group leaders profit by increased awareness of what goes on in the group. Channels of communication between and among groups would be easier to establish and maintain, and it would be easier to avoid the kind of suspicion and destructive secrecy prevalent in schools today, as in any institutions where people are on the defensive because they feel threatened and criticized. As a result of all this, the joint enterprises that would further the education of children in the terms I have specified would certainly prosper.

My own belief is that the educative process works best where teachers (and this includes administrators and supervisors) conceive of themselves as facilitators of learning rather than as imposers of this or that collection of truths. By this concept a teacher (whether of children or adults) would become familiar with the personal style of each individual in his charge and attempt to use the teaching style which best reaches his students. The teacher would use the group to expose differences of motivation, approach and avoidance, and would subgroup according to the needs and pace of the people in each subgroup. The teacher's role then is: to present the task, to erect appropriate boundaries of space and time for the task, and to deal with those forces in the group which interfere with the task and those which, though they may seem like digressions, actually enrich it. In this role the teacher must inevitably use the group, as well as his personal resources, to organize energies so they will work in the direction of learning, and not go too far astray.

Since nearly every aspect of school life is group life, implicitly or explicitly, knowledge based on experience of what happens in groups—their many assets, their frustrations and their difficulties —is essential. This book was written to further that knowledge.

Recommended Readings

Astrachan, B. M., "Towards a Social Systems Model of Therapeutic Groups." *Social Psychiatry* 5 (1970):110–119.

Berne, Eric, *Games People Play*. New York: Grove Press, 1964.

Bettelheim, Bruno, *Informed Heart: Autonomy in a Mass Age*. New York: Free Press, 1960.

Bion, Wilfred R., *Experiences in Groups*. New York: Basic Books, 1961.

Bradford, William, *Of Plymouth Plantation 1620–1647*. Edited by Samuel E. Morison. New York: Alfred A. Knopf, 1952.

Braun, Robert J., *Teachers and Power*. New York: Simon and Schuster, 1972.

Edelson, Marshall, *Sociotherapy and Psychotherapy*. Chicago: University of Chicago Press, 1970.

Erikson, Erik H., *Childhood and Society*. New York: Norton, 1964.

Fowles, John, *The Magus*. Boston: Little, Brown and Company, 1966.

Freud, Sigmund, *Beyond the Pleasure Principle*. London: Hogarth, 1920.

Friedenberg, Edgar Z., *The Vanishing Adolescent*. Boston: Beacon Press, 1959.

Fromm-Reichmann, Frieda, *Principles of Intensive Psychotherapy*. New York: Grune, 1956.

Kennedy, Robert F., *Thirteen Days: A Memoir of the Cuban Missile Crisis*. New York: Norton, 1969.

Kirst, Hans S., *The Night of the Generals*. New York: Harper and Row, 1964.

Long, Nicholas J., Morse, Robert, and Newman, Ruth, *Conflict in the Classroom: The Education of Children With Problems*. California: Wadsworth, 1971.

Menzies, Isabel, *The Functioning of Social Systems as a Defense Against Anxiety*. London: Tavistock, 1967.

Miller, E. J., and Gwynne, G. V., *A Life Apart*. Philadelphia: J. B. Lippincott Company, 1972.

Miller, E. J., and Rice, A. K., *Systems of Organization: The Control of Task and Sentient Boundaries*. New York: Barnes and Noble, 1970.

Mowat, Farley, *Never Cry Wolf*. Boston: Little, Brown and Company, 1963.

Newman, Ruth G., *Psychological Consultation in the Schools*. New York: Basic Books, 1967.

O'Connor, Garret, "The Tavistock Method of Group Study." *Science and Psychoanalysis* 18 (1971):100–115.

Parloff, Morris, "Assessing the Effects of Headshrinking and Mind Expanding." Paper presented at The American Group Psychotherapy Assoc., New York, February, 1969.

Redl, Fritz, and Wineman, David, *The Aggressive Child*. New York: Free Press, 1966.

———, *When We Deal With Children*. New York: Free Press, 1966.

———, *Mental Hygiene in Teaching*. New York: Harcourt, Brace Jovanovich, Inc., 1959.

Rice, A. K., *The Enterprise and Its Environment*. London: Tavistock, 1963.

———, *Learning for Leadership*. London: Tavistock, 1965.

———, *The Modern University: A Model Organization*. London: Tavistock, 1970.

Rioch, Margaret, "All We Like Sheep . . . (Isaiah 53:6): Followers and Leaders." *Psychiatry* 34 (1971):256–273.

———, "The Work of Wilfred Bion on Groups." *Psychiatry* 33 (1970):56–66.

Singer, D. Whiton, M.D., and Fried, M. C., "An Alternative to Traditional Mental Health Services and Consultation in Schools: A Social Systems and Groups Process Approach." *Journal of School Psychology* 8 (1970):172–178.

Slavson, Samuel R., *Analytic Group Psychotherapy*. New York: Columbia University Press, 1950.

Sullivan, Harry S., *The Interpersonal Theory of Psychiatry*. New York: W. W. Norton, 1953.

———, *Conceptions of Modern Psychiatry*. New York: W. W. Norton, 1953.

Thomas, Piri, *Down These Mean Streets*. New York: Alfred A. Knopf, 1967.

Yalom, Irvin D., *Theory and Practice of Group Psychotherapy*. New York: Basic Books, 1970.

X, Malcolm, *Autobiography of Malcolm X*. New York: Grove Press, 1965.